Advanced Information and Knowledge Processing

Yun-Heh Chen-Burger and Dave Robertson

Automating Business Modelling

A Guide to Using Logic to Represent
Informal Methods and Support Reasoning

With 104 Figures

 Springer

Yun-Heh Chen-Burger, MS, MSc, PhD
Dave Robertson, PhD

School of Informatics, The University of Edinburgh, UK

Series Editors
Xindong Wu
Lakhmi Jain

British Library Cataloguing in Publication Data
A catalogue record for this book is available from the British Library

Library of Congress Cataloging-in-Publication Data
CIP data available.

AI&KP ISSN 1610-3947

ISBN 978-1-84996-934-5   e-ISBN 978-1-84628-106-8
Springer is a part of Springer Science+Business Media
springeronline.com

34/3830-543210   Printed on acid-free paper

To my husband, Albert Burger, and my parents, Ching-Liang Chen and Peng-Tzu Chiu.

Yun-Heh Chen-Burger

Preface

This book describes different ways of providing automated support for enterprise modelling. It firstly introduces different Enterprise Modelling methods and their relevance to an organisation. This provides an insight to how Enterprise Modelling methods may benefit organisations that use them. Technical knowledge is explained and illustrated by examples that give practical guidance. This book is therefore suitable for undergraduate students in their senior years and post-graduate students who are studying in business studies, computer science and/or artificial intelligence. It will also be suitable for practitioners in the fields of knowledge management, modelling and software engineering who wish to apply such technologies.

This book has used a business modelling method, IBM's *BSDM's Business Modelling* method, as an exemplar to describe how logical methods may be used to provide automatic support and thus help the modeller to produce higher quality models in a controlled and speedy manner. Although this book focuses on one modelling method, the principles demonstrated in the book are generic and may be used for other modelling methods. Two knowledge based tools, *KBST-BM* and *KBST-EM* have been implemented based on the technology described in the book. They have been used to support 27 different modelling methods in practice.

For learning purposes, this book includes normal exercises and advanced exercises at the end of most chapters. Normal exercises are designed for all readers of the book and most of the knowledge needed to answer these questions are included in the book. Advanced exercises are questions that require more in-depth understanding of the topic and may draw on related knowledge that is outside of the scope of the book (e.g. knowledge in Business and Knowledge Management, Artificial Intelligence, Computer Science and Programming) so these suit those who may be taking related courses at the same time.

The content of this book (with the exception of the introductory chapter to Logic, originally written by Dave Robertson for undergraduate teaching) is an extension and adaptation of Yun-Heh Chen-Burger's PhD thesis. Some additional work is derived from AOEM (Air Operations Enterprise Modelling), AKT (Advanced Knowledge Technologies) IRC, CoAKTinG (Collaborative Advanced Knowledge Technologies in the Grid) and experience from commercial projects.

The authors would like to thank Dr. Albert Burger, Ms. Lyn Imeson and Mr. Michael Koy for their careful proof-reading of the book. They also wish to acknowledge their colleagues for providing an interesting and inspirational environment within which to work, and in particular the following people: Dr. John Mark Agosta, Dr. Stuart Aitken, Mr. Tai-Hung Chen, Mr. Mike Dean, Dr. Hsiao-Lan Fang, Professor Peter Gray, Dr. Kit-Ying Hui, Dr. Peter Jarvis, Dr. Yannis Kalfoglou, Mr. Chris Lin, Dr. Fang-Pang Lin, Ms. Christine Lissoni, Mr. Siu-Wai Leung, Professor Chris Mellish, Professor Enrico Motta, Dr. Steve Potter, Dr. Alun Preece, Dr. Marco Schorlemmer, Professor Nigel Shadbolt, Professor Qiang Shen, Dr. Julian Smart, Professor Austin Tate, Mr. Larry Tonneson, Dr. Chris Walton and Professor Ching-Long Yeh.

Moreover, the authors would like to thank their families for their persistent support and company over the years.

Edinburgh, UK   *Yun-Heh (Jessica) Chen-Burger*
August 2004   *Dave Robertson*

Contents

List of Figures

1

Introduction

1.1 The Wider Context: Enterprise Modelling Methods

Enterprise Modelling (EM) methods are commonly used by entrepreneurs as an analysis tool for describing and redesigning their businesses. The resulting product, the enterprise model, is often used as a blueprint for reconstructing their organisations as part of *Business Process Reengineering (BPR)* or *Business Process Improvement (BPI)* initiatives[28].

The goal of applying an enterprise modelling method is to seek ways to improve an organisation's performance. EM methods are typically informal or semi-formal. They provide notations which enable business persons to describe aspects of their business operations. The notation is normally complemented with semi-formal or natural language descriptions which allows details of the business operations to be described.

Examples of such EM methods are IBM's *BSDM Business Modelling Language* [53], Ould's *Business Process Modelling* language *RAD* [82], Dobson and Strens's *Organisational Modelling language (ORDIT)* [31] , Fox and Gruninger's methods to produce ontologies [39], Eriksson and Penker's *business modelling based on extensions of UML* [34], and *IDEF* methodology's process modelling languages such as IDEF3 [72] and IDEF0 [80] . We distinguish between (enterprise) modelling languages and models: a modelling language is the language that is used to describe a domain, whereas the description of the domain (in that modelling language) is the end product of a modelling exercise and is called a model, or more specifically in this case an *Enterprise Model*.

Although EM methods have proved to be useful in providing a systematic working procedure and structural framework to capture and analyse enterprise-wise information, a key problem that remains is the lack of means to *ensure the quality of the developed models*. This problem is to a large extent due to the fact that models are mostly described using informal or semi-formal languages. To maintain the quality of such models, manual checking by a human modelling expert is required. However, a full-sized model for an enterprise is often so large and complicated that it is too complex a task to be carried out manually. Furthermore, the system dynamics described by the model are often implicit and are very difficult to comprehend by the human mind without appropriate computational aids. All of the above problems are further compounded by the fact that normally only limited time is allowed for a modelling project. Hence, when a model has been constructed, little time is left for quality assurance.

It is clear that conventionally labour-intensive modelling tasks can benefit from appropriate automatic and semi-automatic support. Tools that are currently used to support modelling activities may be grouped into two types: the first type of tools provide primarily capturing and report-generation functions for a specific modelling method, the second type of tools provide documentation and report-generating functions as well as simulation facilities for the described models. Although these tools provide useful facilities in assisting model-building activities, their support is based on the syntax of the model, i.e. its notation. For more sophisticated verification, validation and other inferencing functionalities, tools must also be able to process models at the semantic level. How to achieve this is the primary issue in this book.

This book identifies areas where AI techniques can be usefully applied to provide automatic tool support at a level beyond that of conventional tools. The EM method used for illustration is *BSDM's Business Modelling* method [53]. A support framework that covers the life cycle of modelling exercises – the iterative *plan-build-test-refine* modelling life cycle – has been introduced; and based on the methodologies provided by BSDM, a formal method to represent BSDM Business Models was developed. Based on this formal language, explicit and implicit information described in the model is extracted (and derived) from a business model using various AI techniques.

Relevant modelling knowledge that may be helpful for either building, verifying or simulating an EM model is also captured. Such knowledge may be extracted from, for instance, modelling guidance provided by the modelling method, standard (that may not be formally described) modelling practice that has been commonly deployed in the field, benchmarked standard models and other domain-specific information. Such modelling expertise provides a standard to judge the quality of newly created business models: to achieve this, various techniques have been developed and applied to provide automatic and semi-automatic modelling support and theorem proving for the modellers.

The formalised expertise is used in different parts of a *Three-Layered Framework* (which will be introduced in Section 1.4). Based on this framework the *Knowledge Based Support Tool for Business Models (KBST-BM)* has been developed. The tool's target users are business modellers with a good understanding of IBM's *BSDM Business Modelling* method as well as knowledge engineers who are interested in using BSDM as a modelling tool. Business persons (with fundamental knowledge of the business modelling method) may also wish to use the tool for browsing, demonstrating, communicating with others and refining the business context that has been captured in the business model.

The modelling support framework and the techniques used within it are generic and may be adapted to provide automatic and semi-automatic support for other EM modelling methods as well as methods that are similar to BSDM. *KBST-BM* has been extended to a new tool *KBST-EM (Knowledge Based Sup-*

port tool for Enterprise Models) that currently includes 29 different modelling methods that utilise techniques of similar principles. Examples of how those techniques have been applied to other EM methods will also be illustrated at appropriate places. Before the support framework and its techniques are introduced, a brief introduction to the main EM method, BSDM, is given in section 1.2.

1.2 The Focus: Business System Development Method (BSDM)

BSDM (Business Systems Development Method) [53] was developed by IBM. It provides a business modelling method for developing software systems that are to be used in a business environment, i.e. a company or an organisation. The result of the business modelling activity, a business model, is taken as input for its later activities, *Need, Shape* and *Run*, which include scoping, designing and implementing a business system, including both computing and manual procedures. Although *BSDM's business modelling method* is primarily used to help design better business IT systems, it also can be, and often is, used as a business analysis tool and a communication device amongst managers and between managers and software engineers.

What makes BSDM an interesting method is its provision of a well-documented description of its modelling approach, model-building procedures, rich example models and practical evaluation guidelines for good modelling practice, something that most other EM modelling languages do not have. These EM methods provide the *methodology*, i.e. notation and its meaning, but not a step-by-step *method* of use of the methodology in practice.[1] This makes BSDM particularly valuable because it provides a reliable foundation upon which useful model-building automation can be based.

A further advantage of *BSDM's business modelling method* is its comprehensiveness. It offers coherent guidelines for the whole life cycle, in the natural sequence, of BSDM model development, rather than merely discrete techniques for random stages of the development process. These guidelines are also sufficiently concrete so that they can be easily applied in practice. This provides a basis on which a level of automatic support can be provided by KBST-BM that has previously not been seen in other tools.

In spite of these advantages and its concise yet powerful notation for business managers to capture and analyse a complex business environment, BSDM suffers from one of the key problems of most enterprise modelling methods: the quality of the built model is largely dependent on the experience and knowledge the modellers have of the method (BSDM) and their comprehension about the enterprise they are trying to model, which makes it difficult to provide quality assurance for the model. Additionally, like other EMs, developing a BSDM

---

[1] The distinction between *methodology* and *method* follows the definition given by Wieringa [116].

business model is a labour-intensive task which tends to be error-prone when
the modelled domain is complex. This problem is made worse by typical industrial project time constraints that often leave little time for a comprehensive
iterative process of quality checking and refinement once a model has been
built.

Hence, BSDM shares problems typically found in most enterprise modelling
methods, but has also a number of specific characteristics that make it particularly suitable as a target method for automatic and semi-automatic tool support
through the formalisation of models and model-building knowledge. Interestingly, much of those modelling expertise and automatic support, once fully
understood, can be transferred and adapted to be applied to provide similar
support for other enterprise modelling methods. This is particularly interesting
when several different enterprise modelling methods are used in conjunction to
compliment each other. Common information that is stored in each model may
also be used to check against each other to improve the quality of all models.
This work is described in more detail in [20].

1.3 The Aim: A Different Type of Modelling Support

As outlined in the discussion so far, this book introduces a new level of tool
support for business modellers. Specifically, it aims at incorporating various
sources of knowledge into the tool. This will enable the tool to extend its
scope beyond the more traditional features, such as drawing diagrams and
storing information using natural language (e.g. general English descriptions
of the model). New, advanced semantics-based functionalities, enabled through
the underlying formal representation of models and model-building rules are
proposed. These include automatic and semi-automatic consistency checking
across the whole model,[2] support for the development of new models through
an existing library of previously built models, automatic checking of compliance
with general quality guidelines of new models, and overview and preview of
possible executions of business processes.

In summary, through the proposed approach, tool support shifts from
merely a documentary role to one in which the tool is used to improve model-
building efficiency and model quality. These aims and how they are achieved
are discussed in more detail throughout the book, beginning with an overview
of the modelling context of the support framework in the next section.

1.4 Modelling Context and the Support Framework

The support framework is provided in a context where modelling activities are
carried out. This section therefore looks at the modelling context of BSDM.
BSDM's Business Modelling method provides a two-step activity framework

---

[2] As well as across models, when several models are used.

for developing business models. The first activity is to build an *Entity Model*. During the second activity, processes are added to construct a *Process Model*. A business model captures and represents the given business environment in graphical and textual format. It describes a consensus view of senior managers in the environment and provides a basis on which to build software (and the corresponding manual) systems for that environment.

In a typical business modelling session, managers of key business areas and a BSDM facilitator (expert in BSDM method) work together to create a business model for the organisation. Normally, flip charts and post-it notes are used during these sessions. The information is transferred to a drawing and text-editing tool after the session. An *Entity Model*, which captures the concepts in the business as *entities* and the relationships between them as *dependencies*, is created first. The Entity Model is then extended with information about the *processes* which manage these entities to form a *Process Model*. Information about the life cycle of an entity is described in detail in the corresponding *BSDM Life Cycle Diagrams*. Descriptions of entities, processes and their attributes are included in the *BSDM Definition Forms* using BSDM notation and English.

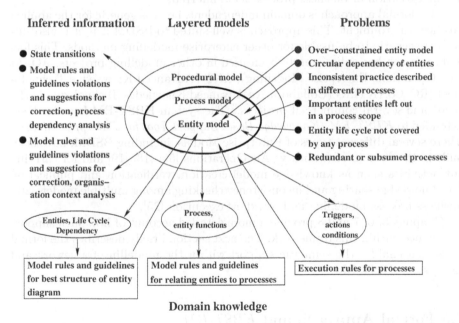

Fig. 1.1. Three-layered modelling support framework

Based on the activity framework that has been provided by BSDM, the modelling support framework described in Figure 1.1 has been introduced as part of this work. Three layers are used: the *Entity, Process* and *Procedural Model*. The *Entity* and *Process* layers correspond to the activities of building *Entity* and *Process Models* as described in BSDM. The *Procedural Model* layer was created to provide the necessary notation to specify the execution details of a BSDM process which provides a basis for executing BSDM processes and carrying out relevant verification and validation support. Since the execution procedure of a process can only be decided after a process has been specified, the *Procedural Model* is a natural extension of the existing BSDM modelling framework.

Figure 1.1 lists example problems that may arise during each modelling activity, the types of domain knowledge that have been extracted and formalised, and example information and automatic support that has been inferred and provided for in each layer. The domain knowledge for each layer is divided into two types: information captured in the business model and (standard) modelling rules for creating these models, shown in Figure 1.1 as ellipses and boxes, respectively. From the Entity and Process Models, violations of modelling rules or guidelines are detected and possible corrections offered. Organisation contextual information may also be inferred to form specific analysis from Entity and Process models. Dependencies and partially-ordered execution sequences between the (distributed) processes are derived from the Process Model. On top of this Process Model is a Procedural Model and the behaviours generated by the execution of business processes are inferred.

This formal approach is domain independent, i.e. it is generic for the applied business environment. This approach is well-suited to BSDM [24], it is also sufficiently generic to be usable for other enterprise modelling methods. This formal approach has subsequently been used in other modelling projects: AOEM (Air Operations Enterprise Modelling), AKT (Advanced Knowledge Technologies) IRC, CoAKTinG (Collaborative Advanced Knowledge Technologies in the Grid) and several commercial projects.[3] The system KBST-BM has also been extended to *KBST-EM (Knowledge Based Support Tool for Enterprise Models)* where several different types of Enterprise Models, including BSDM, have been built in the domain of (military) Air Operations [56] [18] [19] and for carrying out activities such as knowledge model creation, verification and publication [21], knowledge sharing and inconsistency checking among multiple models [20], business process modelling and workflow execution [25].

Chapters 5, 6, 7 and 8 provide a more detailed account of how such support is provided within this framework. The next section briefly describes the formal basis that enables the semantic support within the modelling framework and the system KBST-BM.

1.5 Formal Approach and *KBST-BM*

KBST-BM is based on a formal logical language, the *DEFinition language for Business Models (DefBM)*, which can be used to express the modelling knowledge of the method (BSDM) as well as its models using a lightweight formal approach. This approach helps to obtain and retain BSDM modelling

---

[3] These commercial projects were carried out for Artificial Intelligence Applications Institute (AIAI) and Centre for Intelligent Systems and Their Applications (CISA), The University of Edinburgh.

knowledge and to use this knowledge to guide the model-building process, i.e. in a plan-build-test-refine modelling development life cycle (adapted from [83] and [41]). Because it is a "lightweight" approach, the various benefits are achieved without having to cope with the overhead that is typical for "heavyweight" formal methods.

DefBM is based on an adaptation of the Process Interchange Format (PIF) [62] core class hierarchy, but uses first-order predicate logic to formalise the concepts within it. It is this formalisation that enables the overall objectives of increased model quality assurance and increased modelling productivity. Using *DefBM* it is possible to capture more model semantics and not just notation, thereby opening a wider range of automated reasoning features. Logic-based programming and case-based reasoning techniques are implemented on top of *DefBM*.

The formal representation of a business model can be stored and cross-referenced, as it has a one-to-one mapping to concepts described in the model. A simulation engine, based on the same formal representation, has been developed to explore business model dynamics by executing business processes. It provides the primary support for model validation, but it also allows the modellers to experiment with various "what-if" scenarios.

A *Case-Based Reasoning* inference engine, the *Generic Model Advisor*, has been developed to allow automatic model checking of BSDM modelling rules against new business models and to give error-correction advice, where necessary. Using case-based reasoning techniques and the formalised representation of the models, past business models can be stored in the *Generic Model Library* and be reused for comparison and analysis for when new, but similar, business circumstances are encountered.

1.6 The Use of *KBST-BM*

As mentioned in Section 1.1, two types of users are envisaged for *KBST-BM*: the BSDM modelling experts and modellers/software engineers with fundamental knowledge of BSDM – they have received training on BSDM and understand the methodology to a certain extent. Primarily the tool is intended to be used during business model building working sessions. Either the modelling expert or one of the participating engineers/managers uses *KBST-BM* to document the model as it develops, starting with the Entity Model. At various stages of the work session, the tool can be used to check that the model developed thus far is consistent and does not violate any of the modelling rules. It may also be used to get help in developing the model through the *Generic Model Advisor*. Once a stable model has been completed, the process simulation engine can be used to analyse the dynamic states of the model. This may initially be helpful in identifying remaining errors in the model, but may also later be used to investigate various "what-if" business scenarios.

KBST-BM was initially built based on a business modeller requirements; its capabilities have later on been extended where AI techniques and (generic) modelling needs meet best. To demonstrate its use, we give five different models in this book: the standard and example models provided by the method and its course material, an actual industrial model provided by a company from the automobile industry, a generic industrial model for small and medium-sized restaurants and a model for a real example of processing student marks for academic assessment. Details and rationale for why these different models have been chosen are given in Section 8.6. Most diagrams of these models, described using *KBST-BM*, are available in Appendices A, C, D and E.

1.7 Organisation of the Book

The remainder of this book is organised as follows. Chapter 2 gives a general introduction to Enterprise Modelling methods, including a more detailed summary of BSDM, as well as modelling tools currently available and their uses. Chapter 3 discusses the motivation for a formal framework from the software engineering point of view as well as from the business point of view, and the chosen approach. As the foundation technique used within the proposed support framework is logic based and, in particular, First Order Predicate Logic (FOPL), an introduction to logic is given in Chapter 4. Chapters 5, 6 and 7 give details of the three parts of the layered modelling support as described in Section 1.4. Chapter 8 describes how past model-building knowledge may be stored and reused with case-based reasoning as well as ontology and rule-based techniques. Chapter 9 gives a brief demonstration of the use of the built system, *KBST-BM*, whereas Chapter 10 evaluates the system. Chapter 11 concludes the book.

2

Background Knowledge

This chapter describes the general background that sets the context for the work that is described later. It firstly introduces an overview of various *Enterprise Modelling (EM)* methods which are currently available. It then discusses *Business Modelling* in the *Business System Development Method (BSDM)*, the method for which a formalisation is proposed in this book. An introduction to *Business Process Modelling (BPM)* follows, since some of the extensions to BSDM used in this work are based on techniques developed in the area of BPM. There is also a brief discussion of software systems and other related work.

The purpose of this chapter is not to cover all the background needed in great detail, but to set the scene for the rest of the book. More details of BSDM are introduced in subsequent chapters together with the corresponding formalisation work. We also defer a brief introduction to *Case-Based Reasoning (CBR)* techniques to Chapter 8, where the use of CBR in KBST-BM is explained.

2.1 Why Enterprise Modelling?

The global economy and market in which a business operates and competes has changed so dramatically in the last decade that traditional business management and operational methods are no longer sufficient to manage today's business. Three main driving forces are behind these changes: rapid advances of modern computing technology, intensified competition of the world market, and changing demands from consumers [85].

The advances of modern (computing) technologies have continuously provided companies with new ways to do their business: both internal and external to the organisation. Internally they provide more standardised, efficient and direct control over the working processes which are supported with organised information that is easily sharable among relevant personnel. Externally they provide a revolutionary medium to interact with customers and other businesses. It is no longer necessary to face the customer in person or to provide a shop floor. Communication with customers and other businesses, such as ordering goods and delivering services, can often be done electronically (e.g. through the Internet).

Modern computing technology and the fact that the world market has become more accessible and exploited by businesses have made the world smaller and the competition for customers more acute. It is commonplace that similar kinds of services and goods are produced by companies all over the world. The boundaries set by countries or geographical distance have become less important. Customers can now more easily shop around companies all over the world to get the best product at the best price. To gain a competitive edge, the modern enterprise is a virtual entity which consists of many sub-organisations spread across many different geographical areas each with special functionalities and business advantages. Customer demands have also changed. Customers today are more informed and aware of their power. They are no longer satisfied with mass produced indifferent goods or passive services. Instead they demand more sophisticated and individualised products and better and quicker service. This puts pressure on companies to offer high quality, diversified customer-tailored goods and services, and at the same time to offer them at a reasonable price and delivered within a relatively short time.

All of these demands require a radical change in how a business operates. It not only needs to acquire stronger financial backing to be able to compete on the global market, it also needs to create wider and intense direct contacts with (potential) customers. Some companies achieve this through the Internet, some by gaining more business allies, others by becoming larger companies through merging. More importantly, to cope with these changes, a business needs to introduce and practise brand new sets of management and organisational methods. In fact, these changes have forced many of today's businesses into fundamentally **rethinking and redesigning** their strategies and operations. Instead of adapting various ad-hoc solutions on a trial and error basis, companies seek methods which help them to analyse their businesses as a whole systematically and effectively, which in turn help them improve organisational performance. To address this problem, *Enterprise Modelling* methods have been deployed.

2.2 Enterprise Modelling Methods

A variety of enterprise modelling methods have emerged during the last decade. They provide a structural framework to help an enterprise capture the enterprise-wide knowledge which forms the basis for the targeted analysis and helps the re-shaping and re-designing of a business. A key goal of applying these methods is to seek ways to improve an organisation's effectiveness, efficiency and profitability.

Most enterprise modelling methods are influenced by more than one discipline and often overlap with each other in some aspects. It is therefore difficult to gives an absolute classification for them. Nevertheless, this information is useful in understanding the different EM methods. We therefore try to categorise them in three groups depending on their origin, the application domains that use them actively and the way that they are used in a broad sense. The three types that have been identified are:

- business process modelling,
- business system modelling, and
- organisation context modelling methods.

Business Process Modelling (BPM) methods were initially inspired by process modelling techniques which provide precise formats to capture processes that are practised in a manufacturing environment. By using these techniques, informally practised processes can be made more concrete and formal analysis of processes can be carried out. More importantly, actions and effects of these processes can be demonstrated using simulation techniques. The performance of each process can therefore be predicted and used to choose between competing processes [85].

These techniques have been adapted and extended by *business process modelling* methods to capture and standardise processes practised in a non-manufacturing environment. This has enabled the analysis and re-design of processes in the service sector leading sometimes to radical performance improvements. Representative business process modelling methods are described in the *Handbook of Organisational Processes* [70], *Workflow Reference Model* [49], *Process Interchange Format (PIF)* [62], *Process Specification Language (PSL)* [98],[1] *Integration DEFinition Language (IDEF3)* [72], *Integration DEFinition Language (IDEF0)* [80], *UML's Activity Diagram* (extension) [94], *Event-driven Process Chains (EPC)* [89] and *Petri-Nets* [87].

In addition, based on fundamental (business) process modelling concepts, new process languages are being developed to promote understanding and interoperability of process semantics over the Internet (and the *Semantic Web*).[2] These languages are characterised by their chosen representations that are based on XML, RDF or OWL.[3] They may also provide constructs to assist communication between processes over the Internet. This is a field that is relatively young and languages in flux. Examples of such languages are *Web Services Business Process Execution Language (BPEL)* [4], *ebXML Business Process Specification Schema* [64], *XML Process Definition Language (XPDL)* [117], *Business Process Modelling Language (BPML)* [5], and *OWL-based Web Service Ontology (OWL-S)* [71].

Because some of the process modelling techniques used by the above methods have a strong influence on the work of this book, Section 2.4 will describe

---

[1] PSL and PIF provide a common platform for communications between process modelling languages.

[2] Semantic Web is a (conceptual) layer on the Internet. It consists of data and applications where meaning (or semantics) is encoded to support knowledge sharing.

[3] XML, RDF and OWL are representational languages that have been designed to describe the semantics of data and to support machine processing (vs. human understanding) over the Internet.

them in more detail. As process languages that have been developed for applications over the Internet are often a use of the process modelling concepts that are already included in the fundamental methods, they will not be discussed further in this book. Readers who are interested in more details are therefore referred to the above citations for more information.

The creation of **Business System Modelling (BSM)** methods was inspired by the software engineering community where discrepancies were recognised between the vision of software engineers for the software system to be built and the true need of a business for its procured software system. The motivation for employing *BSM* methods is often to provide a clearer picture and directions for building a better IT system [53].

BSM methods provide the means to describe a business and capture its operations from a business point of view, not confined by technical, specifically Information Technology (IT), considerations. This means that for each business model there are potentially many different ways to implement a software system. Examples of BSM methods and techniques are: *BSDM*'s business modelling method [53], *ORDIT* [31], *Role Activity Diagram (RAD)* [82], *Meta-Model* by Scacchi et al. [75], *Swim-lane Diagram* by Rummler et al. [95], the *Business Modelling* approach using (extended) *UML* notation by Eriksson et al. [34] and by Rational [86], and the reengineering method developed by Jacobson [55].

Organisation Context Modelling (OCM) methods capture and tackle the wider organisational issues within a business. This includes methods which capture the functional, structural and/or cultural aspects of an organisation. It also includes methods which capture the decision making processes as well as the vocabularies and terms that are used in the business context. To promote effective organisational knowledge management and utilisation, Macintosh et al. [67] and Schreiber et al. [99] provide a framework to identify, obtain and maintain the required knowledge and skills for an organisation and the means to make use of them to achieve organisational objectives. Yu, Mylopoulos and Lesperance [118] provide graphical notations to capture business strategies and their rationale in the *Strategic Dependency* and *Strategic Rationale Models* which exploit links between business strategies and the actual operations. To promote better communication via a common language within and between organisations, ontologies have also been developed for businesses. Representative examples of work in this area are the *Enterprise Ontology* developed by Uschold, King, Moralee and Zorgios [113] [114] and *Tove* by Fox, Gruninger et al. [38]. Other OCM methods are *Activity-Based Costing (ABC)* [30], *Simulation Modelling* [100] and *Total Quality Management (TQM)* [29].

In parallel to the development of the above methods, techniques in *Business Process Reengineering (BPR)* have become a popular management tool for rapid enterprise re-structuring and re-design. Example literature includes Hammer et al. [45] and DOD [112]. Instead of using modelling methods, they provide a collection of generic business management principles coupling with software engineering methods. When deploying such BPR techniques, OCM methods, such as ABC and TQM, can also be used as a part of a BPR initiative – although they are often used in their own right. All of the above methods provide the means to record and analyse some aspects of a business environment and therefore all of them can be used to support BPR initiatives. This book focuses on one EM method, the *Business Modelling* method in BSDM, which is described below.

2.3 Introducing the Business System Development Method (BSDM)

The Business System Development Method (BSDM) is an enterprise modelling method which was introduced by IBM [53]. It provides a modelling framework to capture and analyse a business operation and requirements which helps the understanding of the complex business environment as well as providing a basis for strategic analysis and re-structuring of the organisation. It also provides a specification for the design of a software system from an early stage from the business point of view and independent of any information technology considerations which makes the developed software system more "business-need-oriented" rather than "technology-oriented". The ultimate goal for applying BSDM is to improve an organisation's performance.

BSDM consists of four activities: *Map, Need, Shape* and *Run.* BSDM firstly describes business environments, its policies, components and constraints and represents them in a *Business Model* during the *Map* activity. Given this business model, BSDM then provides the means to identify and specify requirements for a business system during the *Need* activity.[4] Based on these requirements, BSDM then allows the user to choose any suitable (software engineering) methods to design and implement the business system during the *Shape* activity.[5] The actual deployment of the system takes place during the *Run* activity. Since the most distinctive and important activity of BSDM is the *Map* or *Business Modelling* activity, this book focuses on that activity.

2.3.1 Business Modelling

The main components of a BSDM *Business Model* are *Entity Model, Process Model, Life Cycle Diagrams*, and their supplemental textual descriptions. At the beginning, business managers together with a BSDM facilitator create an *Entity Model* which captures the concepts (abstract and concrete things) in the business as *entities* and the relationships between them as *dependencies*. The Entity Model is then extended with information about the *processes* which manage these entities to form a *Process Model*. A BSDM process describes the context of a business process, the circumstances which trigger such a process

---

[4] A suitable *business system* may not necessarily involve a computing system; it can be a computing system supported by a manual process, or it can be a purely manual system depending on the business need.

[5] A suitable method for designing and implementing a business system may be a software engineering method suitable for the organisation.

and the effects of its actions. In parallel to the development of entity and process models, *Life Cycle Diagrams* are built. They describe information about
an entity's life statuses and how different processes manipulate these entities to
enable transitions between these life statuses. They also indicate the subtle relationships between processes and the operations used to carry out a particular
task.

BSDM provides step-by-step procedures for building business models with
supporting recommendations, guidelines and example models. A business model
is normally built during BSDM workshops over a few months. Conventionally,
the model is initially paper-based. The graphical information is later recorded
in a graphical tool and the textual information in a text-editing tool.[6] The
quality of the built model relies entirely on the knowledge and experiences of
the participants in the project. In Chapter 3, the kinds of automatic support
which can be provided for such informal modelling methods will be proposed.
The potential benefits of these kinds of automatic support will also be discussed.

2.3.2 BSDM Compared with SE

BSDM can be used in several different contexts, e.g. as a business analysis
tool, a management tool, or as a support method before a software engineering
method is carried out. To show the relation between BSDM and traditional
Software Engineering (SE) methods, a comparison is given below.

The part which distinguishes BSDM from a conventional software engineering method is the *Map* or *business modelling* activity which captures and
specifies business requirements that fills the gap between conventional software
engineering (SE) methods and business modelling needs during the requirements analysis phase. Figure 2.1 shows how BSDM is mapped onto conventional software engineering methods, adapted from the comparison given by
Spurr et al. [103].

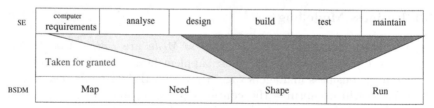

Fig. 2.1. A comparison of BSDM with conventional SE methods

The most significant difference is the lack of *business modelling* activities
in traditional SE that is the mapping area labelled with "Taken for granted".
This missing part represents the activities of identification and analysis done
in *Map*; as well as the activities of evaluating requirements for a business need

---

[6] The graphical tool was not built specifically for BSDM and does not properly
support its notation and use.

in *Need*. Since part of the BSDM *Need* activity is based on the earlier *Map* activity, much of it has no counterpart in SE.

The SE *computer requirements, analyse,* and the early stage of *design*, which include the capturing and analysis of user requirements[7] and the logical and architectural design of a software system, corresponds to the later stage of *Need* and the early stage of *Shape* activities in BSDM. Since the later part of *Need* includes user requirements capturing and analysis (for technical and operational issues), the scoping of a business system as well as the determination of main system functionalities, it corresponds to *computer requirements, analyse* and the early stage of SE *design* activities. The early activities of *Shape* include the logical and architectural design of a business system, and therefore are similar to the early activities of *design* in SE.

The rest of the SE phases, the late activities of *design* and the *build, test* and *maintain* of a software system, are mapped onto the BSDM *Shape* activity. The SE *maintenance* phase correspond to a revisit of *Shape* after the deployment of the system, and sometimes even a revisit of *Need* when necessary. Since *Run* indicates the actual use of a business system, it is not considered an SE activity, therefore it is not mapped onto any phases in the SE method.

The building of a software system is an iterative cycle that is sometimes described in a *Plan-Build-Test-Refine* spiral model. The business modelling activities can also benefit from the same principle. Chapters 3 and 9 illustrate how our automatic support can help this iterative modelling process.

2.4 Introducing Business Process Models

Although *BSDM's Business Modelling Method* is not a "process-oriented" modelling language, nor is it directly influenced by *Business Process Modelling (BPM)* methods, techniques used in BPM can be adapted and used to extend BSDM notations and can amplify and diversify the use of BSDM models. A brief background description of BPM is first given below.

Since the 1960s and 1970s, process modelling has been applied in the manufacturing sector [85]. Motor companies, such as Ford, and aerospace companies, such as McDonnell Douglas Corporation, have used process models to capture the processes of designing and manufacturing products. These process models were also simulated to allow predication and evaluation of trade-offs of current design, and used to guide the construction and selection of alternative designs.

The early acceptance of process models in manufacturing sectors was mainly due to the need for frequent change of products which requires frequent and rapid generation of production processes. It is also due to the fact that working procedures in a manufacturing environment are comparatively clearly defined and sometimes formalised. These useful characteristics initially were not obvious or were believed to be non-existent in the service sector: their procedures being more informal and open to interpretations that differed depending on the person who implemented the tasks.

---

[7] With regard to aspects of IT and the actual working procedure considerations.

This situation changed in the early 1990s when a great majority of informal business processes were found to be similar and repetitive, so they too can be captured, analysed and improved using modelling techniques similar to those of process modelling (Harrington et al. [46], Malone et al. [70]). This discovery encouraged the creation and use of process modelling methods in a more general business environment rather than in a pure manufacturing context.

Enterprise modelling methods which are evidently influenced by this are classified as *Business Process Modelling* methods in this book, as mentioned earlier in Section 2.2, which includes methods such as the *Handbook of Organisational Processes, PSL, PIF* and *IDEF3*. All of these methods treat the processes practised by an organisation as the central focus in their modelling activities. To help understand what a process is, Chris Menzel's definition is given below:

> An objective real world event, described totally as a sequence of events (activities, sub-processes) occurring over time containing certain objects having certain properties standing in certain relations. [98]

This is further elaborated by Jeffery Herrmann:

> A process can be decomposed into other processes. A process begins and ends at points in time. One can view a process from different perspectives that include different things. Objectives or drivers may be part of one perspective but not another: if included, they could be seen as instructions. [98]

The descriptions of a process given above are applicable for processes in many process models including the one described in this book. A process is, therefore, an event which may include many activities where each activity may also be itself a process that is decomposable – this is the *decomposability* property. A process often lasts for a period of time during which it may involve the manipulation of various objects as well as actors who enact or interact with it at some point of time. It is, therefore, necessary to identify and represent those temporal relations between those objects and actors and the corresponding processes in a process model. These characteristics and their representations will be discussed later in the section on PIF and in our formal work in Chapter 7.

In summary, in a (hierarchical) process model,[8] processes described at a higher level can be divided into *sub-activities*. These sub-activities carry out collaborative and complimentary activities so that together they accomplish the higher level task. These sub-activities also provide more implementation details towards the task. In addition, sub-activities may again (recursively) be divided into even smaller tasks and described in further detail. This is the concept of **process decomposition** [72] [70].

In some methods, decomposed (or sub-) processes may include *alternative processes*. Those processes are used to describe a process from different view

---

[8] There are some (and not many) process modelling methods can only describe flat level processes.

points, e.g. from a neutral observation view point, or from a particular actor's view point [72]. This concept has been extended in this book and *FBPML* [25] where **alternative processes** are competing sub-processes that achieve the same purpose as a common generic task, but may involve different working procedures, objects and/or actors. For instance, for a business to receive a payment from its customer, it may receive it using different methods, e.g. over a counter, the phone or via the Internet. Each method may involve different working procedures and objects and may also have different actors. So long as a business receives a payment, regardless of the method used, the more generic process "Receive payment from customer" is accomplished.

In parallel, in the *Process Handbook project* [70], once processes are identified for an organisation, they are classified and represented in a *class hierarchy* (of specialisation). Processes represented at a higher level of abstraction in the class hierarchy may be *specialised* into *sub-typed* processes. For instance, the more generic process of "Sell product" may be specialised into "Sell by mail order" and "Sell in retail store" where more details are added. As in object-oriented programming, processes described at the higher level of the hierarchy describe more generic tasks, and they often possess characteristics and properties that are sharable by processes described at the lower level of the class hierarchy. These common properties can be passed to or *inherited* by the more specialised processes described at the lower level of the hierarchy. This is **process specialization**.

The benefits of *process specialisation* and *decomposition* are essentially in four areas. Firstly, these reduce the work of developing a new process. By identifying an appropriate position in a class hierarchy for a new process, fundamental features of that process can be automatically inherited from existing processes which are at a higher level of the hierarchy. Secondly, they can decrease the work for maintenance: any error only needs to be corrected once at the highest level and all of the more specialised processes are corrected. Thirdly, since all similar processes are grouped together, it is easier to evaluate the trade-offs and select between them. Lastly, by providing a taxonomic structure, process allocation, searching, combining and creating of new processes can be done more systematically and efficiently. This combined use of *process decomposition* and *specialisation* was first identified in a process modelling framework [109][9] and used in the *Process Handbook Project* and was accepted and used in many later developed modelling methods.

In this book, the concept of *process specialisation* has been used to show how BSDM's business processes can be classified and reused by incorporating them as a part of our *Inheritance Class Hierarchy* and will be introduced in more detail in Chapter 5. The concept of *process decomposition* has also been adapted and used in our devised *Procedural Model* which will be described in Chapter 7. By deploying these concepts, our formal architecture is able to enjoy many of the above benefits, such as inheriting properties from a more general process to a more specialised one, ease of maintenance, comparison

---

[9] Through its use in hierarchical planning techniques in AI dates from the mid 1970.

and manipulation of processes. Temporal and other constraints which limit the execution of a task are also included in a process model to describe and prescribe the implementation of the actual working practice. This information may be encoded using dependencies and junctions between processes as well as attributes of processes that will be demonstrated in Chapter 7.

Although it can be used to capture (business) processes, the main purpose of the *Process Interchange Format (PIF)* is to provide a common language that enables different process models to communicate and exchange information through them. PIF identifies a set of concepts that are fundamental to process modelling and is commonly used in many different process models. Based on these concepts, PIF gives precise descriptions for each concept and defines the relationships between them. Formats based on a *frame structure* are also provided by PIF to capture and store information of these concepts – this set of fundamental concepts for process modelling is called *PIF's core*. Specialised processes that are captured in other process modelling languages which cannot be described using only PIF's core may be represented using an extension format that is described in *PIF's Partially Shared View*.

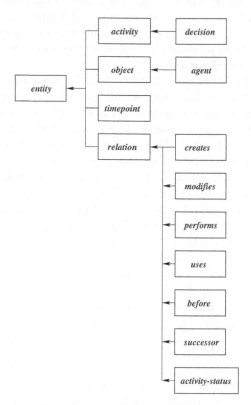

Fig. 2.2. The PIF class hierarchy

Figure 2.2 shows the PIF class hierarchy [62]. Modelling concepts such as *entity, activity, object, agent* and the notion of *time* are captured as PIF classes in the hierarchy. Everything in PIF is a subclass of the root class *entity*. There are four subclasses of *entity: activity, object, timepoint* and *relation.* Each subclass may also have its own subclasses. A subclass is indicated by an outgoing arrow from itself to the corresponding superclass. This relationship between the subclass and the superclass is a *specialisation* relationship. For instance, in PIF, *decision* (making) is a special type of *activity,* and *before* describes a particular kind of (temporal) *relation.*

The benefits of allocating all modelling concepts in a PIF class hierarchy with the property of *inheritance* is similar to that of the *Process Handbook Project.* The conceptual entities are clearly identified and relationships between them specified. New concepts can be added to the hierarchy and fundamental properties can be automatically inherited from their superclasses. This speeds up the process of creating, manipulating and evaluating process modelling concepts.

In addition to the concept of *process specialisation,* the PIF class hierarchy has also been adapted in our formal work to suit BSDM's business modelling method, which enables our work to enjoy all of the above benefits of PIF. Moreover, because we have taken an approach similar to PIF, we enabled BSDM's business models to more easily communicate with any other process languages communicating through PIF. It also enables BSDM models to be translated to other process languages through PIF which already is linked to many other languages.

2.5 Review of Existing Enterprise Modelling Tools

The field of enterprise modelling, especially business process modelling and workflow, is a very active area during the past five years in which new research as well as commercial tools have been built rapidly. This section therefore is not intended to provide a comprehensive review, but discusses example tools currently available and their characteristics. From what has been collected, most modelling tools provide quality related support for some aspects of modelling activities. Based on their functions, such tools are divided into two categories.

The first category of tools provide primarily capturing and report-generating functions for specific modelling methods. Examples of such tools are *RBPL* [108] which provides its own business process modelling language as well as the corresponding documentation facilities; Paradigm Plus [84] supports various modelling methods, such as *Booch* [10], *OMT* [93] and *UML* [11], and exporting facilities for these methods; *BP WIN* [66] provides drawing and report-generation facilities for IDEF0 [80] and *Data Flow Diagrams (DFD); AI0 Win* [60] supports the drawing and documentation of *IDEF0* models and can export its details to other tools, such as *ProSim* [60]; *Win A&D* (or *Mac A&D*) [35] provides documentation and reporting facilities for various modelling languages, such as the *Class Model, Entity Relational* data model and *Data Flow Dia-*

grams; another relevant business process modelling tool is *Procedural Builder* [7] developed by AIAI which allows the user to build an adapted version of *IDEF3* models [72] and can communicate with the *Enterprise Toolset* that is supported by knowledge described in the *Enterprise Ontology* [6].

In addition to providing documentation and report-generation functions, the second category of tools also provide simulation (and/or process execution) facilities for the described models. For example, *ProSim/ProCap* can simulate its own processes and can import processes that have been drawn using other tools, e.g. *AIO Win* and *Visio* [76]. *Simprocess* [17] is an object-oriented process modelling and analysis tool based on its own simulation language *Simscript* for analysing complex, dynamic systems. *BPSimulator* [110] is a discrete event simulation tool which simulates business processes using statistical simulation methods. *iThink* [47] is a tool for simulating system dynamic models – these system dynamic models were initially designed to simulate physical systems, e.g. a fluid system – this technology has been used by *iThink* to model the flow of a business environment. ARIS Toolset [54] provides its own modelling language which supports *Activity-Based Costing (ABC)* and *Balanced Score Card (BSC)* to record and analyse a business performance. Yu, Mylopoulos and Lesperance [118] capture the actors, actors' goals and dependencies between them in a business operation in *Strategic Dependency Models* and *Strategic Rationale Models* which allow simulation of business processes to be carried out and opportunities, vulnerabilities and patterns of dependencies to be explored. SAP R/3 [97] offers a client/server architecture and distributed open system solution whose in-house business processes are under-pinned by the modelling language *EPC (Event-driven Process Chain)*. Other recent work are to provide a workflow system that supports business process definitions and execution, e.g. Oracle Workflow [81] and Staffware [104].

The simulation support given by the tools in the second category is largely of the type that is usually found in performance studies. It allows the user to specify type and frequency of business processes and the company resources required by these processes. Running such simulations can help identify bottlenecks in the company's operations, but also means that the user has to specify numerous input parameters.

In general, there is very little, if any, exploitation of the rich contextual knowledge that is implicit in the models that have been captured through the corresponding documentation features of the above tools. One reason for this is that there is no underlying mechanism to allow such knowledge to be built into and used by these tools. Consequently, they are unable to provide modelling support beyond that based on a model syntax.

Together, KBST-BM and GMA support the basic modelling activities such as drawing, documenting, navigating, summarising and reporting, but they also provide support related to model semantics, such as consistency checking, error-correction advice-giving, alternative visualisation of the model (some based on derived information), simulation of processes, model building and refining guidance (by referring to and comparing with standard or existing models), model verification and validation, and model reuse. In particular, much of the model quality checking work can be automated to such an extent to make it feasible and effective to do so in an applied context.[10] More details about KBST-BM and GMA are given in Chapter 5, 6, 7, 8 and 9.

2.6 Exercises

1. What is an Enterprise Modelling method? Why Enterprise Modelling?
2. What are the different types of Enterprise Modelling (EM) methods? Explain BSDM's relation with EM.
3. What is the relationship between BSDM and generic software development methods in Software Engineering? Can BSDM be useful as a part of software development processes?
4. What are the main concepts in a (business) process model?
5. Describe the process interchange language of PIF, and discuss whether it is useful to have such a language.

---

[10] KBST-BM and its successor KBST-EM have been used in research projects AOEM [56], AKT [1] and AIAI commercial projects.

3

Problems and Overview of Approach

3.1 Introduction

Enterprise Modelling Methods offer a structure and means to describe and analyse a problem domain (the business) as well as tools for constructing solutions for problems. While these methods are invaluable in problem understanding, context analysing and diagnosis, they are also helpful for software system development by providing a framework to understand the organisation in which the software system will be deployed. On the other hand, the process of quality assurance of the products from these methods, which often is paper-based, can benefit from innovation from the software engineering community. In this chapter, we describe a framework which has been inspired by the software system development cycle and an approach that uses formal methods to provide the means of quality assurance for these informal enterprise modelling methods.

3.2 Business Model and Software Engineering

3.2.1 Software Systems Development Cycle

Computer systems are used extensively either to stay competitive or to gain advantages over rival companies. The demand for appropriate software is acute. Software systems are involved in companies' operations at many levels and perform ever more complicated tasks. Furthermore, due to the globalisation of economies and the need to react to market changes quickly, the business organisations in which software systems are deployed are not only more complex but also more dynamic than ever before. This leads to constant requirement changes during system development as well as deployment stages. The challenges to software engineers to develop systems that are timely and appropriate have thus increased tremendously over the last decade.

To ensure appropriate software systems are built, there is real pressure on software developers to find ways of producing high quality software quickly. In the early days, researchers in this area sought to employ various disciplinary procedures in software creation. Royce [92] in 1970 first presented "the waterfall model" which captures a framework for software system development. Figure 3.1 shows the waterfall model proposed by Royce. This model was later seen to be relatively inflexible as software development stages can only traverse between neighbouring stages. The U.S. Department of Defence relaxed those constraints and adopted and created their own version [111]. A more recent variation of the model was proposed by Alan M. Davis in 1993 [27]; see Figure 3.2.

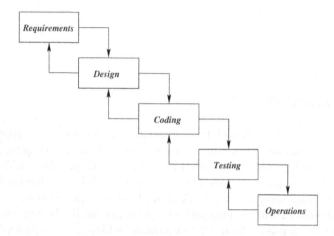

Fig. 3.1. Royce's waterfall model

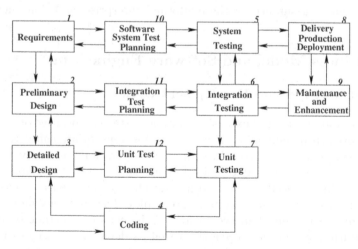

Fig. 3.2. Alan Davis's software system development model

In both Figures 3.1 and 3.2, boxes represent stages of activities which are carried out during the life cycle of a software system's development and deployment. Arrows show the workflow between these stages. When comparing these two models, although Alan's model elaborates somewhat more on the initial stages, both include stages of requirements, design, coding, testing and software deployment. Alan, however, particularly stresses planning and testing activities for **all** stages, as shown in boxes 10, 11, 12, 5, 6 and 7 in Figure 3.2. It is implied by Alan's model that a key factor in producing an appropriate software system is to test it carefully at each stage. These testing activities can also be seen as the verification and validation process of the deliverables at each stage.

Agreeing with the assessment that testing is essential, other scholars offer theoretical and practical techniques in this area. For example, Perry offers a structured method for software testing [83], Friedman and Voas offer techniques in assessing software reliability and safety [41], and Voas and McGraw propose fault injection techniques to discover errors in software [115]. All of these techniques provide guidance and frameworks for ensuring the quality of the built software systems, once what is required from the system has been given. However, in spite of such techniques being available and practised, many software systems still do **not** fit the intended organisations.

3.2.2 Software System Seeks Real Goal

While testing is widely recognised as an important technique to uncover software errors, more and more evidences indicate that most software errors are design errors which in general happen at the early stages of a software development cycle; in fact at the stages of software specification or requirements gathering. Jackson has identified this problem:

> Requirements engineering is about the satisfaction of goals. But goals by themselves do not make a good starting point for requirements engineering. To see why, consider a project to develop a computer-controlled turnstile guarding the entrance to a zoo ... the real goal is to ensure the profitability of the zoo. [119]

Only when one discovers the real goals for developing a software system can one have a chance to develop the "correct" and "appropriate" software application for that business. Unfortunately, it is not always straightforward to understand these goals. To make matters worse, the business in which a software system is to be used may not have clearly defined goals or they may be changing too frequently. Under such circumstances, developing an application to support a company's goals becomes a very difficult task indeed.

Recognising this shortcoming, one approach for discovering these goals is firstly to understand the business context and where necessary to help the business to clarify and formulate its goals. Only then will the software engineers be able to identify and develop appropriate software solutions. To promote a better understanding of the domain of a business, several enterprise methods, including business modelling methods, have been used in the past **prior** to the stage of user requirements elicitation and specifications for a software system,

that is described as "requirements" in Figure 3.2. Although, the use of enterprise modelling methods is not limited to help build sound software systems, it
remains a good motivation for a business to use them prior to the standard software system development process. A brief description of *Enterprise Modelling
Methods* is therefore given in the next section.

3.3 Support for Enterprise Modelling Methods

3.3.1 Problems with Enterprise Modelling Methods

As mentioned in Chapter 2, a variety of enterprise modelling methods have
emerged. For example, there are methods for business modelling: BSDM [53];
process modelling: PIF [62], Malone et al. [70], PSL [98]; enterprise modelling: IDEF [73]; organisational modelling: ORDIT [32] , ISO standard 13407
[37], Rummler-Brache [95]; business process reengineering: Hammer [45], DOD
[111] [112]; management of enterprise knowledge: Fraser and Macintosh [40],
Hollingsworth [49] and ontological work: enterprise ontology [114] and Tove
[38].

   Object-oriented technologies have also been used to depict a business and its
processes: for example, the *activity diagrams* in UML [11], the *Business Models*
offered by *Rational Rose* [86] [108], methods by Jacobson [55] and using UML
for business modelling by Eriksson and Penker [34]. By providing a structural
framework, these methods help an enterprise to capture its enterprise-wide
knowledge which forms the basis for targeted analysis and helps the re-shaping
and re-designing of a business (which normally involves the use of advanced
electronic and computing technologies). These methods also provide a neutral
forum where people of different disciplines can communicate with each other.
The goals of applying these methods are to seek ways to improve an organisation's effectiveness, efficiency and profitability.

   The benefits of a successful application of these modelling methods can
be tremendous for an enterprise. For example, according to a report by the
U.S. Department of Defence in 1997, the application of a business process
reengineering project, leading to a combined utilisation of modernised business
practice and computing technology in its organisation, has led to 1.6 billion
USD in savings in inventory management in 5 years (1993 to 1997) [112]. There
are also other success stories, for example those cases documented in a survey
published by the BPR Online Learning Center [14] in which over 200 companies
across the world have been included; some other success stories are included
in Berztiss' book [9]. The potential benefits offered by each of these enterprise
modelling methods have attracted increasing attention from both industry and
researchers. However, not all applications of these methods have been equally
successful.

   One key factor in the successful application of these methods is the quality
of the produced model, i.e. to ensure that the produced model is the right
one for the organisation. However, it is hard to determine the quality of the

produced model, and often its suitability and applicability are not known until it is actually put into action. There are several problems in ensuring the quality of the produced model, some of which are discussed below.

- *Availability of expertise:* A large enterprise today is a virtual entity which consists of many sub-organisations distributed across different geographical areas, each possessing different expertise. Hence, it may not be possible to have all of the persons with the right expertise (who are normally senior and/or middle-level managers) available for model development. Furthermore, the required expertise may change as companies have to react – adapting their goals and processes – to today's fast-changing global economies.

- *Lack of a comprehensive evaluation method:* Most of the enterprise modelling methods mentioned above provide only semantics for their notations, others provide a procedural description of how to carry out the modelling tasks and some measurement criteria for how well the model fits reality. However, none of them supports a comprehensive and systematic approach with respect to determining the correctness and completeness of a model, both methodology-wise and enterprise-wise. This is not surprising, because guaranteeing the correctness and completeness of enterprise-wide knowledge is extremely difficult. It requires a complete understanding of the enterprise knowledge for the present and in some methods also for its future, that is the very knowledge to be captured with the help of the modelling method in the first place. Guaranteeing correctness and completeness is also complicated by the fact that in order to determine whether a business has been represented correctly and fully using a particular method requires knowledge of the method as well as the business, and few people possess both.

- *Informal or semi-formal modelling context:* The first step in checking whether a model is appropriate for its purpose is to understand the content that a model describes. Many of these enterprise modelling methods are informal methods, some of them are semi-formal and include pre-defined diagrammatic symbols supplemented with natural language text. It is generally difficult or impossible to ensure the correctness and consistency of informal and semi-formal methods, because the checking normally involves a person reading and checking all of the details of the model which for a complete real industrial-sized model is an impossible task.

- *Time pressure:* Very few projects can enjoy the luxury of not having to deal with strict time constraints. When trying to keep the organisation in business and gain a competitive edge over its rivals, time is a critical factor. It is therefore important to make effective use of all of the resources allocated. In the model-building context this means that there is a need to provide an efficient and effective way to maximise the productivity of the modellers in building a model, verifying and validating it, and finding and correcting inadequacies in the model. One way to attempt this is by providing an appropriate software support system. Some such software tools have been offered, but most of them concentrate on model-building, storage and report generation, without support for the important aspect of model validation. This generally means that there is not enough time to carry out the tedious task of validating a model by hand.

- *Lack of modelling support facilities:* An enterprise-sized model is often domain-specific, knowledge-rich and rather complex. In addition, the modellers need to remember the technical details of the method. Again, it needs to be remembered that few people posses good knowledge of both. To achieve an efficient and effective modelling process, a proper (software) tool should ideally support a knowledge base for the specific business domain as well as direct support for the method.

- *Lack of efficient and effective means of knowledge transfer:* As mentioned above, lack of availability of expertise can be a problem. A related issue is the lack of efficient and effective knowledge transfer. Enterprise modelling is intended to help this transfer, but it requires a sufficiently wide use of a particular method so people can communicate through it. Most methods do not have wide usage at this stage and would require additional training of staff. This may be difficult due to internal resistance in the organisation. Furthermore, a complete enterprise model may be too complicated for un-aided human comprehension. A tool which eases the communication (using a particular method) between people could thus be helpful in the transfer of knowledge.

- *Dynamic aspects of a model are complex:* An enterprise modelling method normally captures the static structure of the targeted domain, but it often implies and/or prescribes the actual activities to be carried out, e.g. activities to be carried out in a business process. As many of these dynamic activities may be happening concurrently and interacting with each other, to understand the impact of them becomes in general a task too complex for un-aided human reasoning. Therefore, it is important that these processes can be simulated within the model with the help of a software tool to demonstrate and/or predict their behaviour, to help people understand their implications and restrictions.

> Change is inevitable, except from a vending machine. [1]

To cope with the changes of today's business world caused by the advances of electronic and computing technologies, business organisations must adjust and/or re-shape themselves to thrive in the new Post-Industrial Era.[2] The potentially great rewards offered by applying enterprise modelling methods have encouraged many businesses to use them. Unfortunately, as noted above, these methods have problems. One particular problem is to determine and assure the quality of the model.

In this book, we describe our attempt to provide automatic support in assisting modellers, particularly in providing a "testing" facility for those enterprise modelling methods. We focus on one particular method: the Business System Development Method (BSDM). Before discussing our approach about

---

[1] This is a quote from DOD [112], the original author is unknown.
[2] The term "Post-Industrial Era" is taken from [9].

how to tackle the problems, we look into the BSDM method and identify areas where assistance can be provided to help modelling activities.

3.3.2 BSDM's Business Modelling

The Business System Development Method (BSDM) is an Enterprise Modelling Method. It has been promoted and practised by IBM, as well as its clients, as an effective way to capture a business' static and dynamic environment and its constraints. Furthermore, it is designed to fill the gap between business and IT systems requirements – an area where conventional software engineering methods appear inadequate [23] [51]. BSDM's business modelling acts as a communication tool between software engineers and businessmen who can now describe a complex business environment using only simple notation. This simplicity fosters time efficiency when developing models.

However, it is not sufficient from the point of view of software system development, since BSDM's business modelling uses a single notation (entity) to capture anything that a business would want to manage. It also uses a single notation (dependency) to represent every kind of relationships within a business. This overloading of semantics on a few symbols results in confusion when one wants to use a business model as the basis for constructing software systems, since there is not a direct translation from a BSDM model to an existing requirements engineering model.

Various modelling rules are given by BSDM which describe constraints on the model that is built during the business modelling activity. Some of these model rules are obvious, but others are not. A violation of model rules can lead to an incorrectly structured model. It is, therefore, necessary that these model rules are described explicitly and unambiguously. There are also guidelines recommended by BSDM; these are valid for most business cases, but they are not compulsory to allow flexibility for special circumstances. It is desirable to express these modelling guidelines explicitly and unambiguously.

Since a part of the business model is written in natural language which leads to difficulties for automatic correctness and consistency checking (due to the ambiguities inherent in natural languages), it is, therefore, important to describe business models in a way that is executable and can be used as a basis for model validation.

3.3.3 Providing a Quality Assurance Life Cycle

Most issues mentioned above are rooted in the same basic problem: business models are usually described informally. As is the case for any modelling activity, creating a model is only the first step in a larger cycle. Once a model has been designed, to ensure its quality, it needs to be verified and validated. In our context, *verification* is the process of checking that no modelling rules have been violated. *Validation* is the process of confirming that the model is a true representation of the real world.[3] The lack of a formal representation

---

[3] Or an intended representation, if the modelled domain is in the future.

in methods like BSDM makes verification of a business model a tedious and error prone task. To validate a model, the modeller must as a minimum be able to work through the execution of typical scenarios for business processes and then compare these with the real world. As mentioned earlier for all but very simple business models, this is not achievable through a simple paper and pencil exercise and, hence, detailed validation has not, hitherto, been possible.

Our aim therefore is not to improve the method itself, but help to improve the quality of its products. One may provide support that is closely tied in with the method so that the original practices are not disturbed and no unnecessary unfamiliarities are introduced to the user. It is important not to disturb the use of the original method, as this may cause unwanted distortions in the method and lead to resistance from the practitioners to use the formal method. *The objective of our work is therefore to provide support not only for creating models, but also for automating, as far as possible, the verification and validation of business models in a way that is compliant with the method.* By doing so, we provide the means to complete the modelling cycle, i.e. the modeller can go through several iterations of design, verification and validation until a satisfactory business model has been produced. This iterative machine-aided modelling development cycle is illustrated in Figure 3.3.[4]

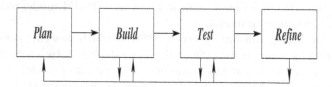

Fig. 3.3. The plan-build-test-refine model development cycle

In formalising BSDM business modelling, the objective is not only to develop an appropriate formal representation of a model, but also to take advantage of the **knowledge** of BSDM about how to build such models and the existing set of rules about how to evaluate the quality of them. Furthermore, the formal representation of a BSDM business model must be able to capture not only the static but also the dynamic aspects of the model.

Although in conventional BSDM the various states of the model can be captured, there is no explicit way of describing how a process is carried out and how entities are manipulated by a process. To enable the execution of a business model, i.e. to simulate the execution of business processes, this knowledge of how to carry out a process is essential. An additional objective was, therefore, the ability to describe and simulate the dynamic aspects of the models; because of this, an explicit representation of time had to be introduced into the formalism. This was not included in the original BSDM model.

---

[4] This verification cycle is small compared with Alan Davis's model in Figure 3.2, as it describes activities in the "Requirements" stage (box 1) and stages before that, i.e. business description and organisation requirements.

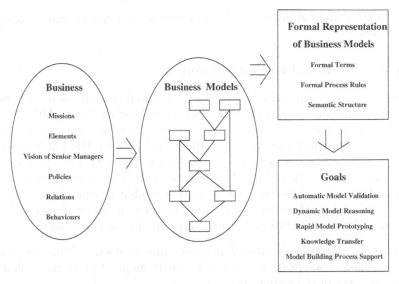

Fig. 3.4. Overview of approach and goals of the research

A formal framework was developed for describing a business model by representing components in the business model in formal terms, and rules written originally in natural language in the BSDM manuals were interpreted as formal process rules. A semantic structure was also devised which classifies and interconnects the many different notations used in business models. An overview of the approach and goals of this work is outlined in Figure 3.4.

The leftmost oval represents a business environment. Items inside this oval are elements and characters of a business which are captured in a business model. The oval in the middle of the figure represents business models which capture the business environment described in the left oval. The boxes in this business model are entities or things in a business, the links between these boxes represent relationships or constraints between these things. The top right box shows how business models are formulated, it indicates the use of logical terms and semantic structures to describe business models. The lower right box itemises the goals that are the aim of this work. The list below gives a somewhat more comprehensive list of these goals:

- to classify and distinguish model primitives;
- to clarify ambiguous model rules;
- to enable automatic model checking;
- to provide automatic/semi-automatic reasoning on dynamic business models;
- to encourage sharing of model-building knowledge;
- to support rapid model prototyping;
- to establish a basis for business strategic planning;
- to bridge business models and software engineering methods;

- to build a foundation towards rapid system generation that is based on business goals.

3.3.4 A Logic-Based Formal Method

As pointed out earlier, formal methods can be used to help assure the quality of informal and/or semi-formal enterprise modelling methods. Although it is desirable to provide these benefits, we do not claim that we can provide all of these benefits, since there is still a great gap between the informal and/or semi-formal enterprise modelling methods (or the description of a problem) and the formal representation of all of its semantics. It is our aim to try to narrow this gap. Fuchs and Robertson, advocators of applying formal logical methods in support of informal modelling methods, pointed out three areas which often cause difficulties in the process of formalisation [43], as given below.

- Concepts, notations, standard practices and problem solving methods in the domain of application may not be easily mapped to, or reconciled with the concepts of the formal method.
- Resistance comes from application specialists in applying a new formal method, other than the one they are already familiar with. This is the case if they have only dealt with informal or semi-formal methods in the past.
- A premature mapping from concepts in the domain of application to the domain of computational logic, caused by incomplete knowledge of the domain of application.

The quality of the built model may be weakened by any of these problems. More importantly, the application of the formal method must not compromise the working practice of the domain experts or distort the initial design. The approach that we have taken is to understand the modelling concepts in BSDM and the relationships between them. We also take a close look at the modelling process in building a BSDM model. The formal method proposed here is intended to be close to and supportive of the basic concepts as well as the normal pattern of using BSDM. This is, in general, a good principle when providing a formal language and/or computational support for any modelling method. This should therefore reduce the unfamiliarity problem and promote acceptance of the new approach. The formal method should also manage the transition from targeted concepts in BSDM to our formal method. Finally, we aim to provide an executable formal representational language.[5]

3.3.5 Lightweight Logical Method

> To be formal or not to be formal is not the question - how formal is.[6]

---

[5] A further publication by Fuchs [42] may be of interest to the reader wanting more details on why it is preferable to have specifications that are executable.

[6] This is modified from one of the well-known quotes of Shakespeare.

Formal logical methods, sometimes referred to as "heavyweight" logical methods, in spite of being able to help achieve many of the benefits that we have described in the previous sections, are rarely practised in the context of enterprise modelling. One major consideration is the low cost-effectiveness implied in applying these formal methods. The application of a "heavyweight" formal method normally requires lengthy involvement of the domain experts concerned, which means high costs for the organisation. The end product, the formal theory and description, is often sophisticated and complicated that it is not easily understood. As a result, the end product cannot easily be put in good use.

To address these setbacks, *lightweight formal logical methods* have been advocated by a group of scholars, Bowen [13] [12], Robertson and Agusti [90] and Saiedian [96]. In contrast to "heavyweight" formal methods, "lightweight" formal theories usually focus on a small number of central issues, their primitives are plainly stated and can be understood intuitively. Their aim is to provide easier access to the models for the user.

The formal method that we have devised and deployed for BSDM is also lightweight. One major concern has been pragmatics. We wanted to devise a formal language which uses logical terms to represent concepts of the business model that can be understood intuitively.[7] Like many other enterprise modelling methods, quality assurance is a major problem for business modelling methods. To provide the facility of quality assurance, a framework has been devised which uses this formal language as a foundation to provide model verification and validation facilities and various other model building support. This book describes the formal language and the built tool, *KBST-BM*, which provides various forms of automated support based on this formal language.

3.3.6 A Layered Framework

IBM's *Business System Development Method (BSDM)* is an informal method for developing business models. As described in Section 2.1, initially a BSDM business model consists of an *Entity Model*, which is later extended to a *Process Model*, both of which are specified in a semi-formal way using diagrams and English text. On top of the Entity and Process Model familiar to conventional BSDM practitioners, we introduce another layer, the *Procedural Model* which extends the Process Model. As previously mentioned, Figure 1.1 illustrates our layered modelling approach. It points out problems which can occur during entity and Process Modelling activities. It also shows which domain knowledge has been formalised for each layer and what kind of information can be inferred through the formalisation process.

An Entity Model describes the key components of a business' operation, e.g. persons, business partners, products, product information, activities and relationships. The constituent elements of a business are captured and denoted

---

[7] This formalism is also generic, as similar principles has been used to create formal representations for many other different enterprise models [18] [20] [21] [25].

as *entities* with dependencies placed between each entity and those others on which it relies for its existence. A Process Model is a collection of business processes crucial to the business' operation. The context of a business process is described, including the involved entities, the circumstances that trigger a process and the consequences of its actions. The Procedural Model was devised on top of BSDM's Entity and Process Model to enable the logical sequences of action for processes to be specified and recorded, thus enabling simulation of business processes in a model.

Problems that can occur while building an Entity Model include methodical issues, application domain related methodical issues, and pure application domain issues. For instance, circular dependency is generally prohibited in many modelling practices, while the fact that an Entity Model should generally only have four or fewer layers is a methodical as well as an application domain issue. Although in general the BSDM method recommends up to four layers in an entity model, it allows exceptions due to specific domain requirements. Since this is an application-dependent issue, in practice its treatment is more flexible [51]. Examples of purely domain-dependent issues are the actual construction of a model or the acceptable boundary of defining an entity. Domain-dependent problems vary between different industries, and are therefore not covered in this book. The generic modelling principles that are considered and applied in all modelling exercises are captured and formalised as rules.

The domain knowledge for each layer can be divided into two types: model components and rules, which are shown in Figure 1.1 as ellipses and rectangles, respectively. From the Entity and Process Models, any violations of modelling rules or guidelines and possible corrections can be inferred. From the Procedural Model, the state transitions of the model caused by the execution of business processes can be inferred. A more detailed description of these layers is given in the following sections and chapters.

3.3.7 Modelling Support Overview of KBST-BM

The support tool, KBST-BM, was built to provide automatic support for BSDM's business modelling activities. Figure 3.5 gives an overview of how KBST-BM can be used to help modellers in developing BSDM's business models. At the beginning the user creates a business model that is described using BSDM notation. From the model, a formal representation is derived, one for the static and one for the dynamic aspects of the model, respectively. In addition, general as well as user-defined modelling rules are formalised. The general rules are method-derived Entity and Process Model rules and guidelines that are considered fixed and hence require no user input. The user-defined rules are domain-specific attributes and business rules created with the help of input from the user.(At this stage, the Procedural Model is not yet needed.)

The formal representation of the model as well as the rules provide the input to a reasoning engine which analyses the business model. An interactive diagnosis report is produced which describes any violation of modelling rules and makes recommendations for how the model can be improved. The user

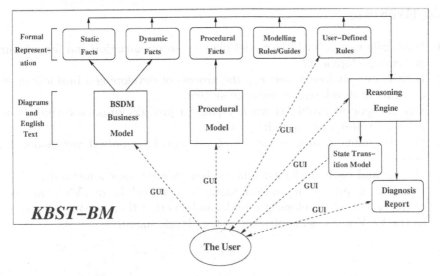

Fig. 3.5. An overview of modelling support by KBST-BM

may modify the business model accordingly and start the next iteration of this process. The cycle is repeated until no further errors and recommendations are produced, or when the user decides not to incorporate any more of the given recommendations.[8] Once no more modelling rule violations are reported by the reasoning engine, verification of the model is complete.

Before the user can simulate and therefore validate the model, they must create the Procedural Model, which can then be formalised and fed into the reasoning engine. During simulation of the model the user interacts directly with the reasoning engine – telling it which process to execute from which starting state. The reasoning engine maintains a state transition model and information about the various states, which the user can compare with the effects of business processes in the real world. If the user decides that some changes in the business model are necessary, these changes must be formalised and then again input to the reasoning engine.

Details of the underlying formal language, *DefBM*, for KBST-BM are introduced and examples illustrated in the following chapters. Before more advanced features are introduced, Chapter 4 gives an introduction to Logic and uses *Prolog* as an example language for representation and programming language to carry out computational and reasoning tasks. Prolog is a natural choice of computing language to provide the intelligent support mentioned in this book, although other languages could be employed for the same purpose. Understanding logic is the basis for mastering all such languages.

---

[8] Although the system does not impose its recommendations on the user, we assume the user would not want to leave any errors in his/her model. This support is provided based on both complete as well as partial information, it is therefore more flexible in design and is suitable for gradual model development.

3.4 Exercises

1. What role may a business model play for an organisation and for software system development?
2. Is there any similarity between the process of developing a business model and that of developing a software system?
3. Discuss general problems when trying to provide automatic support for informal Enterprise Modelling methods.
4. Why is quality assurance for a business model (or indeed any model) important?
5. Discuss and compare lightweight vs. heavyweight logical methods.
6. Describe the process and role of verification and validation (V&V) as a part of the process of developing a model and whether there are any similarities to the V&V process of software system development.

4

Logic

4.1 Introduction

This chapter gives a brief introduction to logic, in particularly, First Order Predicate Logic. It also illustrates how informal domain knowledge may be described using logical languages. This will provide a foundation for the reader to understand the principles and reasoning techniques that are used in the following chapters.

Logic appears under various guises in most branches of Artificial Intelligence (AI), either as a knowledge representation language; as a programming language; or as a tool for analysing AI programs. This chapter connects on its use as a knowledge representation language. It is not intended as a general purpose logic text, nor as a comprehensive guide to the use of logic in the AI community but provides a preliminary sketch of the basic principles, relying primarily on example and informal argument to justify each technique. For more comprehensive readings on logic and AI representation techniques, the reader may be interested in additional literatures to compliment the description here, e.g. [16] [102].

Logic is particularly appealing as a means of representing knowledge because it has several important characteristics:

- It is expressive, within limits. In other words we can use it to make a wide variety of different statements.
- It has a clearly defined semantics. That is, the meaning of the notation is unambiguous and well understood.
- It provides sound rules of inference. This means that given some set of true statements in logic and sound proof rules we can always guarantee that any information inferred from those statements will also be true – i.e. we can trust the inference mechanisms.

The word "logic" has been used as if it referred to a single notation but there are a multitude of different varieties of logic and also different approaches to describing each variety. We have chosen to concentrate on the two most common varieties: Propositional Logic (PL) (Section 4.2) and First Order Predicate

Logic (FOPL) (Section 4.3). Having introduced these notations we demonstrate how they may be used to perform proofs in two different styles: using Natural Deduction (Section 4.4) and Resolution (Section 4.5). This forms a basis for introducing Prolog – a successful application of logic as a programming language (Section 4.6). We conclude, in Section 4.7, by sounding a note of warning to those with the idea that logic provides the last word on knowledge representation. Despite its fine qualities it *is* limited in application and, like any tool, can be counterproductive if misused.

4.2 Propositional Logic

4.2.1 The Notation: Well-Formed Formulae

Theorem 4.1. *A proposition is an atomic statement which is either true or false.*

By "atomic statement" in Theorem 4.1 we mean that the statement is an indivisible unit of information, containing no internal structure. The choice about which statements are atomic in a given formula is up to the person who writes that formula, although there are some rough guidelines (see Section 4.2.3). For example, the following are all valid, atomic propositions:

- it_is_raining.
- dave_gets_wet.
- tweety_is_a_bird.

The important point about these sorts of statement is that, although we can see that there is a good deal of structure within each of them, from the point of view of the logic they are just atomic names. In Section 4.3 we introduce a notation for representing more explicitly the structure of propositions.

Theorem 4.2. *A truth-functional connective is a symbol which is used to build complex formulae from simpler ones. The standard connectives of the Propositional Logic are: and, or, not, → (signifying implication), and ↔ (denoting equivalence).*

The term "truth-functional connective" is used because these symbols connect other formulae and they can be evaluated to be either true or false, depending on the truth or falsity of the formulae which they connect. For example, the *not* connective is attached to a single formula and any formula to which *not* is applied will be false whenever the formula is true and true whenever the formula is false. This means that if we apply *not* to the proposition *it_is_raining* and we know that *it_is_raining* is true, then the statement *not(it_is_raining)* is false. Conversely, if the proposition *it_is_raining* is false then *not(it_is_raining)* is true.

Theorem 4.3. *A well-formed formula in the Propositional Logic is defined according to the following rules:*

1. A proposition is a formula.

2. If P and Q are formulae, then the following are also formulae:

- *not P*
- *not Q*
- *P and Q*
- *P or Q*
- *P → Q*
- *P ↔ Q*

3. Only expressions using rules 1 and 2 are formulae.

Note that different authors may use different symbols to represent the same truth-functional connective. For example: '*not*' is often written as '¬'; '*and*' as '&' and '∧'; and '*or*' as '∨'. These are merely differences in notation and we shall continue to use the English names for illustration in this chapter given in Theorem 4.3 above.

4.2.2 Analysing the Structure of Formulae in Propositional Logic

Formulae in the Propositional Logic can be built by first joining together atomic propositions using one or more truth-functional connectives and then applying the same procedure to construct yet more complex formulae from these components. In this way, "nested" formulae containing subformulae are obtained. When writing such formulae it is essential to show precisely which parts are nested inside others. For example, the formula:

it_is_raininganddave_is_outside → dave_gets_wet

is constructed out of the conjunction *it_is_raining and dave_is_outside*, connected by the implication symbol to the proposition *dave_gets_wet*. In this example the implication arrow, →, is referred to as the *principal connective* in the formula because it binds together the entire formula. To indicate explicitly this nesting of formulae, the example above could be written as follows:

1 - (*it_is_raining and dave_is_outside*) → *dave_gets_wet*

where the round brackets enclosing *it_is_raining and dave_is_outside* show that it is to be considered as a "unit" in the formula. There is an alternative way of bracketing our example, namely:

2 - *it_is_raining and* (*dave_is_outside → dave_gets_wet*)

Notice that the meanings of 1 and 2 are different. Formula 1 says that *if* we know that it is raining and we know that Dave is outside then we also know that Dave gets wet. Formula 2 says that we *do* know that it is raining and if we know that Dave is outside then we also know that Dave gets wet. In other words, 1 tells us nothing about whether or not it is raining, while 2 tells us that it definitely is raining. This demonstrates the importance of knowing how formulae are nested but how can we avoid having to put brackets around every nonatomic formula? The solution to this problem is to adopt fixed conventions about which operator will be principal in any unbracketed formula. This is referred to as establishing the **precedence** of operators, where operators of lower precedence are applied before those of higher precedence in the structure of a formula. In the absence of explicit bracketing, the operator with the highest precedence will be the principal operator in a formula.

The standard precedence ordering is normally:

- $\rightarrow$ and $\leftrightarrow$ have highest precedence.
- *and* and *or* have next highest precedence.
- *not* has lowest precedence.
- In cases where two operators of equal precedence appear in a formula and there is no bracketing to impose an explicit ordering on the operators, then the operator furthest to the right is taken as the principal operator[1].

If we apply these precedence rules to the unbracketed example at the beginning of this section then the bracketing given in formula 1 turns out to be correct. If we really wanted the nesting shown in formula 2 then we would have to include the brackets. Below are some examples of more complex, unbracketed formulae along with the equivalent, fully bracketed formulae.

Unbracketed formula	Equivalent bracketed form
A and B and C	*(A and B) and C*
not A or A	*(not A) or A*
A or B and C $\rightarrow$ D	*((A or B) and C) $\rightarrow$ D*

4.2.3 Representing Real World Problems in PL

It is often difficult to decide how to represent, using the Propositional Logic, the information necessary to solve some problem in the real world. The reasons for this difficulty include the following:

1. Propositional Logic is of limited expressive power so some things just can't be said (more about this in Section 4.3).
2. We want our formulae to be accurate descriptions of some portion of the real world. It is therefore necessary to talk about the truth of a formula in some interpretation. For example the proposition *dave_gets_wet* is a symbol which denotes that some object, Dave, gets wet. What do we really mean when we say that Dave gets wet? Does he get wet to the skin or is it sufficient for his clothes to become wet? This distinction is important because if we interpret *dave_gets_wet* as denoting that Dave is wet to the skin then the formula:
   it_is_raining and dave_is_outside $\rightarrow$ dave_gets_wet
   might not be true if *it_is_raining* denoted very light rainfall (insufficient

---

[1] There are alternative conventions for establishing the precedence of operators but these need not concern us here.

to wet Dave to the skin). Frequently, the *interpretation* in which particular formulae are assumed to be true is not explicitly stated, relying on the reader to form their own "common-sense" interpretation.

3. It is difficult to decide what should be the atomic propositions in a given problem. Taking the running example from Section 4.2.2, we wanted to say that if it was raining and Dave was outside then Dave would get wet. In Section 4.2.2 we chose to represent this information using the formula:

it_is_raining and dave_is_outside → dave_gets_wet

but we *could* have simply represented the precondition as *one* atomic proposition, thus:

it_is_raining_and_dave_is_outside → dave_gets_wet

Intuitively, the first representation is more appealing because we know that *and* has a special significance in the logic. Unfortunately, it is not always so easy to find an intuitively obvious representation.

4. Having decided on the atomic propositions, it is still easy to get the meanings of the formulae wrong by applying the logical connectives in the wrong order. Recall the marked difference in meaning of formulae 1 and 2 in Section 4.2.2, caused by differences in bracketing of the "same" formula.

To become proficient at the representation of knowledge in Propositional Logic (or any other form of knowledge representation notation) takes practice. The following are some guidelines which might make your task easier:

- Try to retain maximum expressive power. The above discusses two different ways of representing the same statement: one with an explicit conjunction (*'and'*) of propositions and the other with this conjunction buried as part of a larger atomic proposition. It is usually better, in such cases, to choose the version in which the logical operator (in this case the *and* operator) is explicit because this gives more information about the logical structure of the statement.

- Look for smaller propositions within larger ones and represent these separately. This is closely linked to the point above since, by teasing out propositions into smaller and smaller fragments and (using the logical connectives) reconnecting these fragments to form appropriate nested formulae, one provides the maximum amount of structure within each formula.

- Look for key words in English which suggest use of one or more of the logical connectives. The following are some helpful hints for each connective, although there are no hard and fast rules:

  - The '*not*' connective: Look for negatives like "doesn't", "no" or "never". For example:

Phrase	Possible formula
"does not contain nil value"	*not contains_nil_value*
"never exceed level 4"	*not exceeds_level_four*
"have no selflinks"	*not have_selflinks*

– The '*and*' connective: Look for phrases like "also", "as well as" or "in addition to". For example:

Phrase	Possible formula
"Entity is a class and model primitive"	*entity_is_a_class and* *entity_is_a_model_primitive*
"Thing is a class as well as a rootclass"	*thing_is_a_class and* *thing_is_a_rootclass*

– The '*or*' connective: Be careful to distinguish between the use of *inclusive* and *exclusive or* connectives. The table below gives two examples using inclusive *or* and then two examples using exclusive *or*.

Phrase	Possible formula
"has one or (sometimes) two parentclasses"	*has_one_parentclass or* *has_two_parentclasses*
"is named process, or activity"	*named_process or* *named_activity*
"dead or alive"	*(dead or alive) and* *not(dead and alive)*
"is either one or zero"	*(one or zero) and* *not(one and zero)*

Note that in some cases of exclusive *or* it is possible to avoid the necessity of excluding explicitly the coexistence of both disjuncts by being careful about which propositions are used. Taking the "dead or alive" example from the table above, this could be represented using the more complex expression: *dead or (not dead)*. We can then use the general theorem that for any formula P, the statement P *and* (*not P*) is contradictory in that P *and* (*not P*) cannot be true at the same time to prevent the coexistence of the two disjuncts.

– The '$\rightarrow$' connective: Look for phrases such as "If X then Y", "Given X, then Y" or "Whenever X then Y". For example:

Phrase	Possible formula
"If large organisation then business modelling"	*large_organisation* $\rightarrow$ *business_modelling*
"Automation makes modelling easy "	*automation* $\rightarrow$ *easy_modelling*

It is also possible to find implication statements from English statements which do not, on first glance, look like implications. Consider, for example, the statement that: "Either the witness can't see properly or she identified the burglar correctly". This could be represented directly as the formula below:

not witness_can_see_properly or witness_identified_burglar but we could also convert it into an equivalent implication by using the proven equivalence between $(not(P)\ or\ Q)$ and $(P \to Q)$ (see Section 4.2.4). This gives us the implication below.

$$witness\_can\_see\_properly \to witness\_identified\_burglar$$

- The '$\leftrightarrow$' connective: Look for phrases such as "X is true if and only if Y" or "X is a necessary and sufficient condition for Y". For example:

Phrase	Possible formula
"You will only shift this nut with a spanner"	$shift\_nut \leftrightarrow use\_spanner$

Be careful not to use equivalence when you mean only implication. If A and B are equivalent then whenever one of them is true the other will be true as well. Expressing this more formally: the formula $A \leftrightarrow B$ has the same meaning as the formula $(A \to B)\ and\ (B \to A)$.

4.2.4 Determining the Truth of Formulae by Analysis of their Structure

In Sections 4.2.1 to 4.2.3 we have been concerned with the use of Propositional Logic as a representation language and haven't bothered much about using it to solve problems. The key property which logic provides in this respect is the ability to determine the truth or falsity of a well-formed formula, given appropriate data in the form of other well-formed formulae. In this section we consider a simple means of performing this task by analysing the structure of a formula. In Section 4.4 we consider a more sophisticated proof technique using proof tactics.

Recall that the truth-functional connectives are so called because they evaluate to either true or false, depending on the truth values of the subformulae which they connect. We can enumerate all the possible results of this evaluation for each of the connectives, as shown in the table in Figure 4.1. This table is normally referred to as a *truth table*. To form this table, we write down (in the first two columns) all possible combinations of truth values for formulae P and Q. We then make a column for each connective applied to P and/or Q and enter the appropriate truth value for each row. We use the letter 't' to represent truth and 'f' to denote falsity.

P	Q	$\neg P$	$P\ and\ Q$	$P\ or\ Q$	$P \to Q$	$P \leftrightarrow Q$
t	t	f	t	t	t	t
t	f	f	f	t	f	f
f	t	t	f	t	t	f
f	f	t	f	f	t	t

Fig. 4.1. A Truth Table for Logic Formula

The truth values allocated to some of the operators are intuitively obvious. For example, it is not surprising that P *and* Q is true only when both P and Q are true; nor is it surprising that P *or* Q is false only when P and Q both are false. However the results for $P \to Q$ may seem counter intuitive: why is this true whenever P is false?

Consider a specific example: suppose that the statement we want to represent is "If it is raining then the ground is wet", which we represent formally as *raining* $\to$ *ground_wet*. Given that the implication arrow ($\to$) always makes *ground_wet* true whenever *raining* is true, then we can safely say that either it isn't raining or the ground must be wet (assuming, as we must in Propositional Logic, that statements must be either true or false). In formal terms we can say that *raining* $\to$ *ground_wet* is equivalent to *not*(*raining*) *or* *ground_wet*, or more generally:

For any two propositions, P and Q: $(P \to Q) \leftrightarrow (not\ P\ or\ Q)$.

Given this equivalence, we can now switch our attention to the formula *not* P *or* Q in the knowledge that its truth values should be the same as those for $P \to Q$. Now we know that *not* P *or* Q will be true whenever either *not* P or Q is true, and we know that *not* P will be true whenever P is false. Therefore if P is false, the formula *not* P *or* Q is always true.

Since we can now allocate truth values to all the connectives of the Propositional Logic, we are able to determine the truth or falsity of any formula in the logic, given the truth values of all the atomic propositions contained in it. This is done by progressively evaluating the truth of each subformula, starting with the connectives joining atomic propositions and propagating the truth values "higher up" in the structure of the formula. Using this method we can distinguish several useful categories of formula:

- **Tautologies**: where the formula is always true regardless of the truth values of the propositions that it contains. The simplest form of tautology is P *or not* P. An example formula $(P\ and\ (P \to Q)) \to Q$ is also a tautology, as we shall demonstrate later.
- **Contradiction or Inconsistent formulae**: where the formula is always false regardless of the truth values of the propositions that it contains. For instance, the formula P *and not* P is always inconsistent.
- **Contingent formulae**: where the formula is sometimes true and sometimes false, depending on the truth values of the propositions that it contains. The formula P *and* $Q \to R$ is an example.

Figure 4.2 contains a detailed example of this method of establishing truth values. The goal is to prove that $(P\ and\ (P \to Q)) \to Q$ is a tautology. To do this, we enumerate each possible combination of truth values for P and Q (giving four combinations in all) and, for each combination, propagate the truth values up through the structure of the formula. The curly braces show the truth values assigned to each part of a formula during this process. The final truth value assigned to each of the four formulae is 'true' so this formula is a tautology.

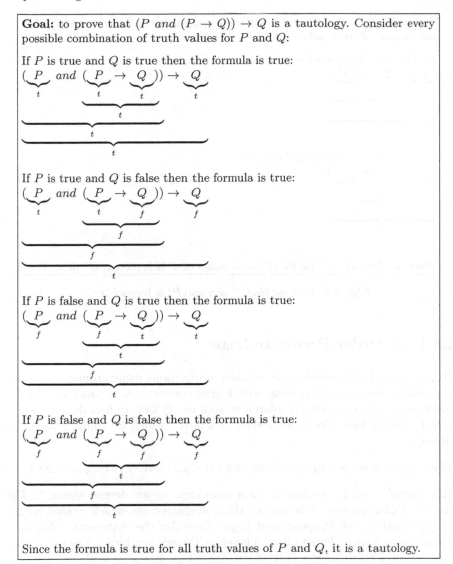

Fig. 4.2. Proving that $(P\ and\ (P \to Q)) \to Q$ is a tautology

Proving that a formula is inconsistent is also quite straightforward. An example appears in Figure 4.3. Again, we establish the truth value for the entire formula, given each truth value for P. Whatever truth value we assign to P the formula is false so it is inconsistent. For more details of Propositional Logic and of the First Order Predicate Logic which we discuss in the next section the reader should consult a general introductory textbook such as [63].

Goal: to prove that *P and not(P)* is inconsistent. Consider every possible assignment of truth values for *P*:

If *P* is true then the formula is false:

$$P \text{ and } not(P)$$

t t

f

f

If *P* is false then the formula is false:

$$P \text{ and } not(P)$$

f f

t

f

Since the formula is false for all truth values of *P* it is a contradiction.

Fig. 4.3. Proving that *P and not(P)* is inconsistent

4.3 First Order Predicate Logic

Propositional Logic enables one to make propositions using atomic statements or atomic statements connecting with logical connectives. It provides a formal notation in which to perform inferences such as "If Tweety flies then Tweety is a bird. Tweety flies. Therefore Tweety is a bird", which we could write as the formula:

((tweety_flies → tweety_is_a_bird) and tweety_flies) → tweety_is_a_bird

This formula can be proved to be a tautology, as we demonstrated in Figure 4.2. Unfortunately it is easy to think of statements which cannot readily be expressed in the Propositional Logic. Consider the statement: "Anything which flies is a bird. Tweety flies. Therefore Tweety is a bird." The only difference between this and the previous statement is that a general rule has been introduced, stating that any flying thing is a bird.[2] Now, we *could* represent this general rule using simple propositions but the problem is that this makes it impossible to prove that Tweety flies. To convince yourself of this, try proving that the following representation of our example statement is a tautology (you won't succeed).

((anything_flies → anything_is_a_bird) and tweety_flies) → tweety_is_a_bird

The reason this happens is that there is no way of knowing that *anything* could refer to *tweety*: in the Propositional Logic the two are *completely different* strings of symbols, buried within different propositions. We require a way of

[2] We ignore, for our present purposes, the fact that this rule isn't always true.

unpacking the structure of propositions, thus enabling us to identify more easily those which are similar. First Order Predicate Logic (FOPL)[3] is a standard notation in which to provide this facility. As a taste of what is to come, our example expressed in FOPL turns out to be:

$((\forall X\ flies(X) \rightarrow bird(X))\ and\ flies(tweety)) \rightarrow bird(tweety).$

4.3.1 The Notation: Well-Formed Formulae

Many of the techniques which are employed in the Propositional Logic are also used in First Order Predicate Logic (FOPL) (though sometimes in augmented form). The difference in the two notations is that in FOPL propositions can contain substructure and, in particular, may contain variables. We now provide a simplified definition of well-formedness in the FOPL. A word of warning: although this definition is adequate for our current purposes some important details have been sacrificed for the sake of explanation. For a complete definition refer to [16].

Theorem 4.4. *A well-formed formula in the First Order Predicate Logic is defined as follows:*

1. *A constant can be any number or any unbroken sequence of symbols beginning with a lower-case letter.*
2. *A variable is any unbroken sequence of symbols beginning with an upper case letter.*
3. *A predicate is a term consisting of a functor, the predicate name, and an ordered set of 0 or more arguments. Predicates with 1 or more arguments are written in the style: $F(A_1, \cdots, A_N)$, where F is the functor and N is the number of arguments (or arity) of the predicate.*
4. *Predicate names must be constants.*
5. *Arguments may be either constants or variables. Variables may be quantified using either universal or existential quantifiers, i.e. $\forall$ or $\exists$, respectively.*
6. *If P and Q are formulae, then the following are also formulae:*
   - *not P*
   - *not Q*
   - *P and Q*
   - *P or Q*
   - *$P \rightarrow Q$*
   - *$P \leftrightarrow Q$*
7. *Only expressions using rules 1 to 6 are formulae.*
8. *If P is a well-formed term then $\forall X\ P$ and $\exists X\ P$ are terms quantified over X. Any variables not quantified using either $\forall$ or $\exists$ are referred to as free variables in P.*
9. *A sentence contains no free variables.*
10. *Only expressions using rules 8 and 9 are sentences.*

---

[3] Also often referred to as First Order Predicate Calculus.

Theorem 4.4 (above) introduces some new terminology. To understand what it all means, we first examine in detail an example of a well-formed formula in this notation. We return to the statement we introduced earlier, that "all flying things are birds":

$$\forall X(flies(X) \rightarrow bird(X)).$$

This formula contains two predicates, $flies(X)$ and $bird(X)$, joined using the connective '$\rightarrow$'. The variable, X, is quantified using the universal quantifier, the $\forall$ operator (read as "forall"). Note that the variable X could refer to *any* object that we wanted to talk about. For example, it could be *tweety*. Why is the introduction of variables with quantification so important? Recall that in the Propositional Logic it is possible to determine the truth or falsity of a formula simply by examining its structure, given the truth values of the propositions it contains (see Section 4.2.4). This simple technique will not always work in FOPL because it deals with quantification over variables.

To understand why this creates a problem, consider the problem of deciding whether the formula $\forall X \; devious(X)$ is true. Suppose, for the moment, that we know the set of all possible objects which might be substituted for X in this formula and that it is $[fred, dave, george]$. If this is the case then we need only establish that $fred$, $dave$ and $george$ are devious in order to establish that any object (in this problem) is devious. This above formula therefore may be rewritten into a conjunction in Propositional Logic as below:

$devious(fred)$ *and* $devious(dave)$ *and* $devious(george)$.

But what happens if we *cannot enumerate all the possible objects* that we want to talk about (e.g. if we want to establish the truth of $\forall X \; devious(X)$ for all of the people in the world)? We can no longer form a conjunction of instances of the formula because we don't know what these are. At this point we need to reason with universally quantified formulae without specifying all the objects to which they apply.

Turning now to the existential quantifier, what if we wanted to establish whether there existed some devious person (i.e. $\exists X \; devious(X)$)? Once again, if we know that the complete set of objects we are concerned with is $[fred, dave, george]$ then we could establish the truth of this statement if we know that either $fred$, $dave$ or $george$ are devious. This corresponds to the disjunction:

$devious(fred)$ *or* $devious(dave)$ *or* $devious(george)$.

But, again, what happens if we don't know which particular objects we are dealing with (e.g. we know that someone is devious but we don't know who)? One answer is to develop ways of reasoning with existentially quantified formulae. Another way, which we shall explore in Section 4.5.1, is to replace existentially quantified variables with "typical instances" of the objects which they represent.

4.3.2 Representing Real World Problems in FOPL

We have presented FOPL as an extension of Propositional Logic and, as such, many of the points made in Section 4.2.3 with respect to the Propositional Logic still apply. Therefore we shall restrict our attention to the influence of the new structures which FOPL provides - namely structured terms and quantification. It is difficult to provide precise guidelines on how to encode statements in FOPL but here is a rough procedure:

1. First try to identify the things which are **objects** in the statements you want to represent. For example, in the statement "If Dave's alarm clock rings Dave gets up" there are two objects: *daves_alarm_clock* and *dave*. Note that these are both constants – i.e. they refer to a particular alarm clock and a particular person.

2. Having identified the objects involved, try to identify the **relations** which apply to those objects. Continuing the example begun above, the relations are: for the alarm, that it rings; and, for Dave, that he gets up. Therefore we have two predicates: *rings(daves_alarm_clock)* and *gets_up(dave)*. We say that *rings* is a predicate applying to the object *daves_alarm_clock* and that *gets_up* is a predicate applying to *dave*.

3. Given suitable definitions of predicates, apply the appropriate **logical connectives**, in a similar manner to that described in Section 4.2.3. To complete our running example, this gives the formula:

$$rings(daves\_alarm\_clock) \rightarrow gets\_up(dave).$$

4. If variables appear in the expression which you are constructing then these have to be quantified using either the universal and/or existential quantifiers. Consider these separately.

   The universal quantifier: Look for phrases such as "All X are Y" or "It is always true that X". For example, the statement "All politicians are devious" means that for any object, X, if that object is a politician then it will be devious. In FOPL this becomes below.

   $$\forall X \; politician(X) \rightarrow devious(X)$$

   The existential quantifier: Look for phrases such as "There is an X such that Y" or "Some X is Y". For example, the statement "There is a/some politician who can be trusted" might be represented using the formula below.

   $$\exists X \; politician(X) \; and \; trustworthy(X)$$

It is quite common to have a mixture of universal and existential quantifiers in a statement. For instance, we might want to say that "If all politicians are devious then none of them are trustworthy":

$(\forall X \; politician(X) \rightarrow devious(X)) \rightarrow$
$\qquad not(\exists Y \; politician(Y) \; and \; trustworthy(Y))$

This example can be used to illustrate several important points:

- It is sometimes necessary to restrict quantification to parts of the formula, rather than to the whole thing. In this example, universal quantification over X occurs only in that part of the formula which is to the left of the second implication arrow.
- Care must be taken to distinguish variables which can represent different objects. Thus, although all the variables in the statement refer to politicians, it is necessary to have a separate variable name (X) for devious politicians and for trustworthy politicians (Y).
- The meaning of a formula can be changed just by altering the scope of the quantifiers. If we shift the existential quantification of Y in our example to apply to the whole formula, rather than just the part on the right of the implication arrow, then we get the formula:

$\forall X \; \exists Y \; (politician(X) \rightarrow devious(X)) \rightarrow$
$\qquad not(politician(Y) \; and \; trustworthy(Y))$

which means that for any X, there is some Y such that if X is devious because he/she is a politician then Y is not a trustworthy politician. This would allow a *single* untrustworthy politician, whose lack of trust was dependent on the deviousness of all the others (and so there could be some trustworthy politicians). Compare this with the meaning of the original example, which says that if being a politician implies deviousness then *none* of the politicians are trustworthy.

- As an antidote to the previous point, it is sometimes possible to change the quantification of a formula without altering its meaning. For instance, there is a proven equivalence between the statement $not(\exists X \; F(X))$ and the statement $\forall X \; not(F(X))$ (i.e. saying that there isn't an instance of some object with some property is the same as saying that all objects don't have that property). We can use this equivalence to replace the existential quantifier in our original example with a universal quantifier, thus:

$(\forall X \; politician(X) \rightarrow devious(X)) \rightarrow$
$\qquad \forall Y \; not(politician(Y) \; and \; trustworthy(Y))$

- The precedence of the quantifiers (see Section 4.2.2) may be important in determining the meaning of the formula. For example, we might have a predicate of the form: $votes\_for(X, Y)$ which is true if person X votes for person Y in an election. Suppose that we quantify this as follows:

$\forall X \; \exists Y \; votes\_for(X, Y)$

To understand what this really means we need to know the precedence
of the quantifiers (i.e. which is dominant in the formula). If the existential quantifier were dominant then the fully bracketed formula would be:

$$\exists Y (\forall X \; votes\_for(X,Y))$$

or, stated in English: "There is some person for whom everyone votes."
Alternatively, the universal quantifier might be dominant, giving the
bracketed formula:

$$\forall X (\exists Y \; votes\_for(X,Y))$$

which is read as: "Everyone votes for someone." *The normal convention
is that, in the absence of explicit bracketing, a quantifier further to the
left in a formula will dominate those quantifiers to its right.* This makes
the latter of our bracketed examples the correct one.

4.3.3 Unification

In the Propositional Logic of Section 4.2 there was no difficulty in deciding whether two propositions were the same: all that was necessary was to
check that the names of the propositions were identical. Thus the propositions
dave_hates_someone and *someone_hates_fred* are not the same. In FOPL the
method by which we determine whether two terms are the same needs to be
more sophisticated because one or more of the terms may contain variables
and/or constants. The word used to describe this test for matching between
terms is *unification*. For example, we might want to unify the two FOPL terms
$hates(dave, X)$ and $hates(Y, fred)$, which is possible if X is *instantiated* to
fred and Y is instantiated to *dave*. The resulting term, after unification is:
$hates(dave, fred)$. We provide below a description of a *simple* unification algorithm. For a (comparatively) gentle introduction to more complex unification
algorithms the reader is referred to [58].

Theorem 4.5. *Two terms, P and Q, in the FOPL <u>unify</u> when:*

1. *P and Q are both constants, and the names of P and Q are identical.*
2. *Otherwise, if P and Q are both variables then P and Q are denoted to be
   the same variable.*
3. *Otherwise, if P is a variable and Q is a nonvariable then P is made equal
   to Q. We say that Q is <u>substituted</u> for P.*
4. *Otherwise, if Q is a variable and P is a nonvariable then Q is made equal
   to P. We say that P is substituted for Q.*
5. *Otherwise, if P is a term with principal functor F_P and Q is a term with
   principal functor F_Q then the names of F_P and F_Q are identical and their
   corresponding argument pairs are unified. To find out how to unify the two
   lists of arguments of P and Q follow the procedure below:*

- *Find the set, $[A_1, \cdots, A_N]$, of arguments for P, in the order in which they appear in that term.*
- *Find the set, $[B_1, \cdots, B_N]$, of arguments for Q, in the order in which they appear in that term.*
- *For each pair of arguments, (A_I, B_I), where I denotes the position of the argument in each term, unify each A_I and B_I pair using all of the above procedures as applicable.*

To illustrate how the unification algorithm given in Theorem 4.5 works, consider its application to the example we supplied earlier. The task is to test whether $hates(dave, X)$ and $hates(Y, fred)$ unify. These terms correspond to P and Q in Theorem 4.5. The terms are not both constants or variables, so steps 1 and 2 do not apply. Neither are they a variable-and-constant pair, so steps 3 and 4 do not apply.

However, step 5 can be applied, since both $hates(dave, X)$ and $hates(Y, fred)$ have $hates$ as their principal functor. The ordered sets of arguments for $hates(dave, X)$ and $hates(Y, fred)$ are $[dave, X]$ and $[Y, fred]$, respectively. We now try to unify each pair of arguments in these two sets. First take the pair of corresponding arguments $(dave, Y)$. These unify using step 4 in Theorem 4.5, making Y equal to $dave$. Next take the pair of arguments $(X, fred)$, which unify using step 3, making X equal to $fred$. We can now say that $hates(dave, X)$ and $hates(Y, fred)$ unify, with $dave$ substituted for Y and $fred$ substituted for X. Below are some more examples of unification between terms.

Terms		Result of unification
$hates(X, fred)$	$hates(dave, Y)$	$hates(dave, fred)$
$hates(X, X)$	$hates(dave, Y)$	$hates(dave, dave)$
$hates(dave, fred)$	$hates(X, X)$	Don't unify
$hates(dave, X)$	$hates(X, fred)$	Don't unify

4.4 Natural Deduction Proofs

The method of establishing the truth or falsity of a propositional formula using truth tables (see Section 4.2.4) is useful but suffers from several limitations. In particular:

- It doesn't provide us with fine control over the tactics which we use to prove a particular formula – it offers a single "shotgun" approach.
- It will not scale up to problems involving quantification over possibly infinite sets of objects because truth values cannot be assigned to every instance of the formula.

An alternative method, which we describe in this section, is to use **proof rules**. A proof rule provides a strategy for establishing the truth of a formula, given the truth of other formulae. For example, we know that *A and B* is true given some set of assumptions, S, if we can prove that A is true, given S and that B is true, given S. Before performing proofs using rules we must introduce a new operator '⊢' which connects a set of assumptions to the formula which is to be proved using those assumptions, called a **Sequent**. The operator '⊢' has a higher precedence than operators → and ↔.[4]

Theorem 4.6. *We write the sequent $S \vdash C$ to denote that the formula, C, can be proved from the list of assumptions, S. If S is empty, then C is a theorem (i.e. its truth depends on no assumptions).*

Some examples of valid sequents, some of which are expressed as theorems, are shown in Figure 4.4. Some of these will be referred to in later sections – particularly when discussing conversion to normal forms in Section 4.5.1.

Commutativity of '*and*'	$[] \vdash (A \text{ and } B) \leftrightarrow (B \text{ and } A)$
Associativity of '*and*'	$[] \vdash (A \text{ and } (B \text{ and } C)) \leftrightarrow ((A \text{ and } B) \text{ and } C)$
Transitivity of '→'	$[(A \rightarrow B) \text{ and } (B \rightarrow C)] \vdash A \rightarrow C$
Equivalence →, *or*	$[] \vdash (P \rightarrow Q) \leftrightarrow (not(P) \text{ or } Q)$
Equivalence *and*, *or*	$[] \vdash not(P \text{ and } Q) \leftrightarrow (not(P) \text{ or } not(Q))$
Equivalence *or*, *and*	$[] \vdash not(P \text{ or } Q) \leftrightarrow (not(P) \text{ and } not(Q))$
Equivalence ↔, →	$[] \vdash (P \leftrightarrow Q) \leftrightarrow (P \rightarrow Q) \text{ and } (Q \rightarrow P)$
Distribution of *or* over *and*	$[] \vdash (P \text{ or } (Q \text{ and } R)) \leftrightarrow ((P \text{ or } Q) \text{ and } (P \text{ or } R))$

Fig. 4.4. Some useful sequents in classical logic

For reasons which will become clear, a thorough understanding of the subtleties of Natural Deduction proof techniques is not essential to an understanding of the topics which we shall discuss later. However, they do provide a useful link between "traditional" logic and the more specialised forms of logic used by AI practitioners. We could explore this topic in the context of more traditional "Lemmon style" proof rules but we believe that these are not ideally suited to the task in hand. Instead we introduce a simplified proof technique, inspired by Roy Dyckhoff's implementation of Gentzen and Prawitz's **Sequent Calculus**. The proof rules which we shall use in this section are shown in the table in Figure 4.5. Each row of this table corresponds to a particular proof rule, consisting of a name, for easy reference; a sequent for which the rule provides proof; and the supporting proofs which are necessary in order to establish the truth of this sequent. Below, we restate each of the proof rules in English.

- equiv_elim: allows us to prove a formula, $A \leftrightarrow B$, given some assumptions if we can prove $A \rightarrow B$ from those assumptions and $B \rightarrow A$ from those assumptions.

---

[4] See Section 4.2.2 for explanation on precedence of operators.

Rule name	Sequent	Supporting proofs
equiv_elim	$\mathcal{F} \vdash A \leftrightarrow B$	$\mathcal{F} \vdash A \rightarrow B,\ \mathcal{F} \vdash B \rightarrow A$
and_intro	$\mathcal{F} \vdash A\ and\ B$	$\mathcal{F} \vdash A,\ \mathcal{F} \vdash B$
and_elim	$\mathcal{F} \vdash C$	$A\ and\ B \in \mathcal{F},\ [A, B\|\mathcal{F}] \vdash C$
or_intro_left	$\mathcal{F} \vdash A\ or\ B$	$\mathcal{F} \vdash A$
or_intro_right	$\mathcal{F} \vdash A\ or\ B$	$\mathcal{F} \vdash B$
or_elim	$\mathcal{F} \vdash C$	$A\ or\ B \in \mathcal{F},\ [A\|\mathcal{F}] \vdash C,\ [B\|\mathcal{F}] \vdash C$
imp_intro	$\mathcal{F} \vdash A \rightarrow B$	$[A\|\mathcal{F}] \vdash B$
imp_elim	$\mathcal{F} \vdash C$	$A \rightarrow B \in \mathcal{F},\ \mathcal{F} \vdash A,\ [B\|\mathcal{F}] \vdash C$
contradiction	$\mathcal{F} \vdash C$	$\mathcal{F} \vdash false$
neg_intro	$\mathcal{F} \vdash not(A)$	$[A\|\mathcal{F}] \vdash false$
neg_elim	$\mathcal{F} \vdash C$	$not(A) \in \mathcal{F},\ \mathcal{F} \vdash A$
double_neg	$\mathcal{F} \vdash A$	$\mathcal{F} \vdash not(not(A))$
immediate	$\mathcal{F} \vdash A$	$A \in \mathcal{F}$

Where: $\mathcal{F}$ is some list of assumptions.

A, B and C are well-formed formulae.

$X \in Y$ denotes that X is an element of set Y.

$[X|Y]$ is a list with first element X and remaining elements Y.

Fig. 4.5. Proof rules (Sequent Calculus after Roy Dyckhoff)

- and_intro: states that we can know $A\ and\ B$, given some assumptions if we can prove A from those assumptions and also prove B from those assumptions.
- and_elim: allows us to prove a formula, C, from some assumptions if we can find a conjunction, $A\ and\ B$, among those assumptions and obtain a proof of C from the assumptions with the addition of A and of B.
- or_intro_left: gives a proof of a formula, $A\ or\ B$, from some assumptions if A can be proved from those assumptions.
- or_intro_right: gives a proof of a formula, $A\ or\ B$, from some assumptions if B can be proved from those assumptions.
- or_elim: allows us to prove a formula, C, from some assumptions if we can find a disjunction, $A\ or\ B$, among those assumptions and obtain a proof of C from the assumptions with the addition of A, and then obtain a proof of C from the assumptions with the addition of B.
- imp_intro: states that we can know $A \rightarrow B$, given some assumptions if we can prove B from those assumptions with A added.
- imp_elim: allows us to prove a formula, C, from some assumptions F if we can find an implication, $A \rightarrow B$, among those assumptions. We then obtain a proof of A from the assumptions F; then find a proof of C from the assumptions with B added.

- contradiction: says that any formula C can be proved from some assumptions if we can prove that the assumptions are inconsistent (i.e. if we can prove *false* from them).
- neg_intro: provides a proof of $not(A)$ from some assumptions if we can prove *false* from those assumptions with the addition of A.
- neg_elim: says that any formula C can be proved from some assumptions if $not(A)$ appears in those assumptions and we can also prove A from those assumptions. Since the ability to deduce both $not(A)$ and A indicates that the assumptions are inconsistent, this is similar to the *contradiction* rule.
- double_neg: provides a proof of a formula A from some assumptions if those assumptions yield a proof of $not(not(A))$ (i.e. that the negation of A is false).
- immediate: provides a proof of a formula A from some assumptions if A is one of the assumptions.

To understand how these rules are used, consider the following example. Suppose we want to prove that the proposition, b, is true given the assumptions a and $a \rightarrow b$. This corresponds to the sequent: $[a, a \rightarrow b] \vdash b$, which we shall refer to as a goal to be proved. To prove this sequent we must first select a rule from those available in Figure 4.5. Assume that we choose the *imp_elim* rule, unifying the sequent, $[a, a \rightarrow b] \vdash b$, with the rule sequent, $\mathcal{F} \vdash C$, and thus instantiating $\mathcal{F}$ to $[a, a \rightarrow b]$ and C to b. This gives us the instantiated set of subgoals:
$[A \rightarrow B \in [a, a \rightarrow b], [a, a \rightarrow b] \vdash A, [B|[a, a \rightarrow b]] \vdash b]$. We then attempt to satisfy each of these subproofs in turn. First we establish that $A \rightarrow B \in [a, a \rightarrow b]$ which instantiates A and B to the propositions a and b. We then look for a proof of $[a, a \rightarrow b] \vdash a$, for which we need to select a rule. The *immediate* rule is chosen, which possesses the single, satisfiable condition: $a \in [a, a \rightarrow b]$. This leaves the third of our original subproofs: $[b, a, a \rightarrow b] \vdash b$ which can be satisfied by again applying the *immediate* rule to generate the final satisfiable condition: $b \in [b, a, a \rightarrow b]$. The proof is now complete.

Although this proof takes some time to explain, it can readily be represented in diagrammatic form, as shown in Figure 4.6. This figure shows a trace of the completed proof in the form of a *tree diagram*. At the root of the tree (at the top of the diagram!) is shown the initial sequent. The line below this sequent represents the application of the *imp_elim* rule. At this point the tree splits into three branches, one for each of the subgoals introduced by the *imp_elim* rule. The first of these is just a membership test (these tests are enclosed in boxes to distinguish them from other goals in the proof tree) so there are no further branches beneath it. However, the other two each have a subbranch corresponding to the application of the *immediate* rule. This form of tree is referred to as an *and tree* because if there is a set of branches $[B_1, B_2, \cdots, B_N]$ arising from a given sequent then it is necessary to satisfy B_1 *and* B_2 *and* $\cdots$ *and* B_N. Using this diagram, one can reconstruct the temporal sequence of steps taken to perform the proof by starting at the root node; moving downwards; and always exploring left-hand branches before those to the right. This form of search is

known as *depth-first, left-to-right search* because all branches are explored out
to their tips, starting with those farthest to the left.

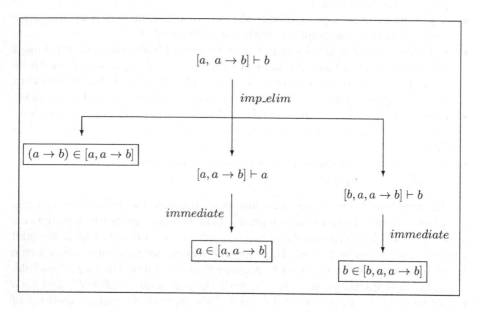

Fig. 4.6. Proof tree for $[a, a \rightarrow b] \vdash b$

The proof shown in Figure 4.6 was quite straightforward because it involved
only two proof rules. More commonly, a wide range of rules are necessary and
we shall demonstrate this by providing two more examples. The first of these
is shown, using a tree diagram, in Figure 4.4. The proof is of the sequent:
$[b \rightarrow c] \vdash (a \; or \; b) \rightarrow (a \; or \; c)$. Intuitively, this seems valid because if c follows
from b then if some other proposition, a, is true then $(a \; or \; c)$ is true; on the
other hand if b is true then c is true and so $(a \; or \; c)$ is true. To prove this
formally it is first necessary to apply the *imp_intro* rule to insert $(a \; or \; b)$
among the set of assumptions. We then apply the *or_elim* rule which allows us
to prove $(a \; or \; c)$ given the presence of $(a \; or \; b)$ in the set of assumptions and
independent proofs of $(a \; or \; c)$ from a and from b.

Our second example of the application of proof rules is shown in Figure 4.8.
This example is interesting because it involves proof by contradiction – in
particular, we want to prove the sequent: $[a, not(a \; and \; b)] \vdash not(b)$ and do this
by adding b to the set of assumptions and proving that this is inconsistent (using
the *neg_intro* rule). Therefore, since the formula, a, is inconsistent, $not(a)$ must
be true.

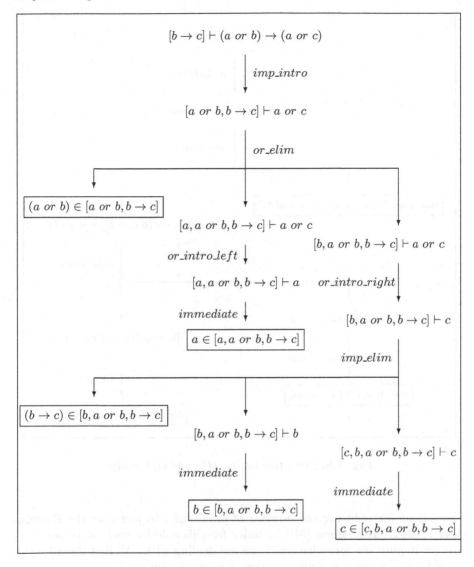

Fig. 4.7. Proof tree for $[b \to c] \vdash (a \ or \ b) \to (a \ or \ c)$

4.5 Resolution: A Simplified Proof Mechanism

The natural deduction proofs of Section 4.4 are rigorous and (some might say) intellectually stimulating. Unfortunately, they are also quite complex. In particular, it is difficult to know which proof rule to apply at a given stage in the proof. If the proof process is to be automated it would seem advantageous to reduce the number of proof rules as far as possible (provided that this doesn't restrict the range of sequents which we can prove). In this section, we describe

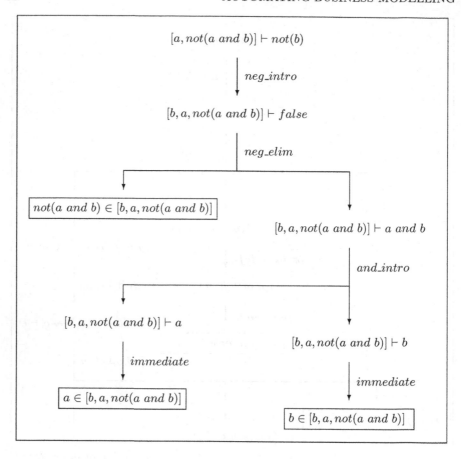

Fig. 4.8. Proof tree for $[a, not(a\ and\ b)] \vdash not(b)$

a technique for reducing the number of proof rules to just one: the **Resolution Rule of Inference** [91]. In order for this rule to work, it is necessary also to simplify the formulae which we are dealing with. We first describe this simplification process and then explain how resolution works.

4.5.1 Normal Forms

In making various statements using Propositional Logic and FOPL we have made use of a variety of operators – namely *not, and, or,* $\rightarrow$, $\leftrightarrow$, $\forall$ and $\exists$. We know that all of these operators are not strictly necessary – for example, the $\rightarrow$ operator can always be "rephrased" in terms of the '*not*' and '*or*' operators by employing the equivalence: $(P \rightarrow Q) \leftrightarrow (not(P)\ or\ Q)$. By progressively rewriting a formula in this way, it turns out to be possible to represent any FOPL formula using *only* the '*and*', '*or*' and '*not*' operators. Furthermore, it is possible to further simplify the formula by breaking it up at each '*and*' symbol;

converting the resulting propositions (which we shall call *literals*) into sets; and
finally placing these sets themselves into a set. The result is therefore a set of
(implicitly "and"ed) sets of (implicitly "or"ed) literals. The formula is then said
to be in *clausal form*. The conversion procedure is described in Theorem 4.7
below.[5]

Theorem 4.7. *The algorithm for conversion of a FOPL formula to <u>clausal form</u>
is as follows:*

- *Eliminate any $\leftrightarrow$ and $\to$ operators by rewriting using the following equivalences (where the expression on the left side of the '$\leftrightarrow$' can be rewritten as the statement on the right side):*
  - $(P \leftrightarrow Q) \leftrightarrow ((P \to Q) \text{ and } (Q \to P))$
  - $(P \to Q) \leftrightarrow (not(P) \text{ or } Q)$
- *Convert to <u>prenex form</u> by moving all quantifiers to the left-hand side of the formula, using the following equivalences (where X is a quantified variable and A and B are sub-expressions in the formula):*
  - $not(\forall X\ A) \leftrightarrow (\exists X\ not(A))$
  - $not(\exists X\ A) \leftrightarrow (\forall X\ not(A))$
  - $((\forall X\ A) \text{ and } B) \leftrightarrow (\forall X\ A \text{ and } B)$
  - $((\exists X\ A) \text{ and } B) \leftrightarrow (\exists X\ A \text{ and } B)$
  - $(A \text{ and } (\forall X\ A)) \leftrightarrow (\forall X\ A \text{ and } B)$
  - $(A \text{ and } (\exists X\ A)) \leftrightarrow (\exists X\ A \text{ and } B)$
  - $((\forall X\ A) \text{ or } B) \leftrightarrow (\forall X\ A \text{ or } B)$
  - $((\exists X\ A) \text{ or } B) \leftrightarrow (\exists X\ A \text{ or } B)$
  - $(A \text{ or } (\forall X\ A)) \leftrightarrow (\forall X\ A \text{ or } B)$
  - $(A \text{ or } (\exists X\ A)) \leftrightarrow (\exists X\ A \text{ or } B)$
- *Eliminate all existential quantifiers as follows:*
  - *Those outside the scope of any universal quantifier are replaced with Skolem constants (arbitrary names which don't appear anywhere else). For example, the formula: $\exists X\ happy(X)$ might be converted into happy (someone), where "someone" is a Skolem constant representing some arbitrarily selected person.*
  - *Those inside the scope of any universal quantifier are replaced with Skolem functions, whose arguments are the universally quantified variables within whose scope the existential occurs. For instance, the formula:*

    $$\forall X\ \exists Y\ hates(X, Y)$$

    might be converted into $hates(X, enemy\_of(X))$ where $enemy\_of(X)$ is a Skolem function which obtains some enemy for any X.
- *Remove all universal quantifiers, on the understanding that all the variables are implicitly universally quantified. The formula is now free of quantifier symbols.*

---

[5] The full conversion procedure is slightly more complex. We have simplified it in
order to bring out the important features.

- *Drive negation in to the individual predicates, using the equivalences:*
  - *not(P and Q) ↔ (not(P) or not(Q))*
  - *not(P or Q) ↔ (not(P) and not(Q))*
  - *not(not(P)) ↔ P*
- *Distribute disjunction over conjunction, using the equivalence:*
  - *(P or (Q and R)) ↔ ((P or Q) and (P or R))*
  - *The formula is now said to be in <u>conjunctive normal form</u>.*
- *Convert each group of disjunctions into a set of atomic formulae and place each of these sets into an implicitly conjoined set of disjunctions.*
- *Rename all variables so that the same variable name doesn't appear in different disjunctive sets.*

To illustrate how this procedure works, suppose that we have the following formula:

$\forall X$ *(lecturer(X) and not(ai_lecturer(X)) → kindly(X))*, and
lecturer(dave), and
not(kindly(dave))

This corresponds to the English statement: "Any lecturer who is not an AI lecturer is kindly. Dave is a lecturer. Dave is not kindly." We can convert this formula into clausal form by applying the sequence of transformations shown in Figure 4.9. We end up with the final normalised formula:

[[*not(lecturer(X))*, *ai_lecturer(X)*, *kindly(X)*],
  [*lecturer(dave)*],
  [*not(kindly(dave))*]]]

which comprises a set of three subsets. These subsets are implicitly *conjoined*, i.e. all three sets must be true. The elements within each subset (where there is more than one element in a set) are implicitly *disjoined*, e.g. the first subset represents the formula:

not(lecturer(X)) or ai_lecturer(X) or kindly(X).

This example highlights some important points:

- The ordering of literals within each subset is unimportant, since they are all "or"ed together and any one would be sufficient to prove the truth of a subset.
- The ordering of subsets is unimportant because they are all "and"ed together and all must be proved to prove the truth of the formula.
- It would not be possible to reconstruct the original formula, with all the logical operators back in place, just by looking at its clausal form. The same clausal form could have been produced from many different combinations of logical operators.
- The clausal form is quite difficult for a human to read. By imposing uniformity on our representation we have sacrificed some of its intelligibility.

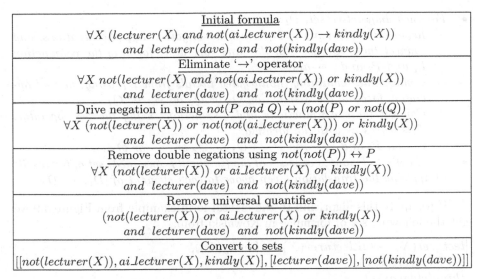

Initial formula
$\forall X$ $(lecturer(X)$ and $not(ai\_lecturer(X))$ $\rightarrow$ $kindly(X))$ and $lecturer(dave)$ and $not(kindly(dave))$
Eliminate '$\rightarrow$' operator
$\forall X$ $not(lecturer(X)$ and $not(ai\_lecturer(X))$ or $kindly(X))$ and $lecturer(dave)$ and $not(kindly(dave))$
Drive negation in using $not(P$ and $Q)$ $\leftrightarrow$ $(not(P)$ or $not(Q))$
$\forall X$ $(not(lecturer(X))$ or $not(not(ai\_lecturer(X)))$ or $kindly(X))$ and $lecturer(dave)$ and $not(kindly(dave))$
Remove double negations using $not(not(P))$ $\leftrightarrow$ P
$\forall X$ $(not(lecturer(X))$ or $ai\_lecturer(X)$ or $kindly(X))$ and $lecturer(dave)$ and $not(kindly(dave))$
Remove universal quantifier
$(not(lecturer(X))$ or $ai\_lecturer(X)$ or $kindly(X))$ and $lecturer(dave)$ and $not(kindly(dave))$
Convert to sets
$[[not(lecturer(X)), ai\_lecturer(X), kindly(X)], [lecturer(dave)], [not(kindly(dave))]]$

Fig. 4.9. A conversion to clausal form

To counter the problem of unintelligibility of formulae in clausal form, it is possible to apply a further set of transformations which will reintroduce the '$\rightarrow$' operator. This is done for each of the subsets in the formula and, once again, makes use of the equivalence: $(P \rightarrow Q) \leftrightarrow (not(P)$ or $Q)$. Every subset of literals in clausal form is composed of two sorts of elements: those which are negated (assume that these consist of the literals $[not(P_1), not(P_2), \cdots, not(P_M)])$ and those which are nonnegated (assume that these consist of the literals $[Q_1, Q_2, \cdots, Q_N])$. Since these are implicitly disjoint, we can replace the 'or' operator between all terms, giving us the formula:

$(not(P_1)$ or $not(P_2)$ or $\cdots$ or $not(P_M))$
or $(Q_1$ or Q_2 or $\cdots$ or $Q_N)$

Now, we can use the equivalence: $not(A$ and $B)$ $\leftrightarrow$ $(not(A)$ or $not(B))$ to convert the first of these two "or"ed bundles to an "and"ed bundle enclosed by a negation. Our new formula is therefore:

$not(P_1$ and P_2 and $\cdots$ and $P_M)$
or $(Q_1$ or Q_2 or $\cdots$ or $Q_N)$

Since we now have a formula of the form $not(A)$ or B, we can use the equivalence: $(A \rightarrow B) \leftrightarrow (not(A)$ or $B)$ to introduce the '$\rightarrow$' operator, thus:

$(P_1$ and P_2 and $\cdots$ and $P_M) \rightarrow (Q_1$ or Q_2 or $\cdots$ or $Q_M)$

This formula is now said to be in *Kowalski form*. A more formal definition of this procedure is given in Theorem 4.8 below.

Theorem 4.8. *Given a formula in clausal form, $[D_1, \cdots, D_N]$, where D_1 to D_N are sets of disjunct literals (see Theorem 4.7), this can be converted into Kowalski form by applying the following sequence of transformations:*

- *For each disjunctive set, D_I:*
  - *Remove the elements of D_I which are negated; drop the negations; and connect these literals with the 'and' operator, forming the conjunction P_1 and P_2 and $\cdots$ and P_J.*
  - *Connect the remaining, nonnegated literals from D_I using the 'or' operator, forming the disjunction Q_1 or Q_2 or $\cdots$ or Q_K.*
  - *Connect these conjunctions and disjunctions using the '$\rightarrow$' operator. This leaves us with the formula:*
    P_1 and P_2 and $\cdots$ and $P_J \rightarrow Q_1$ or Q_2 or $\cdots$ or Q_K.
- *The final set of clauses consists of the (implicitly conjoined) set of the results of applying the translation given above to each element of $[D_1, \cdots, D_N]$.*

If we apply this algorithm to the clausal form example from Figure 4.9 we get the following set of formulae in Kowalski from:

$[lecturer(X) \rightarrow (ai\_lecturer(X)$ or $kindly(X))$,
$\rightarrow lecturer(dave)$,
$kindly(dave) \rightarrow]$

Notice in this example that the second formula: $\rightarrow lecturer(dave)$ would have been considered ill-formed according to our definition of well-formedness for FOPL (Theorem 4.3). In Kowalski form these are well-formed and our example would be interpreted as "$lecturer(dave)$ is true" (i.e. it is a fact, with no preconditions). By contrast, the third formula: $kindly(dave) \rightarrow$ is interpreted as "$kindly(dave)$ is false" (i.e. since it is false, you could conclude anything from it).

An important subgroup of Kowalski formulae are those with a single literal as a conclusion. These are referred to as *Horn clauses*.[6] For example, the following are Horn clauses:

$\rightarrow lecturer(dave)$
$shifty(X)$ and $devious(X) \rightarrow politician(X)$

but this isn't: $lecturer(X) \rightarrow (ai\_lecturer(X)$ or $kindly(X))$. Horn clauses form the basis for the "logic programming language" Prolog because it turns out that the resolution rule of inference, when applied to Horn clauses, can be used to run practical programs with reasonable efficiency (see Section 4.6).

Theorem 4.9. *A __Horn clause__ is a formula in Kowalski form (see Theorem 4.8) which has no more than one literal on the right-hand side of the '$\rightarrow$' operator.*

4.5.2 Resolution

Resolution provides us with a simple way of establishing the truth of a formula in clausal form, given a set of assumptions also in clausal form. It relies upon a single proof rule, called the resolution rule of inference. A definition of this rule appears below.

---

[6] After the person who first recognised their importance.

Theorem 4.10. *The* <u>*resolution rule of inference*</u> *permits the following procedure:*

- *if we have two sets of literals, R and S which are implicit disjunctions in clausal form (see Theorem 4.7),*
- *and if we can extract from R an element, P, leaving the remaining elements R′,*
- *and if we can extract from S an element, not(Q), leaving the remaining elements S′,*
- *and if Q unifies with P, under some consistent substitution for variables in Q and P (see Theorem 4.5),*
- *then we can derive the new clause obtained by merging R′ and S′.*

As an illustration, consider the two clauses:

[not(lecturer(X)), ai_lecturer(X), kindly(X)] and
not(kindly(dave))

from our running example. Applying the resolution rule to these two clauses allows us to "cancel out" *kindly(X)* and *not(kindly(dave))* (in the process of substituting *dave* for *X*), leaving us with a clause consisting of the remaining elements from both sets – namely:

[*not(lecturer(dave)), ai_lecturer(dave)*].

Proving the truth of a formula by resolution employs a technique similar to the "proof by absurdity" approach described in Section 4.4. A (simplified) restatement of this rule is that the conjunction *P and not(P)* is inconsistent. If we convert this into clausal form then we can say that [[P], [not(P)]] is inconsistent. Furthermore, we know that the resolution rule allows us to resolve [P] with [not(P)] to obtain the empty clause, []. Therefore, if we can resolve any of the sets in our set of clauses to obtain the empty clause we have proved that our clauses are inconsistent. This allows us to prove the truth of a clause, given some set of assumptions, by *negating* it; proving that the negated clause, when combined with the set of assumptions, is inconsistent by resolving until an empty clause is obtained; and thus concluding that since the negation of the clause is inconsistent (and therefore false) the original, nonnegated clause must follow from the truth of the set of assumptions.

Theorem 4.11. *A formula, F, in clausal form is true, given a set, A, of assumptions in clausal form if its negation, F′, can be proved inconsistent with A by resolution. F′ is inconsistent with A when an empty set of literals can be found by some sequence of applications of the resolution rule (see Theorem 4.10) to the set formed by adding F′ to A.*

Figure 4.10 gives an example of a resolution proof applied to our running example, in which all lecturers except AI lecturers are kindly; Dave is a lecturer;

and Dave isn't kindly. We set out to prove that Dave is an AI lecturer: formally *ai_lecturer(dave)*. To do this we negate the formula; add it to the set of assumptions; obtain an empty clause using resolution – thus establishing that the negated formula causes a contradiction; and so conclude that the original formula is true.

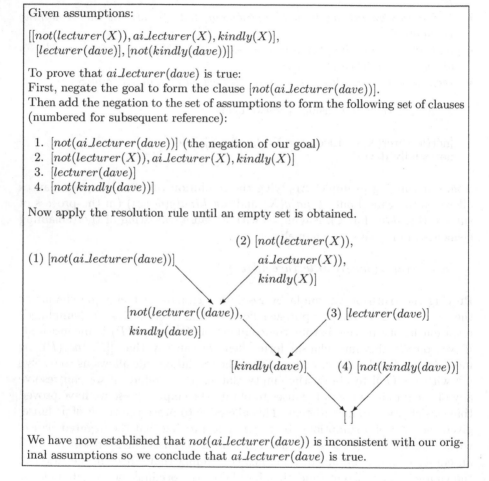

Given assumptions:

$[[not(lecturer(X)), ai\_lecturer(X), kindly(X)],$
$[lecturer(dave)], [not(kindly(dave))]]]$

To prove that *ai_lecturer(dave)* is true:
First, negate the goal to form the clause $[not(ai\_lecturer(dave))]$.
Then add the negation to the set of assumptions to form the following set of clauses (numbered for subsequent reference):

1. $[not(ai\_lecturer(dave))]$ (the negation of our goal)
2. $[not(lecturer(X)), ai\_lecturer(X), kindly(X)]$
3. $[lecturer(dave)]$
4. $[not(kindly(dave))]$

Now apply the resolution rule until an empty set is obtained.

$(2)\ [not(lecturer(X)),$
$(1)\ [not(ai\_lecturer(dave))]$ $ai\_lecturer(X)),$
                                          $kindly(X)]$

$[not(lecturer((dave)),$ $(3)\ [lecturer(dave)]$
$kindly(dave)]$

$[kindly(dave)]$ $(4)\ [not(kindly(dave))]$

$[\ ]$

We have now established that $not(ai\_lecturer(dave))$ is inconsistent with our original assumptions so we conclude that $ai\_lecturer(dave)$ is true.

Fig. 4.10. An example of resolution

It turns out that the resolution procedure can be proved to be both *sound* and *complete*. By "sound", we mean that the inference mechanism is guaranteed not to produce any false conclusions from a set of true assumptions. By "complete" we mean that all conclusions which can logically be derived from a set of assumptions will (in theory) be found using resolution. In practice, there is a caveat to this statement, which we shall introduce in Section 4.7.2.

The main application of Resolution theorem proving is in the programming language, Prolog, but users of Prolog do not have to think about their programs directly as resolution proofs. It is easier to think about Prolog in terms of Natural Deduction proofs, despite the fact that what goes on "underneath" is Resolution. In the next section we describe the bare bones of Prolog in terms of proof rules, similar to those of Section 4.4.

4.6 Prolog

In Section 4.4 we described quite simple proofs which turned out to be complex to work out in detail. This complexity was, in part, caused by the variety of proof rules which could be applied at each stage of the proof. One answer to this problem is to reduce the range of proof rules which are available. The logic programming language, Prolog, can be viewed as adopting this strategy and in this section we shall describe a basic Prolog interpreter using an adapted set of proof rules from Figure 4.5.

First it is necessary to introduce the basic Prolog notation [15]. Prolog clauses are Horn clauses (see Theorem 4.9) – that is, they have only one literal in the conclusion of an implication. Prolog clauses also have the implication arrow going from right to left (i.e. '←') instead of from left to right as we have drawn it previously. This is merely a notational variation; all you have to remember is that the arrow always points at the conclusion from the preconditions. A more formal definition of the basic Prolog notation appears below:

Theorem 4.12. *Basic Prolog clauses must be in one of the following forms:*[7]

- *A Prolog rule signifies that some conclusion P is true given that some precondition C is true. It is written as P ← C. The conclusion must always be a literal. The precondition may be either:*
  - *A literal.*
  - *A conjunction of formulae: A and B, where A and/or B may themselves be conjunctions or disjunctions.*
  - *A disjunction of formulae: A or B, where A and/or B may be conjunctions or disjunctions.*
- *A Prolog fact denotes that some literal, L, is always true. This may be expressed as a rule: L ← true, where the name, true, is a special symbol which is always true.*[8]

The definition above uses symbols which have been introduced earlier in order to emphasise the connection between logic and Prolog. In real Prolog programs the notation is slightly different. The symbol ':−' is used instead of the '←' operator; a comma replaces the 'and' operator; and a semicolon replaces

---

[7] This notation does not correspond exactly to that of Prolog but conforms to the basic principles on which it depends.

[8] In practice, facts are normally written as simple assertions but this need not concern us here.

the '*or*' operator. For our present purposes, we shall ignore these notational differences and retain our own logical notation.

Figure 4.11 shows the set of rules necessary to implement our basic Prolog interpreter. The first three rules shown in the table (*and_intro*, *or_intro_left* and *or_intro_right*) are copied directly from those in Figure 4.5 and give us procedures for establishing a conjunction and disjunction of goals. The remaining two rules did not appear in Figure 4.5 but are straightforward. The first of these, the *truth_symbol* rule, allows us to conclude the truth of the statement, *true*, at any point in the proof. The second rule, *implication*, allows us to prove a statement, A, if our sequent contains the rule $A \leftarrow B$ and we can prove B from that sequent.

Rule name	Sequent	Supporting proofs
and_intro	$\mathcal{F} \vdash A$ and B	$\mathcal{F} \vdash A$, $\mathcal{F} \vdash B$
or_intro_left	$\mathcal{F} \vdash A$ or B	$\mathcal{F} \vdash A$
or_intro_right	$\mathcal{F} \vdash A$ or B	$\mathcal{F} \vdash B$
truth_symbol	$\mathcal{F} \vdash true$	unconditional
implication	$\mathcal{F} \vdash A$	$A \leftarrow B \in \mathcal{F}$, $\mathcal{F} \vdash B$

Where: $\mathcal{F}$ is some list of assumptions.
A and B are well-formed formulae.
$X \in Y$ denotes that X is an element of set Y.

Fig. 4.11. Proof rules for basic Prolog

Now that we have a set of proof rules for basic Prolog we need some method of choosing which rule to apply at any given stage in a proof. Most Prolog systems use a simple algorithm which is given below:

Theorem 4.13. *The basic Prolog search strategy can be defined as a procedure for selecting an appropriate proof rule from those in Figure 4.11. Given some sequent to be proved, of form $\mathcal{F} \vdash P$:*

- *If P is the special symbol, true, then establish it directly using the rule named truth_symbol.*
- *If P is of the form A and B then use and_intro.*
- *If P is of the form A or B then first try to prove it using or_intro_left but, if that fails or you need another proof, then try using or_intro_right.*
- *Otherwise, apply the implication rule with the first member of $\mathcal{F}$ which is of form $P \leftarrow C_1$. If no proof can be found using this implication statement then take the next statement, $P \leftarrow C_2$, and apply the implication rule again. Repeat this procedure until either a proof is found or all the implication statements have been used.*

Let us now consider how this search strategy is applied to a particular problem. Suppose that we want to establish the sequent:

$[a \leftarrow b, a \leftarrow (d \ or \ e), e \leftarrow (f \ and \ g), f \leftarrow true, g \leftarrow true] \vdash a$

The sequence in which Prolog would search for a proof is shown in Figure 4.12, where the sequence of application of rules is from top to bottom of the page and indentation indicates which proofs are subproofs of others. For more details of the relationship between logic and Prolog see [105].

Problem : $[a \leftarrow b, a \leftarrow d \ or \ e, e \leftarrow f \ and \ g, f \leftarrow true, g \leftarrow true] \vdash a$
Agree to represent the set of assumptions using the symbol $\mathcal{F}$

Goal: $\mathcal{F} \vdash a$
    Apply *implication* given $a \leftarrow b \in \mathcal{F}$
    New subgoal: $\mathcal{F} \vdash b$
        No proof rule can be applied to this goal.
    So reapply *implication* given $a \leftarrow d \ or \ e \in \mathcal{F}$
    New subgoal: $\mathcal{F} \vdash d \ or \ e$
        Apply *or_intro_left*
        New subgoal: $\mathcal{F} \vdash d$
            No proof rule can be applied to this goal.
        So apply *or_intro_right*
        New subgoal: $\mathcal{F} \vdash e$
            Apply *implication* given $e \leftarrow f \ and \ g \in \mathcal{F}$
            New subgoal: $\mathcal{F} \vdash f \ and \ g$
            Apply *and_intro*
            First new subgoal: $\mathcal{F} \vdash f$
                Apply *implication* given $f \leftarrow true \in \mathcal{F}$
                New subgoal: $\mathcal{F} \vdash true$
                Apply *truth_symbol*
            Second new subgoal: $\mathcal{F} \vdash g$
                Apply *implication* given $g \leftarrow true \in \mathcal{F}$
                New subgoal: $\mathcal{F} \vdash true$
                Apply *truth_symbol*

Fig. 4.12. Searching for a Prolog proof

4.7 Problems

At first glance, logic might seem like the solution to all knowledge representation problems. It provides inference mechanisms with highly desirable properties, such as soundness and correctness. It has a long history of development and so is comparatively well understood. Unfortunately, there remain a large number of reasons why logic isn't always the best choice of knowledge representation language. In this section we draw attention to some of these problems, starting with the problem of initially converting a problem description into logical notation. For more details of these and other problems see [44].

4.7.1 Ambiguity

If presented with some description of a real world problem, it isn't always possible to represent this as an unambiguous statement in logic. A domain where this problem surfaces frequently is that of natural language interpretation. Consider the following statement:

"Visiting Aunts can be a nuisance."

Does this mean that if some person is visited by an aunt then he/she is inconvenienced – formally:
$visits(Aunt, Person)$ and $aunt\_of(Aunt, Person) \rightarrow inconvenienced(Person)$
or does it mean that if a person goes to visit an aunt then he/she is inconvenienced – formally:
$visits(Person, Aunt)$ and $aunt\_of(Aunt, Person) \rightarrow inconvenienced(Person)$
Although these two representations differ only in the placing of the two arguments to the *visiting* predicate, their meaning is completely different and there isn't enough information in the English statement to allow us to decide which is the correct representation. The fault here is not with the logic but with the ambiguity which is often present in everyday speech. Humans are accustomed to glossing over such ambiguities but logic forces us to be more precise about what our statements mean.

4.7.2 Search Problems

The Natural Deduction proofs which are performed in Section 4.4 demonstrate an essential requirement for successful theorem proving: the theorem prover must know *when* to apply each proof rule during the construction of a proof. For human theorem provers, the strategy of proof construction can be left to "experience" and "intuition" but to obtain proofs by computer it is necessary to represent formally the method by which a correct proof is obtained.

Having introduced a proof style which is well suited to the representation of proofs as trees, we now consider the problems involved in constructing these proof trees. Our first observation is that there are a large number of different proof trees for the same sequent. Consider, for example, an alternative proof tree for the sequent, $[a, a \rightarrow b] \vdash b$, shown in Figure 4.13. This proof commences by applying the same rule as in Figure 4.6 but, instead of solving the third subproof ($[b, a, a \rightarrow b] \vdash b$) using the *immediate* rule, the *double_neg* rule is used to introduce the new subproof: $[b, a, a \rightarrow b] \vdash not(not(b))$. This, in turn, requires a sequence of application of the *neg_intro*, *contradiction* and *neg_elim* rules in order to complete the proof.

In retrospect, the proof tree of Figure 4.6 is preferable to that of Figure 4.13, since it is more compact. However, it is not always easy, when in the midst of performing a proof, to decide on the optimum search strategy. In Figure 4.13 the

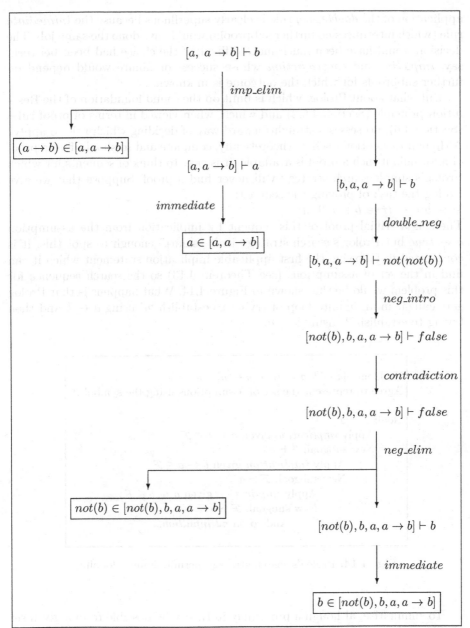

Fig. 4.13. A more complicated proof tree for $[a, a \rightarrow b] \vdash b$

application of the *double_neg* rule is clearly superfluous because the *immediate* rule (which introduces no further subproofs) would have done the same job. The decision would have been much more difficult if the choice had been between, say, *imp_elim* and *contradiction* whose success or failure would depend on further subproofs for which the outcome is unknown.

But what about Prolog, which is built on the sound foundation of the Resolution principle (Section 4.5.2) and which, when viewed in terms of proof rules (Section 4.6), possesses a straightforward way of deciding which rule to apply? Although Resolution itself is, theoretically, complete and so should find a proof of a formula if such a proof is available, it is easy to think of sequents for which Prolog's simple search strategy will never find a proof. Suppose that we give Prolog the task of proving the sequent:

$[a \leftarrow b, a \leftarrow true, b \leftarrow a] \vdash a$

There is a trivial proof of this sequent by implication from the assumption $a \leftarrow true$ but Prolog's search strategy isn't "smart" enough to spot this. It is committed to following the first applicable implication statement which it can find in the set of assumptions (see Theorem 4.13) so the search sequence for this problem would be that shown in Figure 4.14. What happens is that Prolog gets caught in an infinite loop of trying to establish 'a' using $a \leftarrow b$ and then trying to establish 'b' using $b \leftarrow a$.

Problem : $[a \leftarrow b, a \leftarrow true, b \leftarrow a] \vdash a$
Agree to represent the set of assumptions using the symbol $\mathcal{F}$

Goal: $\mathcal{F} \vdash a$
    Apply *implication* given $a \leftarrow b \in \mathcal{F}$
    New subgoal: $\mathcal{F} \vdash b$
        Apply *implication* given $b \leftarrow a \in \mathcal{F}$
        New subgoal: $\mathcal{F} \vdash a$
            Apply *implication* given $a \leftarrow b \in \mathcal{F}$
            New subgoal: $\mathcal{F} \vdash b$
                And so on *ad infinitum...*

Fig. 4.14. Prolog's search strategy permits infinite looping

To summarise, although a proof may in theory be possible from a given set of assumptions, whether it is actually found may depend on the search strategy used to perform the proof.

4.7.3 Representational limitations

Our discussion of logic has been confined to Propositional Logic and First Order Predicate Logic. These are the most commonly used logics because their proof theory is well understood and robust, comparatively efficient proof mechanisms are available for them. Unfortunately, there are many facilities which might be useful for knowledge representation which Propositional Logic and FOPL don't provide. Consider, for example, the statement:

"John hates everything about Mary."

The most natural way to represent this statement is to say that any characteristic possessed by Mary will be hated by John – formally:

$\forall P \; characteristic(P) \; and \; P(mary) \rightarrow hates(john, P)$

Unfortunately this takes us beyond FOPL because we have used a variable, P, as a predicate name. Logics which allow variables as predicate names in this way are referred to as *second order* and yet higher order logics are also possible. These higher order logics are more difficult to automate and are likely to be less efficient (for one thing, the unification process is more complex). Of course, we *could* get around this representational problem by making P in our example an argument to some "more general" predicate, for example:

$\forall P \; characteristic(P) \; and \; property\_of(P, mary) \rightarrow hates(john, P)$

but this just glosses over the problem without addressing the basic cause of it.

A further problem with the logics which we have described is that they lack facilities to deal directly with the use of *hypothetical arguments*. For instance, we might make the following argument:

"If Dave ruled the world he would make everyone his slave. Anyone who enslaves another is hateful. Therefore, Dave is hateful."

We could try to represent this as the sequent:

$\otimes$ $[\forall X \; rules\_world(dave) \rightarrow enslaves(dave, X),$
$\quad \forall Y \; \exists X \; enslaves(Y, X) \rightarrow hateful(Y)] \vdash hateful(dave)$

but this is *not* a provable sequent[9] because it includes no evidence that Dave rules the world. We could make it provable by adding the extra formula: $rules\_world(dave)$, obtaining the sequent:

$[rules\_world(dave), \; \forall X \; rules\_world(dave) \rightarrow enslaves(dave, X),$
$\quad \forall Y \; \exists X \; enslaves(Y, X) \rightarrow hateful(Y)] \vdash hateful(dave)$

Unfortunately, if we want our logical description to maintain integrity with the real world we are not allowed to add this formula because Dave, in reality, doesn't rule the world. We must move beyond FOPL in order to deal with this sort of hypothetical argument in a principled way.

Another failing of Propositional Logic and FOPL is their inability to handle directly the notions of *sequences of events* and *temporal change*. We shall present two examples which demonstrate different aspects of this problem. The first example concerns reasoning about a sequence of events. Suppose that we have the following simple problem:

"John gave Mary his lecture notes and Mary gave them to Dave. Who ends up with the lecture notes?"

---

[9] We shall adopt the convention of tagging invalid sequents with a $\otimes$ symbol.

The answer to this problem is obviously "Dave" but how can we represent this using FOPL formulae? We could try proving:

$\otimes$ [gives(john, mary, lecturenotes), gives(mary, dave, lecturenotes)] $\vdash$
      has(dave, lecturenotes)

but this is of little use because there is no general mechanism which relates the *gives* predicates to the *has* predicate; nor is there a way of detecting that the *gives* predicates form a temporal sequence. Temporal logics have been developed with the specific aim of representing this sort of inference.

Our final example concerns what has become known as the *frame problem*. Imagine that we want to describe, in simple terms, what happens when something is on fire. For one thing, we can say that it will be hot. It will also be charred if it is made of the appropriate material. These statements can be made using FOPL, as shown below:

on_fire(X) $\rightarrow$ hot(X)
on_fire(X) and can_char(X) $\rightarrow$ charred(X)

We now can add the information that Dave's chair is on fire and that Dave's chair can char and prove the following sequents:

[on_fire(chair), on_fire(X) $\rightarrow$ hot(X)] $\vdash$ hot(chair)
[on_fire(chair), can_char(chair), on_fire(X) and can_char(X)
$\rightarrow$ charred(X)] $\vdash$ charred(chair)

Now suppose that we want to follow through the time sequence to a point after which the fire on Dave's chair has gone out, so on_fire(chair) is no longer true. This means that neither hot(chair) nor charred(chair) can be inferred. The loss of the former conforms to our ideas of what happens in the real world (the chair wouldn't normally be hot after the fire had stopped) but we didn't want to lose the ability to deduce that the chair was charred, since this is a property which should persist between time frames. The problem is how to decide which parts of a description should persist over time and which should be transient. This problem has been tackled by many researchers in various contexts but a universally acceptable solution has yet to emerge.

4.8 Exercises

Section 4.2.1: Which of the following are well-formed formulae in the Propositional Logic?
  1. *a not b*
  2. *a and not(b and) c*
  3. *(a or b → not(c and d)) or e*
Section 4.2.2: Write each of the following as a fully bracketed formula:
  1. *a and b or c*
  2. *a or b and c → not a or b*

   3. $a \rightarrow b$ *or* $c \rightarrow d$ *and* e

Section 4.2.3: Convert the following English statements into the Propositional Logic:

   1. "Either Dave is crazy or AI is the world's most interesting subject."

   2. "If Maggie was shy she wouldn't be Prime Minister. Maggie is Prime Minister. Therefore she isn't shy."

   3. "Anyone who is Scottish likes Haggis. Dave is Scottish. Therefore Dave likes Haggis."

Section 4.2.4: Show which of the following are tautologies and which are inconsistencies.

   1. $(not(P)$ *or* $Q) \leftrightarrow (P \rightarrow Q)$

   2. $(P \rightarrow Q)$ *and* P *and* $not(Q)$

   3. $not(not(P))$ *and* $not(P)$

   4. $not(P$ *and* $Q) \leftrightarrow (not(P)$ *or* $not(Q))$

   5. $not(P$ *or* $Q) \leftrightarrow (not(P)$ *and* $not(Q))$

   6. $(P$ *and* $Q)$ *and* $(not(P)$ *or* $not(Q))$

Section 4.3.1: Which of the following are well-formed formulae in the First Order Predicate Logic?

   1. $\forall X \; flies(X) \rightarrow submarine(X)$

   2. $flies(X) \rightarrow bird(X)$

   3. $\forall X \; \forall Y \; property\_of(X, Y) \rightarrow X(Y)$

   4. $not\_true(\forall X \; flies(X) \rightarrow submarine(X))$

Section 4.3.2: Convert the following English statements into the First Order Predicate Logic:

   1. "All politicians are devious. Dave isn't devious so he isn't a politician."

   2. "All Scots are British. Some Scots are stingy. Therefore some British people are stingy."

   3. "All Scots are British. Not all Scots are stingy. Therefore some British people are not stingy."

Section 4.3.3: Which of the following formulae unify and, if they do, what is the resulting unified term?

   1. $p\_name(a, A, B, b) \; p\_name(C, C, D, D)$

   2. $p\_name(a, A, b) \; p\_name(B, B, B)$

   3. $p\_name(a, A, b, A) \; p\_name(B, C, C, D)$

Section 4.4: Prove the following sequents using the proof rules from Figure 4.5:

   1. $[] \vdash (a$ *and* $(a \rightarrow b)) \rightarrow b$

   2. $[P \rightarrow Q, P \rightarrow not(Q)] \vdash not(P)$

Section 4.5.1: Convert the following formulae into clausal form:

   1. $\forall X \; scottish(X) \rightarrow british(X)$

   2. $\exists X \; scottish(X)$ *and* $stingy(X)$

   3. $not(\exists X \; british(X)$ *and* $stingy(X))$

Section 4.5.2: Use the normalised formulae from your answers to Exercise 4.5.1 (above) to provide a resolution proof of the formula below:

$\exists X \; british(X)$ *and* $stingy(X)$, given the assumption:

$\forall X \; scottish(X) \rightarrow british(X)$, and the assumption:

$\exists X \; scottish(X)$ *and* $stingy(X)$.

Section 4.6: Using the diagrammatic notation from Section 4.4, draw the final
  proof tree produced by the search shown in Figure 4.12. Then describe the
  sequence of search for the proof:

  $[a \leftarrow b \ and \ (c \ or \ d), b \leftarrow c \ or \ e, d \leftarrow e, e \leftarrow true] \vdash a$

5

Formal Support for Data Modelling

Based on the modelling support framework provided in Figure 1.1, this chapter and the following ones describe how automatic support may be constructed to help develop BSDM's Business Models. This chapter focuses on the means to provide such support for the *Entity Model*. Chapters 6 and 7 describe the formalisation and reasoning of the *Process* and *Procedural* models.

The automation of this modelling support framework described in Figure 1.1 is based on manipulation of a formal logical language *DefBM* that has been developed using a lightweight approach as described in Section 3.3.5. Before we go into detail about *DefBM* and the automated support, we should firstly understand the domain within which we are working: BSDM's business models.

BSDM business models are *informal* models. To clarify what we mean by an *informal* or a *semi-formal* model, one may describe an informal model as a model that does not have precise semantics, in particular computational semantics. Such models hence may result in different understanding and interpretations. Consequently, inconsistent or error interpretations of a model may occur. A *semi-formal* model provides formal or precise definition for parts of a model but not all of it. The ambiguity caused by an informal model is similar to the one that may exhibit in natural language text (e.g. English) that sometimes an English sentence may be interpreted differently by different persons and under different circumstances, see Section 4.7.1 for more detail. The cause of ambiguity in an informal model is rooted in the ambiguity of the modelling language used. There are two causes: the informal nature of notations used in a method and the allowance of describing a domain using informal representations. The former indicates imprecise semantics of modelling notations that allows different interpretations and use of the same notation. The latter refers to the use of natural language.

In Section 3.3.5, we advocated a **lightweight formal approach** that focuses formalisation effort on selective aspects of a domain that are of importance to our task, as opposed to a heavyweight approach. In the context of formalising an informal model, it translates to formalising the notation, or **modelling primitives**, of a modelling language rather than formalising the entire methodology of a modelling language. In doing so, there are a few general rules of thumb that readers may wish to follow when they formalise an informal or semi-formal model using a lightweight approach. These are described below:

- To identify the main modelling primitives used in the language that are used to capture concepts in an application domain. For instance, if the modelling language is a type of organisational model, then the main modelling primitives are perhaps notations that capture different types of organisations. On the other hand, if it is an activity model, then perhaps the main modelling primitives are nodes that capture activities, actors and objects.

- To identify relationships between the main modelling primitives and understand the boundary for each relationship. One important relationship to look out for is the *subtype* or *subclass* relationships that enable one to describe a concept to be a *specialisation* of another concept in a model. To find out the boundary of a relationship, for instance, the relationship "followed-by" in an activity model defines that an activity A can only be followed-by another activity B, and that it is a one-to-one relationship. The boundary of this relationship is therefore a binary one and can only be used to connect two activities given a definite (temporal execution) semantics.

- To identify properties for each modelling primitive described above. This includes the names of the properties, the allowed data types and/or range for values for the property.

- To identify instances (or occurrences) for each modelling primitives described above, when applicable. Modelling primitives are often used to capture the type of things[1] rather the actual "things" themselves. It is sometimes, however, necessary to be able to describe the actual instance instead of its type only. In this book we use terms "type" and "class" interchangeably to mean a classification that describe a set of instances that shares some common properties. Some representation languages choose not to represent instances, as they are not used in their (reasoning) applications.

- To identify attributes for each instance with its type defined using the modelling primitives as described above. Similarly, this includes the names of the attributes, the allowed data types and/or range of its values. Some representation languages may choose not to distinguish between instance attributes and class properties. The decision about whether to make this distinction often depends on the application of the representation language.

- To identify other auxiliary modelling primitives, the relationships between them and other modelling primitives and their attributes. Auxiliary modelling primitives are primitives that are used during a modelling process but often only served for annotation or navigation purposes. Example auxiliary modelling primitives are the annotations for a model (that is often written in natural language and of no particular format or required content), indexes between different parts of a model (e.g. labelling of diagrams in a model). Such auxiliary modelling primitives, although important as a part of the modelling process, may not be essential for automation tasks.

---

[1] Those things are sometimes called instances or occurrences.

Once the modelling primitives and their semantics are identified and clari-
fied, the next task of formalisation is **Knowledge Representation**. The task
of Knowledge Representation is concerned with finding an appropriate representation of concepts in a domain. To judge whether a representation is appropriate for a modelling language, in addition to correctly represent semantics of
the language, it often involves a close examination of the desirable reasoning
mechanism.

As this book focuses on predicate calculus, we will restrict ourselves to representations using first order predicate calculus. Detailed representation techniques have been discussed in Chapter 4, particularly Sections 4.2.3 and 4.3.2.
Generally speaking, the types of concepts (classes) as well as the types of relationships and attributes are represented as predicates. The domain concepts
that are described by the concepts/classes/relationships/attributes are represented as arguments of a predicate. In the context of representing a modelling
language, the modelling primitives may be represented using predicates and
the content that a modelling primitive described as arguments. For instance,
the modelling primitive "activity" may be described using the predicate:

activity(X)

where X is used to defined an activity (class). The predicate activity('Accept
Customer Order') therefore denotes that "Accept Customer Order" is an activity. On the other hand, the predicate

attribute(Class, Attribute, Att_value)

is used to denote a particular attribute of a class. For instance, attribute('Accept
Customer Order', precondition, null) indicates the class "Accept Customer Order" does not have a precondition. Combining our knowledge of the previous
activity predicate we know that "Accept Customer Order" is an activity that
does not have a precondition. Also note that the allowed types of the arguments for each predicate are fixed and predetermined that form a part of the
definition of a predicate.

Using this approach, this chapter and the following ones describe the formal
language *DefBM* and how it has been used in practice to provide automated
support for business models. This formal work has been implemented in the
tool KBST-BM, as depicted in Figure 3.5.

5.1 Defining a Formal Language: *DefBM*

The formal representation of modelling concepts in BSDM is organised in an
Inheritance Class Hierarchy (ICH) where a concept is modelled in a *class*. It
was inspired by the core class hierarchy of the *Process Interchange Format
(PIF)* [62]. As mentioned in Figure 2.2, PIF is a formal "translation" language
which aims at providing a communication channel for concepts captured in
process models built in different formats and schemas. Since a BSDM's business

model includes a process model and exhibits similarities to a business process model, it is advantageous to make use of this format when constructing a formal language. However, since BSDM is different from PIF in several aspects, the initial hierarchy has been modified and extended. Figure 5.1 shows the inheritance class hierarchy, on which the formal language *DefBM* has been defined.

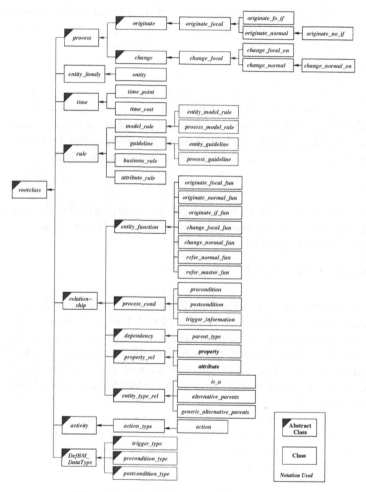

Fig. 5.1. The Inheritance Class Hierarchy (ICH) of *DefBM*

Our aim is not to define the semantics of the BSDM method, but to use it as an example to provide a framework that makes use of the knowledge embedded in the method to demonstrate various kinds of automated support. The aim of this inheritance hierarchy, therefore, is two-fold: (1) to provide a structure to identify and relate concepts which are used in a business modelling context; (2) to support an appropriate automated inference mechanism.

Two types of classes are included in this hierarchy: the *Abstract Class* and the *Normal/Concrete Class*, shown respectively as a rectangle with a shaded corner and a plain rectangle in the figure. An *abstract class* is a class which is matched to an aggregate and/or abstract concept in a BSDM business model, except for *rootclass* which was devised as a class to include all concepts that are described in the business modelling context. The main purpose of an abstract class is to provide a structure to identify and distinguish different concepts in a business model, that each concept is modelled as a class in the class hierarchy, and to allow the classification of the more specialised subclasses. Therefore, members of an *abstract class* are other abstract classes (to enable further specialisation) or *normal classes*.

An *abstract class* describes a primitive concept in a BSDM business model, but it may or may not have a one-to-one mapping to modelling primitives in a conventional BSDM business model because we have added extra class types which are used for the model but are not prescribed by the BSDM model primitives. Added classes are, for instance, the class *time* which is an important concept in the description of the dynamics of the model and therefore useful for our purposes, but it is not a primitive found in the BSDM manual. The classes *process_cond*, *rule* and *activity* are mentioned and used in BSDM but are not explicitly captured in a business model: BSDM does not define notations and structures to record them. The classes *entity_family* and *abstract_entity* are classes applicable to BSDM but not used by BSDM: we include them in the formal language to enable some of the automated support that we intend to provide. With these extended classes, various aspects of an instantiation of a business model can now be explicitly represented and handled by this class hierarchy and the defined formal language.

A *normal class* maps to a set of concrete or abstract things described in a business model. The members of a normal *class* are other *normal classes* as described in Figure 5.1, or instances that may occur in a business world. For example, the members of class *action_type* is another class *action* which defines all of the possible actions that may happen in a business process; whereas the members of class *attribute* (of an entity occurrence/instance) are all of the attributes that any entity occurrence may have, e.g. the name, address and birthday of a person. Again, a *normal class* may or may not have a direct mapping to the existing model primitives in a BSDM model due to the added classes to the formal language, *DefBM*.

The *DefBM* language was defined to represent the architecture and meaning of a business model in BSDM. It is based on first order predicate logic and follows the same convention of the Prolog syntax for arguments, i.e. we use any words starting with a capital letter to denote a variable and any words starting with a lower case letter to denote a constant. *DefBM* has also been used to represent the model rules and guidelines which are described in BSDM.

In *DefBM*, the predicate *abstract_class* indicates an abstract class in the Inheritance Class Hierarchy. For example, the root of the hierarchy, *rootclass*, is denoted as

abstract_class(rootclass).

There are (currently) in total 17 abstract classes and each one of them is represented in an *abstract_class* predicate. A normal class is denoted by a predicate *normal_class*. For example, the class *originate_focal* is represented as

normal_class(originate_focal).

The predicate *super_class* is used to denote the membership of a subclass to a superclass in this inheritance hierarchy: the class *Super* is a superclass of the class *Sub*, as shown in the predicate below.

super_class(Super, Sub).

An example instantiation of predicate *super_class* is that *rootclass* is a superclass of *process*. This is formally represented below.

super_class(rootclass, process).

In this class hierarchy, both super and subclasses can be abstract classes; or a superclass can be an abstract class and its subclass can be a normal class; or both of them can be normal classes. It is not allowed that a normal class has an abstract class as a subclass because this is conceptually incompliant with the class hierarchy convention. The top-down allocation of classes is partly to ensure that the more general and higher level of abstraction always appears first in the hierarchy before the more specialised and concrete concepts are introduced.

Similar to the PIF class hierarchy, properties associated with a superclass are passed on to its subclasses through the inheritance hierarchy. Unlike the PIF hierarchy, however, *this hierarchy not only captures the facts about a business model, but also includes classes that represent modelling rules.* For example, classes *model_rule* and *guideline* are the formalised modelling practice recommended by the method, whereas *business_rule* and *attribute_rule* are domain-dependent rules which are constructed by the modellers.

A rule may be applied to a class anywhere in the hierarchy and may be associated with one or more classes. *Because of the class hierarchy, subclasses inherit the association with rules from their parents.* For example, if a particular rule has been associated with a particular class *originate* (process), then that rule applies to all subclasses of *originate*. Modelling these rules as their own set of classes allows for easier identification of the modelling rules that apply to a particular domain.

Later in this chapter and in Chapters 6 and 7 we describe in detail about how this formal language has been used to represent things that are described and implied in the context of business modelling. Before taking a closer look at the use of this language, a brief summary of the concepts of a BSDM Entity Model is given.

5.2 Entity Model

A BSDM business model gives an integrated view over various important aspects of an organisation. This overview is captured in a so-called *master map*. Its content is divided into the different business operations within an organisation. Each of the local business functions is called a *local map*. In other words, a complete business model consists of many local maps: although each local map is responsible for describing a different operation of the business, as a whole they should be consistent and form a converged view of a company.

Figure 5.2 shows part of an example BSDM business model, a local map, as it appears in our system *KBST-BM*, in which we named a local map a *view*. The notation used in the tool is that described in the BSDM manuals [51] so existing BSDM practitioners should be conversant with the notation. This simplified model describes the selection and evaluation of modules at a university.

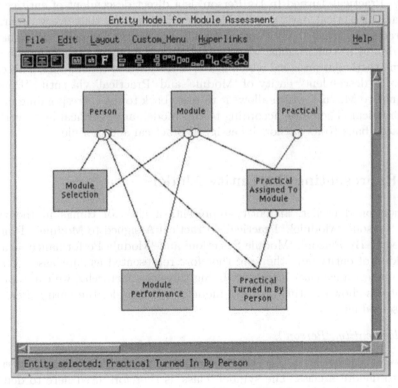

Fig. 5.2. A BSDM Entity Model

Boxes show the entities involved: 'Person', 'Module', 'Practical', 'Practical Assigned to Module', 'Practical Turned In By Person', 'Module Selection' and 'Module Performance'. An entity denotes a class of things in the described world. In this case, 'Person' denotes the class of the individual persons who are in connection with the university, and 'Practical Turned In By Person' denotes the group of all practical homeworks turned in by every (known) person for a (known) assigned practical and a (known) module.

Lines with a circle at one end denote a *dependence* relationship between two entities: the entity with the circle ending is the "parent" entity, whereas the line ending entity is the "child" entity. As it is named, a *dependence* relationship places a "dependent" relationship to the "child" entity. Every occurrence of a "child" entity can only exist if the occurrence of the corresponding "parent" entity exists. For instance, in this example, the entity 'Module Selection' has two parent entities: 'Person' and 'Module'. This means that it is impossible to select a module (i.e. to create an occurrence of entity 'Module Selection') without knowing the particular person and module involved.

The dependence constraint is transferable to child entities (connected by dependencies) and to further "descendent" entities, which also provides tractability between occurrences in the different layers of the model. For example, the entity 'Practical Turned In By Person' is a direct descendent of entities 'Person' and 'Practical Assigned To Module' which means that every occurrence of 'Practical Turned In By Person', namely every recorded practical homework turned in by a student, must identify the particular person (student) who did it and the particular practical which has been assigned to the module. This entity is also a "descendent" entity of 'Module' and 'Practical' via entity 'Practical Assigned to Module' which allows it to trace back to the corresponding module and practical. Therefore, according to this model, any practical homework can be traced back to its author, its assigned practical and module.

5.3 Representing the Entity Model

As mentioned earlier, an entity represents a class of things in the world. Each 'Person', 'Module', 'Practical', 'Practical Assigned to Module', 'Practical Turned In By Person', 'Module Selection' and 'Module Performance' is a specific kind of entity, and they are therefore represented as subclasses of *entity* in the inheritance class hierarchy. Using this class hierarchy, we can represent all entities shown in this business model. For example, the entity 'Person' is represented as:

$$class(entity, \text{'Person'}).$$

Recall that earlier in this chapter we mentioned that a predicate is normally used to denote a class. The symbol 'class' is therefore used here to denote a class. As we also wish to specify the different types of classes in a predicate, i.e. Entity and the different types of Processes, one additional argument was added to indicate the types of classes. In this case, the symbol 'entity' was used to denote an entity class. Representation for different process classes will be illustrated in Chapter 6. To represent the dependence relationship between entities, the predicate *parent_type(Entity, Set_of_Parents)*

is used, where *Entity* denotes the child entity and *Set_of_Parents* is the set of parent entities of this entity. For example, 'Person' does not have a parent entity, therefore, its *Set_of_Parents* is empty as shown below; whereas 'Practical Assigned To Module' has two parent entities, therefore these two entities are enclosed in the set, also shown below.

parent_type('Person', [])
parent_type('Practical Assigned to Module', ['Module', 'Practical'])

BSDM gives a static and sharable set of properties to each entity: *(entity) name, parents preposition, definition, (occurrence/instance) examples, inclusions, exclusions, query, notes, identifier, originated by, originated date, last revised by, last revised date, controller* and *status*. Conventionally, the values of the properties are recorded in a BSDM form: the *Entity Definition Form*. During construction of the business models, the modellers need to fill in values for these properties. These are usually written in natural language and some in structured natural language.

A *property*, as described above, is a definition or characteristic of an entity and is shared by every occurrence of this entity (class). For instance, the property *definition* defines the meaning and boundary of an entity type, therefore every occurrence of this entity must be bound by this definition. It is represented in the *property* predicate below, where *Entity_Name* is the corresponding entity, *Property_Name* is the name of the property, and *Property_Content* is the value of the property.

property(Entity_Name, Property_Name, Property_Content).

Occurrences of an entity also have their own attributes. These are the characteristics of the individual occurrence and are not shared with other occurrences. Examples of attributes of an occurrence are the name of an occurrences or a certain date relevant to a particular occurrence. For instance, an entity *person* may have several occurrences whose individual names are *mary, john* and *mike*, etc. Hence, a predicate *attribute* is used in the formalism to represent attributes of a particular occurrence.

attribute(Entity_Name, Att_Name, Attribute_Type)

Similar to the *property* predicate, *Entity_Name* represents the name of an entity, *Att_Name* represents the name of an attribute, and *Attribute_Type* stores a set of allowed types of values for the attribute. Unlike *properties*, *attribute names* are not provided by the method, but given by the modellers after an entity has been created. The information about an attribute is recorded in a conventional BSDM *Attribute Definition Form*.

The actual value of an attribute for an entity occurrence is not recorded in the definition form, and is only meaningful when a particular occurrence of an entity has been created which is normally not part of the Entity Model building exercise. However, because we provide a simulation facility to demonstrate the dynamic aspects of a model, attribute values are also formalised which will be described in Chapter 7.

Since an attribute value is dynamic and manipulated by other components (processes) of the model, it is useful to define its value types using *Attribute_type*. The types of values are 'STRING', 'INTEGER', or a predetermined finite set of "landmark" values. A landmark value is a value which shows the representative state of the system. Since we are only concerned with values which are significant to the modeller, we will only record landmark values. A good example of using landmark values is the specification of *life statuses* of an entity occurrence, which is illustrated in the following section. While landmarks are expressed in linear and discrete values, it is also possible to show a value that is between two landmark values in the form of *[landmark_value_1, landmark_value_2]* to show a value that is greater than *landmark_value_1* and smaller than *landmark_value_2*.

A qualitative approach has been deployed for assignment of attributes values. This approach has enabled KBST-BM to derive finite states of the model. Each derived state is significant in its meaning to the modeller, and is distinctive from other states which include entity occurrences with representative attributes. Attributes which are not restricted are mostly used for documentation (e.g. STRING) and with limited computational usage.

5.4 Representing the Life Cycle Diagram

The instantiation of an entity, an entity occurrence, has a life cycle which starts when it is "created" (or originated) and ends when it is "terminated" in a model. When an occurrence is "terminated", it becomes a history record in the model and will be used for reference only. It no longer plays any active role or may be treated as an active instance in the model. BSDM uses *Life Cycle Diagrams (LCD)* to capture this information.

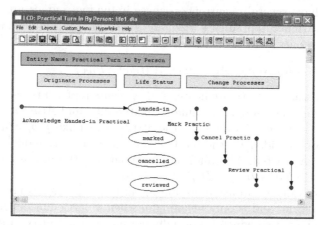

Fig. 5.3. The Life Cycle Diagram for "Practical Turned In By Person"

Figure 5.3 shows an example *Life Cycle Diagram* for the entity *Practical Turned In By Person* as it is used in BSDM. According to this diagram, occurrences of this entity may have four different possible life statuses: *handed-in, marked, cancelled and reviewed*. This means that the work of a practical assignment can be 'handed-in' (by a student), 'marked' (by a first marker), or become 'cancelled' (e.g. in the case of a new submission of a practical from the same student which automatically cancels the previous submissions) and the grade of the practical work can be 'reviewed' by a second marker after it has been 'marked' by the first marker. The diagram does not limit the situation to where the first marker and the second marker are the same person, but it points out that a grade has to be reviewed. Had there been a policy that all practical work has to be reviewed by a different marker, it would have been documented as a business rule.

The left-to-right arrows in a Life Cycle Diagram point to the allowed starting statuses for any occurrence of the corresponding entity type. Figure 5.3 specifies that when an occurrence of *Practical Turned In By Person* is created, its life status is 'handed-in'. This example gives only one starting life status, though in other situations there may be more than one starting status for an entity which would be denoted by the additional left-to-right arrows in the corresponding *LCD* diagram.

The top-down arrows in a Life Cycle Diagram define the possible transitions between life statuses: with the beginning of line aligned to the "begin" or "start" life status and the arrow ending aligned to the designated life status. For example, in Figure 5.3, the two left top-down arrows start with status "handed-in", but one ends with status "marked" and the other ends with status "cancelled", denoting that when a practical work has been handed in by a student, it can either be marked or cancelled afterwards. The right-most top-down arrow denotes that a practical is reviewed after it has been marked. Note that there is no arrow which leads from status cancelled downward; in fact, a cancelled practical is an *inactive* instance and is only stored for reference. Also note that in this figure any marked practical cannot be cancelled and any reviewed practical stays the way it is. This reflects the marking policy of the university.

The definition of life cycle status and the allowed transitions between life statuses of an entity is an important attribute of an entity which not only reflects the policies of an organisation, it also decides the dynamic state of an entity occurrence and that of the whole model. Therefore, it is important that they are represented and handled in the formal language.

The predicates *life_cycle_start_status, life_cycle_end_status* as well as *life_cycle_transit*, are used to represent three different kinds of life status information respectively. Predicate *life_cycle_start_status* stores a possible life status in *Life_status* of an entity occurrence when an occurrence of the corresponding *Entity_name* has been created; whereas predicate *life_cycle_end_status* stores a possible life status in *Life_status* of an entity occurrence when an occurrence of the corresponding *Entity_name* has been terminated; the predicate *life_cycle_transit* records one directional transition, going from the *From_status* to the *To_status*. These predicates are shown below.

> *life_cycle_start_status(Entity_name, Life_status)*
> *life_cycle_end_status(Entity_name, Life_status)*
> *life_cycle_transit(Entity_name, From_status, To_status)*

Therefore, Figure 5.3 can now be formally represented using the predicates below.

> *life_cycle_start_status('Practical Turned In By Person', handed-in)*
> *life_cycle_end_status('Practical Turned In By Person', cancelled)*
> *life_cycle_end_status('Practical Turned In By Person', reviewed)*
> *life_cycle_transit('Practical Turned In By Person', handed-in, marked)*
> *life_cycle_transit('Practical Turned In By Person', handed-in, cancelled)*
> *life_cycle_transit('Practical Turned In By Person', marked, reviewed)*

5.5 Representing Domain Knowledge

BSDM provides advice on how to build good business models. We extract this advice and formalise it under the abstract class *rule* in the class hierarchy shown in Figure 5.1. Some pieces of advice are applicable to Entity Models and others to process models. Each piece of advice is recommended with different strength. According to the degree of enforcement on a model, we classify them in two categories: model rules and guidelines. A model rule is a rule which must be followed if the model is to be sound. Model guidelines are recommendations for a model of good style. They are classified in the classes of *entity_model_rule*, *process_model_rule*, *entity_guideline* and *process_guideline* which are subclasses of *model_rule* and *guideline* which are subclasses of *rule* in the class hierarchy in Figure 5.1.[2] To distinguish these two different strengths of enforcement, two implication operators are deployed in our formalism: '⇒' is used to represent a model rule and is read as 'must be'; '▷' is used for model guidelines and is read as 'should be'. Formula 'P ⇒ Q' reads 'if P is true then Q must be true', and formula 'P ▷ Q' reads 'if P is true then Q should be true'. More details about this naming convention are in Appendix F.

The advice that is given by the method can be categorised into three kinds: general methodical issues, application domain related methodical issues, and pure application domain issues. The advice of purely methodical issues is the advice which is normally associated with the strongest recommendation which when violated often leads to an error in the model. We classify this type of advice as model rules. Advice of application domain related methodical issues is more flexible. This type of advice provides guidelines for standard practice for most organisations. However, since the final decision of design very often depends on the particular circumstances and requirements of the organisation

---

[2] The classes *business_rule* and *attribute_rule* are introduced in Chapter 6.

concerned, exceptions are also acceptable. We classify this type of advice as model guidelines. Advice regarding purely domain-dependent issues is general advice about the construction of a model or the acceptable boundary of defining of an entity, or an error checking mechanism for spotting model inappropriateness. Such advice is mostly used to judge the discrepancy between the built model and business reality. Since the final recommendation for any particular circumstances for an organisation cannot be pre-determined without knowing the particular organisation in depth, this type of advice is not (and cannot be) formalised as rules and guidelines. (However, some such knowledge can be obtained by comparing with similar business models. We deploy *Case-Based Reasoning* techniques to store and reuse business models to provide additional support. Chapter 8 provides more details.)

The text below gives an illustration of how an entity guideline and model rule can be formalised using our formal language *DefBM*.

Example Entity Model Rule

A *dependence* in BSDM means that occurrences of a parent entity must have already been created or are created at the same time as occurrences of its child entities are created. A natural deduction of the above observation is a model rule which states that any circular dependence relationship (a parent being dependent on its child) must not be allowed in a business model.

To describe this rule, we introduce a predicate *ancestor(P, Q)* to mean that P is an *ancestor entity* of Q, if P is a parent entity of Q, formally defined by the *parent_type* predicate, or that it is an ancestor entity of Q through the transitivity property of the *parent_type* predicate. The *ancestor* predicate can be described formally in the two expressions below:

$$\forall X, Y, E. parent\_type(X, Y) \wedge E \in Y$$
$$\Rightarrow$$
$$ancestor(E, X)$$

$$\forall X, Y, E, Z. parent\_type(X, Y) \wedge E \in Y \wedge ancestor(Z, E)$$
$$\Rightarrow$$
$$ancestor(Z, X)$$

The circular dependence rule is then represented by the expression below which can be read as "if X is an entity, then X cannot be its own ancestor".

$$\forall X. class(entity, X) \Rightarrow \neg ancestor(X, X)$$

Example Entity Guideline

BSDM recommends that the depth of an Entity Model should normally be no more than four layers, i.e. four steps through the dependency links. It also provides the types of entities which should be placed in each layer, they are collectively called *Entity Families*. The recommendation for the number of entity layers is to prevent a model from being over-constrained by several layers of dependencies through levels of entities. Since this is only "soft" advice and the final decision very much depends on the application, it has been formalised as a guideline in our formal language.

If we define *property(Entity, level, N)* to mean that an entity *Entity* is located at level N in the business model, then this "4-layer" guideline can be described as:

$$property(Entity, level, N) \rhd N < 5.$$

Folklore Rule

In addition to advice given explicitly in BSDM manuals, there is a small number of the rules which are not mentioned in the method but are natural consequence of the method itself and, therefore, must be followed to create a sound model. These rules are also identified and captured as part of the formalisation. An example of this kind of folklore rule is the "circular dependency rule" that we have shown in the example above. Since these rules are derivable from the method itself and they do not require any treatment which differs from the explicit ones, we do not use separate classes to accommodate them.

Entity Families

Within the domain of an Entity Model, BSDM provides guidance about the structure and example entities to be used in an entity model. They are collectively called *Entity Families*. This information is formalised in our *Entity Conceptual Hierarchy* and represented in *DefBM*. This information is used as background knowledge in our system, *KBST-BM*, for understanding the semantics of an entity and to assist in determining the appropriateness of the selection of an entity during automated Entity Model verification and consultation sessions. A detailed discussion of *Entity Families* and their representation is given in Section 8.7.

Obviously, there are more aspects in an Entity Model that have been formalised but are not described in this chapter. A list of the Entity Modelling rules and guidelines used in the system is given in Appendix G.

5.6 Inference

As different Entity Model rules and guidelines may verify different aspects of the model, similar rules and guidelines are grouped together in *KBST-BM* to enable an iterative, systematic and topical verification process. It gives the user the freedom to either run a complete check on the model or to choose to work on a particular aspect of the model, i.e. to use certain rules/guidelines only, in a smaller *"Plan-Build-Test-Refine"* cycle. This helps the user to focus on a particular design issue and not be overloaded by too much advice which is of no immediate concern.

Each of these model rules and guidelines are also implemented modularly and therefore can operate independently. This enables the user to verify the model in his/her preferred order. It is also advantageous if the rule base is to be modified or extended in the future.

There are in total eleven sets of Entity Model rules and six sets of guidelines. Based on these sets of rules and guidelines and (partial) information about an Entity Model, so-called *critiques* are inferred. These *critiques* provide help to the modeller during model verification. They do not replace the manual verification process entirely, because not all errors and solutions can be standardised or made available, as has been mentioned in the previous section. Instead, partial verification and validation is provided to complement human efforts. In fact, due to the common lack of automatic verification and validation methods for informal methods, partial verification and validation methods can be especially interesting and helpful in quality assurance.

Several types of critiques are provided.

- *Correctness* critiques detect structural, syntactical and semantic errors.
- *Completeness* critiques identify incomplete information in the model and suggest which missing concepts may need to be included.
- *Consistency* critiques point out discrepancies in different parts of the model.
- *Appropriateness* critiques show deviations from standard practices.
- *Presentation* critiques highlight awkward use of naming style which can lead to misunderstandings or conceptual errors.
- *Alternative* critiques search for similar standard and past models and present them as alternatives to a given modelling decision. This critique makes use of a case library of business models (see Chapter 8 for more comments on the use of *Case-Based Reasoning* techniques).

To provide these critiques, each of the above logic expressions are translated into semantically equivalent CLIPS rules [79] which use the above introduced representation of primitives (such as *class*, *parent_type* and *ancestor*) in the model.[3]

For example, logical expressions of the form below:

- $property1(X) \Rightarrow property2(X)$ *(must always be true), and*
- $property3(X) \triangleright property4(X)$ *(should always be true)*

are firstly negated and formalised into a standardised *Conjunction Normal Form*. For instance, the above model rule and guideline is negated and formalised respectively as the formula below.

Model rule: must always be true
$\neg(property1(X) \Rightarrow property2(X))(negation)$
$= \neg(\neg property1(X) \lor property2(X))(normalisation)$
$= property1(X) \land \neg(property2(X))$

---

[3] Because the system that we have chosen for our implementation uses CLIPS, our formal expressions are translated into CLIPS rules. These formal rules can also be programmed in Prolog, as we have done in our first version of the system, or any other suitable language.

Model guidelines: should always be true

$$\neg(property3(X) \rhd property4(X))(negation)$$
$$= \neg(\neg property3(X) \vee property4(X))(normalisation)$$
$$= property3(X) \wedge \neg(property4(X))$$

If any of the normalised formulae are true, a violation is found. This forms the precondition part of a model rule or guideline in CLIPS which checks a model by searching for instances *satisfying* the precondition (it can consecutively find all instances). If any instance is found, then the corresponding model rule and guideline is violated. The CLIPS rule below can be implemented, where *rule_n* and *guideline_n1* denote the identifiers of the corresponding model rules and guidelines.

$$property1(X) \wedge (not(property2(X)))$$
$$=>$$
$$advise(rule\_n, X)$$

$$property3(X) \wedge (not(property4(X)))$$
$$=>$$
$$advise(guideline\_n1, X)$$

In response to the user's request to verify a business model, the inference engine dynamically represents the user model using the formal language and tries to prove each *rule_n* and *guideline_n1* to be true by actively searching all violation instances in the model. If any violation has been found for a *rule* or *guideline*, the corresponding modelling rule or guideline has been broken in the model, and explanation and advice are given to the user, via the function *advise(Violation_id, Source_data)*.

Having the knowledge about these rules and guidelines embedded in the system, the inference engine can provide information which it has found is the cause of the violation. It is also able to give advice on how to correct the error. For instance, if the system has found a cyclic dependence in the model, a warning is given to the user containing information about this violation. It provides a list of entities which are involved in the cycle and suggests possible dependence links to be erased. An example use of KBST-BM for model verification is given below.

5.6.1 Model Verification Consultation Example

Figure 5.4 modifies the example Life Cycle Diagram shown in Figure 5.2. In this figure, one additional top-down arrow '(1)' is added. Arrow (1) is incorrect because it is initially intended that a 'cancelled' practical from a student should not be processed any further. However, this intention may have been lost during a complex modelling exercise and arrow (1) was added at a later stage.

Terminating life statuses of all entities are specified in two ways: by the modellers during model-building activities, normally leading to a status which is only applicable to a particular entity; or as a standard terminating life status

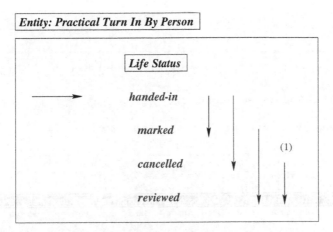

Fig. 5.4. A Life Cycle Diagram with error

which is applicable to all entities, such as "cancelled" and "closed" provided by BSDM. This knowledge can be used to support parts of the checking to determine whether an entity's life cycle has been defined correctly. For instance, if there exists a transition out of a known terminating life status, as indicated by arrow (1), an error has been made and the system should detect it and give appropriate advice.

The model rule which can be used to detect this error uses this knowledge is described formally in the expression below (the two types of terminating life statuses are each formally represented as *life_cycle_end_status* and *terminated_life_status*). Although this rule is sufficiently self-explanatory, a more detailed description is given in Appendix G.

$life\_cycle\_transit(Entity, From\_life, To\_life)$
$\Rightarrow$
$\neg terminated\_life\_status(Entity, From\_life) \wedge$
$\neg life\_cycle\_end\_status(From\_life)$

An example model verification and consultation window for this error is shown in Figure 5.5. The top left slot labelled 'Verify Model Type' indicates the type (or the part) of the business model that the system will be checking: there are currently two types of models that can be checked: an entity or a process model and in this case it is the Entity Model that the system is verifying. The second slot 'Verify Rule/Guideline' indicates that either a set of the modelling rules (R) or guidelines (G) is used: as 'R' is given it means a set of modelling rule is applied. Slot 'Verify Rule/Guideline Set(1-11/6)' indicates that there are 11 sets of modelling rules and 6 sets of guidelines which can be used for verification: as illustrated it is the Entity Modelling rule set 11 that is used. When all of this information has been given, the user can press the button 'Verify NOW' to activate the verification process.

After checking the Entity Model, 5 violations have been found and are shown in the 'Rule/Guideline Violation List' Window. The user can now highlight any

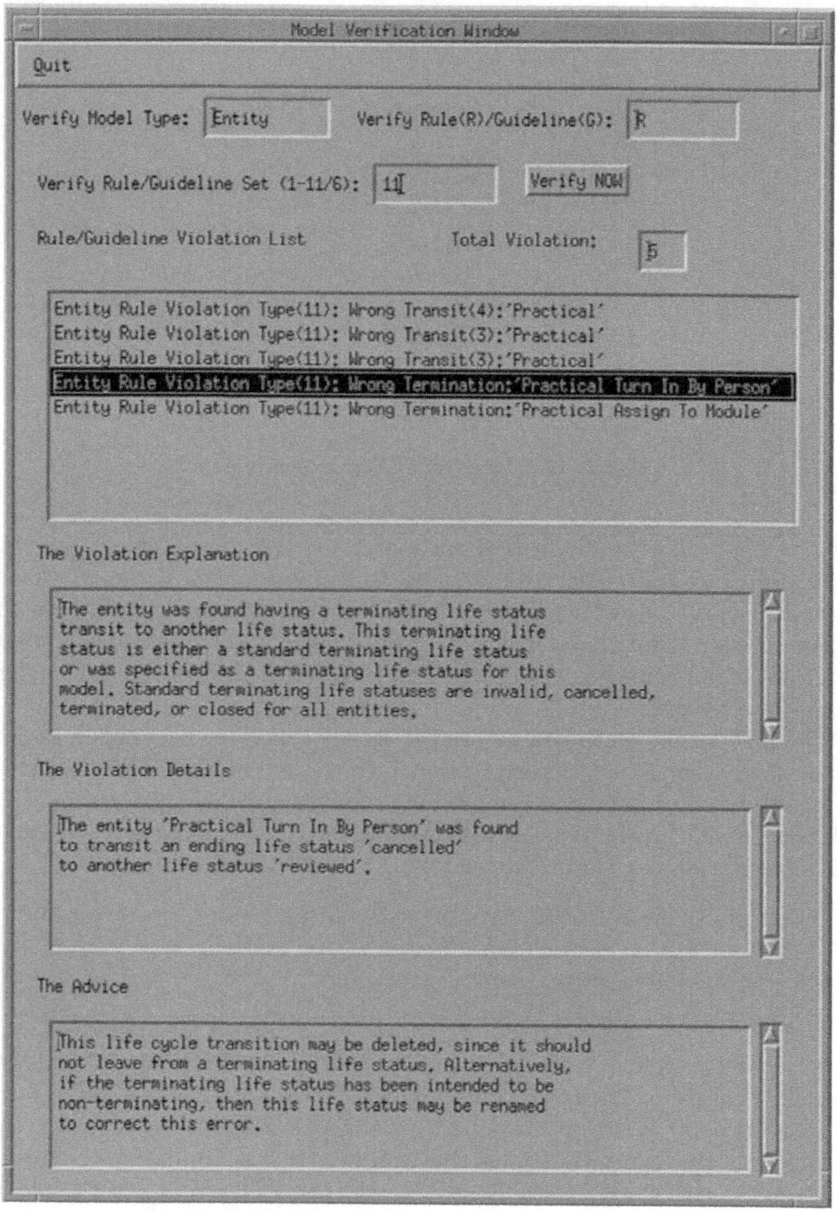

Fig. 5.5. A consultation window in KBST-BM

particular violation to see more details. Figure 5.5 shows that the user has high-
lighted the violation 'Wrong Termination' which involves the entity 'Practical
Turn In By Person'. A detailed explanation about this violation, the violated
instance and the suspected erroneous properties, and the corresponding advice
for the user to correct this error are given in the following three sub-windows

in the consultation window. Similar violation instances are grouped together and displayed in the same "list" window, therefore making it easier to work with as has been shown in this example. To see all of the violations listed in this window, the user can highlight any instance to see more details.

5.7 Conclusion

This chapter demonstrated how an informal or semi-formal method, such as *BSDM's Business Modelling Method*, can benefit by applying a formal method. To capture the knowledge of a business model a formal language, *DefBM*, has been devised which is based on an inheritance class hierarchy. This inheritance hierarchy acts as a meta-model which provides a backbone of categories for distinguishing different types of model concepts allowing attributes to be passed on and model rules and guidelines to be applied to similar types of model primitives.

A BSDM Entity Model can be formalised and represented using *DefBM*. Knowledge, model rules and guidelines are formalised and embedded in a knowledge-based support tool, called *KBST-BM*. Standard and generic knowledge of the method and the business domain is stored as facts in the database of *KBST-BM*; modelling rules and guidelines are stored as rules. Together they are used by *KBST-BM* to infer and inspect the user Entity Models and provide advice for errors. This capability of *KBST-BM* supports the iterative *Plan-Build-Test-Refine* model development cycle, it also allows relevant parts of the model which may be scattered within the model to be examined collectively and systematically using the original method. Compared with many EM tools which are little more than "electronic paper", *KBST-BM* provides useful additional assistance to modellers.

5.8 Exercises

1. Discuss benefits and limitations of knowledge representation techniques. Is it possible (or useful) to represent all the knowledge there is to know?
2. Describe the overall modelling support process and how a formal language may play a part in that.
3. Describe steps in creating a formal language. Can all informal models be formalised?
4. Given different goals, different formal languages are created. Can you illustrate the different goals and how the design of a language should be altered accordingly?
5. Represent the business model in Figure 5.6 using *DefBM*.
6. Discuss the requirements when designing a model support tool and give examples of how a design may meet such requirements.
7. Discuss the different types of verification and validation (V&V) techniques that may be offered for a formalised Enterprise Model. What are the considerations when providing such support to the user?

8. Verification and validation must be based upon existing knowledge. Discuss the potential sources of such knowledge.

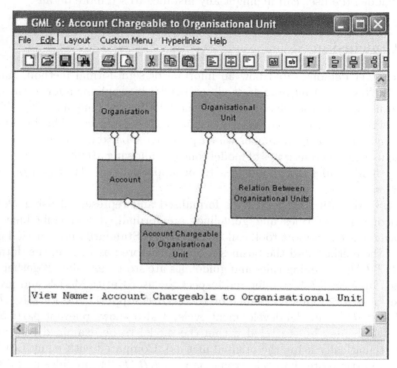

Fig. 5.6. A business model for business account and organisation

5.9 Advanced Exercises

1. This chapter includes two different types of inference rules: model rules and guidelines. Explain their semantics and discuss whether this approach complies with First Order Logic (FOL).
2. Continuing from the previous question, explain how the different types of inference rules may (or may not) differ, in terms of implementation, when compared with the normal inference connectives in FOL. Refer back to Sections 4.2 and 4.3 for more details on FOL.
3. Take the three example Entity Model rules of Section 5.5 and implement them using an appropriate programming language, such as Prolog, Lisp, Clips or Java, using the formal language *DefBM*.

6

Formal Support for Process Modelling

When an *Entity Model* is completed, the next BSDM activity is to build the *Process Model*. Following the same formal framework which has been used for the *Entity Model* (illustrated in Figure 5.1), one will be able to formally represent model primitives and properties of a Process Model using the devised formal language *DefBM*. As previously, advice for building business models in BSDM has been extracted from the user manuals to construct model rules and guidelines. Extensions of modelling rules and guidelines in connection with the execution of business processes have also been derived from BSDM and formalised. These formalised modelling rules and guidelines form the basis for automatic verification and validation facilities in our support tool *KBST-BM*. This chapter describes the components of a Process Model, their formal representation, and the corresponding automatic modelling support which is provided in *KBST-BM*. An example verification and consultation session using *KBST-BM* is illustrated at the end of this chapter. An extensive description of all of the captured and formalised modelling rules and guidelines can be found in Appendix H.

6.1 Process Model and Process-Entity Matrix

Modellers can extend an *Entity Model* with information about how a business operates to form a *Process Model*. Instead of describing the detailed current practice to accomplish certain goals, a process model captures the necessary logical steps, in business terms, to achieve these goals. Things which need to be known or managed in a process are represented as entities and are normally already identified during the Entity Model building activity, though additional entities can be added by revisiting this activity. The set of relevant entities are included in a *Process Scope*. Figure 6.1 shows a screen-shot of our system describing an example Process Model which was built on top of the Entity Model, previously shown in Figure 5.2. Two example processes are shown: 'Acknowledge Handed-In Practical' and 'Module Performance Assessment'. Each includes four entities in its scope.

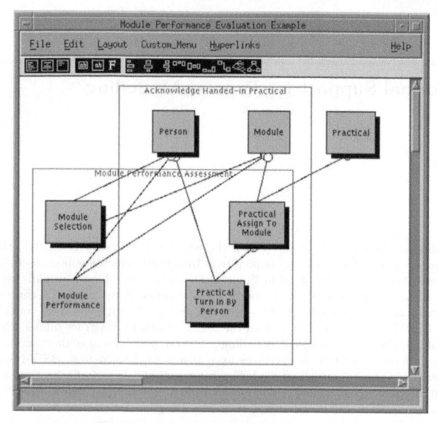

Fig. 6.1. An example BSDM Process Model

Before we go into more details about BSDM's Process Model, it may be a good time to introduce the concept of classes and occurrences in a Process Model. As has been described in Section 5.2 for BSDM's Entity Model, that an entity in BSDM denotes a class of things in the described world and that each entity includes a set of things.[1] Similarly, in a BSDM Process Model, a process denotes a type of *process instances* or *occurrences* so that each process may include a set of actual processing events being carried out in the described world.

A BSDM process includes at least one entity in its scope. The relationship between a process and an included entity is specified by the role that an entity plays in the process. This relationship is called an *entity function* and is normally summarised in matrices like the one in Figure 6.2. There are seven entity functions in BSDM:

- *originate focal,*
- *originate normal,*
- *originate in-flight,*

---

[1] They are often called occurrences or instances.

Process-Entity Matrix		
	Ack. Handed-In Practical	Module Performance Ass.
Person	refer normal	
Module	refer normal	
Practical Assign to Module	refer normal	refer normal
Practical Turn In By Person	originate focal	originate in-flight
Module Selection		refer normal
Module Performance		originate focal

Fig. 6.2. A Process-Entity Matrix

- *change focal,*
- *change normal,*
- *refer normal,* and
- *refer master.*

An entity function which includes the key word "focal", i.e. *originate focal* or *change focal,* indicates that the main purpose of the process is to create an *originate focal* entity occurrence (instance) or to modify attributes of the *change focal* entity occurrence. The originate type of entity functions, such as *originate focal, normal* and *in-flight,* specify the creation of occurrences of the entity type. The change type of entity functions, such as *change focal* and *normal,* represent update operations carried out on the properties of the entity. The refer type of entity functions, such as *refer normal* and *master,* capture the referencing of an entity during process execution. The three types used in our example are *originate focal, refer normal* and *originate in-flight.* The matrix in Figure 6.2 shows the relationships (entity functions) between the processes and entities shown in Figure 6.1.

The BSDM modeller specifies the role of each entity in a process. The primary purpose of the process 'Acknowledge Handed-in Practical' is to acknowledge the fact that the practical work which has been handed in by a person (student) is received, i.e. its purpose is to create an occurrence of the *Practical Turn In By Person* entity (the *originate focal* entity). To create the occurrence, information stored in relevant entities, i.e. *Person, Module* and *Practical Assign to Module,* is used. These entities, hence, are *refer normal* entities. In the process of *Module Performance Assessment,* the entity *Practical Turn In By Person* is an *originate in-flight* entity. This indicates that records of practical must be known before *Module Performance* can be calculated. Otherwise, the corresponding practicals must be recorded and relevant marks assigned,[2] as part of the assessment process, before the overall *Module Performance* can be determined.

---

[2] The mark is null if a practical has not been handed in.

6.2 Representing the Process Model

There are two main kinds of processes in a BSDM model: *originate* and *change*. For the *KBST-BM* system, we classify these two kinds of processes respectively as *originate* and *change* classes in the inheritance hierarchy (Figure 5.1). They are subclasses of *process*. We further distinguish each process into subcategories, according to the functions that they carry out. Similar to the representation of an entity, a process is formally represented through a *class* predicate:

class(Process_type, Process_name).

In the example given in Figure 6.1, the process *Acknowledge Handed-In Practical* is an *originate_focal* process, because its main function is to originate an entity which is its focal entity. On the other hand, the process *Module Performance Assessment* is an *originate_focal_if* process, because its main function includes not only to originate its focal entity but also to manage its *in-flight* entity. The class *originate_focal_if* is a subclass of *originate_focal*, which is a subclass of *originate_process* in the inheritance class hierarchy. The example's two processes can be formally represented as follows:

class(originate_focal, 'Acknowledge Handed-In Practical')
class(originate_focal_if, 'Module Performance Assessment')

A process is a class described by a set of common characteristics which are shared by a collection of business processes. As was the case for entities, these common characteristics are recorded through the use of a *property* predicate: *property(Process_name, Property_name, Property_Content)*. The values of these properties are static, i.e. they remain unchanged during the simulation of the model.[3]

As mentioned earlier, entity functions are relationships between processes and entities. They are therefore modelled as subclasses of *relationship* and *entity_function* in the inheritance class hierarchy. To represent entity functions, a predicate *Entity_function(Process_name, Entity_name)* is used. The formal representation of the three entity functions which are used in the example Process Model (Figure 6.1, *refer normal, originate focal* and *originate in-flight*) for process 'Module Performance Assessment' is given below.

refer_normal_fun('Module Performance Assessment',
                  'Practical Assign to Module')
refer_normal_fun('Module Performance Assessment',
                  'Module Selection')
originate_focal_fun('Module Performance Assessment',
                  'Module Performance')

---

[3] Dynamic aspects, i.e. issues dealing with the execution of a business model, are covered in Chapter 7, when we discuss the *procedural model*.

originate_if_fun('Module Performance Assessment',
'Practical Turn In By Person')

Since each entity in a process must play a role in a process, i.e. has an entity function, the collective information of entity functions define the process scope. This derived process scope can be used to check the drawing of a Process Model. It can also be used to understand the purpose of a process which forms the basis for checking whether two processes can be merged or whether one is subsumed by the other.

6.3 Representing the Life Status of a Process

Based on the *Life Cycle Diagram* completed during the Entity Model building sessions, BSDM allows the modellers to further specify the relationships between entities, their life statuses and processes. For example, Figure 6.3 adds information about which processes are involved in the calculation of a practical mark by extending the *Life Cycle Diagram* which was initially built during the Entity Model building activity (see Figure 5.3).

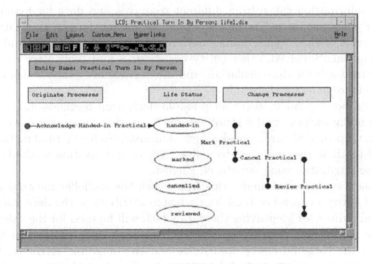

Fig. 6.3. An extended BSDM *Life Cycle Diagram*

As one can see, four processes have been identified: one originate process *Acknowledge Handed-In Practical* and three change processes *Mark Practical, Cancel Practical* and *Review Practical.* To represent this new process information, we use predicates *orgprocess* and *chgprocess.*

orgprocess(Process_name, Entity_name, Life)
chgprocess(Process_name, Entity_name, Start, End)

The *orgprocess* states that process *Process_name* is an *originate* process, and that its actions include the creation of occurrences for entity *Entity_name* with a (starting) life status *Life*. The *chgprocess* predicate states that process *Process_name* is a *change* process, and that its actions include the changing of life statuses for occurrences of entity *Entity_name* from a life status *Start* to another life status *End*.

This information is used to help safeguard a complete and appropriate transit of an entity life cycle. Furthermore, it can be used to derive information needed for cross-checking the design of process scope. Part of this checking is carried out as a part of automatic Process Model verification, which is described in Section 6.6, another part is implemented via the *procedural model* and its simulator which is described in Chapter 7.

6.4 Representing User-Defined Attribute Rules

BSDM allows *derivable attributes* for entity occurrences. The value of a *derivable attribute* is the result of a calculation based on one or more attribute values of itself or other entity occurrences. *Derivable attributes* normally provide aggregate information taken from different resources and data for management and analytical purposes. The function used to derive values for these attributes must consist of three types of information: the derivable attribute and the entity occurrence involved, other entity occurrences and their attributes which provide the basis for the calculation, and the derivation method which provides the means to generate the result.

We do not intend to cover all possible derivation methods, because they come in many varieties and it is not feasible to provide comprehensive coverage. Instead, we provided a framework which demonstrates how formal methods can be used to allow the modellers to define their own derivation methods for the derivable attributes using structured English.

As mentioned above, under this framework the modeller must specify the targeted entity occurrence (and its derivable attributes), the derivation function, and indices for identifying the data which will be used for the calculation. The first piece of information is given when through the user interface the user identifies the targeted entity occurrence and the derivable attribute. For the second part, two mathematical functions, summation and average, which are normally used in a derivation method are built into *KBST-BM*. The modellers can choose to use these derivation functions or build their own functions using Prolog expressions.

As not all data items can be identified directly, some searching and identifying methods must be provided. Since entities are linked by dependencies throughout the model, entity occurrences are also connected by dependency occurrences. Following the structure of dependency occurrences, relevant entity occurrences can be found and identified. The third part of the information, therefore, is for the user to provide the identifying information which enables the system to search for and identify the individual data items which are used as a basis for calculating the attribute value. We call the identifying information an *index* because it is used as an index to identify entity occurrences. The following explains in more detail.

6.4.1 Predicate for User-Defined Attribute Rules

All of the relevant information is described by the predicate *derive_att_rule* given below.

```
derive_att_rule(Ent_name, Ent_ID, Ent_parents
                Att_name, Att_value,
                List_of_index_entities,
                List_of_data_items,
                Derivation_method,
                Attribute_rule_content).
```

The information of entity name (*Ent_name*) and entity ID (*Ent_ID*) together identify a particular entity occurrence. *Ent_parents* stores the occurrences of the corresponding entity parents. *Att_name* is the name of the derivable attribute, whereas *Att_value* stores the (eventually) derived attribute values. *List_of_index_entities* gives the set of all entity occurrences which are used as *indices* to identify the referring entity occurrences. An index can be a particular entity occurrence or an ancestor entity occurrence of the referring entities. *List_of_data_items* specifies the pairs of entity (type) and attribute name of the referring entity occurrences which hold the necessary data for deriving the result. *Derivation_method* is either an empty list which indicates that a built-in function of *KBST-BM* has been used, or a list containing the user-defined functions. *Attribute_rule_content* specifies the derivation and search method which generates the final result.

Four types of statements can be used in the *Attribute_rule_content*. The underlying grammar for these statements is described next, followed by some examples of how the *derive_att_rule* predicate is used.

6.4.2 Grammar for User-Defined Attribute Rules

BSDM mentions entity occurrences and their attributes, and the need to specify attribute rules which specify how attribute values can be derived from other attributes, but it does not specify how the relevant information that is scattered in different parts of the model can be put together to generate values for the derivable attributes, nor does it describe how the attribute rules are used in a process. We need to provide a mechanism which can capture this information and produce the corresponding answers. We first try to understand BSDM attribute rules in an attempt to draw the necessary requirements and design structure for representing them:

- Not all information needed is known even at run-time: to generate a derivable attribute value, attribute values of other entity occurrences are often needed. However, those values are often generated dynamically during the simulation, therefore cannot be obtained when the attribute rules are defined. Furthermore, it is also common that the referred entity occurrences themselves are not known, since they are also created dynamically. There is, therefore, a need for a mechanism which relates the known information to the unknown to help identify and retrieve the set of "base" values needed for calculation at run-time.

- Several types of base/referred data items may be included in a derivation function: known distinctive and particular values enumerated by the modeller; entity attributes which share common characteristics; results of other derivation methods; or a combination of any of the above situations.

- The derivation or calculation function is often application domain and case dependent. Since the calculation function may come in any arbitrary form (arithmetic or not), the design must be as flexible as possible, in fact preferably completely open-ended to allow the user's own design, but supplied with some commonly used functions.

- The attribute rule must be easy to read: since most of the modellers are not familiar with formal languages, describing attribute rules using formal notations is not appropriate. The more desirable descriptions should be easy to design, understand and use.

To accommodate the above requirements for BSDM attribute rules, we have used the approach below:

- To allow the dynamic identification of referring attributes which are not known to the modellers when derivation methods are specified, an indexing and searching mechanism is provided to enable the automatic identification of those attributes during process execution. Since all BSDM entity occurrences can be identified through dependency links, we have used this property for searching and navigation in the dynamic business model.

- To accommodate and capture the diversified relationships between the referring data and the calculation functions, we have provided a grammar (for *Attribute_rule_content*) which allows the user to specify the *parent* or *ancestor entity occurrences* as *indices* to search for the desirable referring entity occurrences and attributes. It is also possible to use a combination of complex and compound sentences and phrases to obtain inter-medium results from the collected entity attributes and use the results as an input to the derivation function.

- To provide the maximum flexibility for calculation functions, commonly used functions are provided in the system and can be called by the calculation function. We also allow the user to design their own functions using *Prolog* expressions which will be used by *KBST-BM*.

- For easier design, use and understanding of attributes rules, we use structured English to express these rules. The aim of being "easy to design" is somewhat contradictory to the previous aim of "maximum flexibility" which inevitably requires more skills from the user. One compromise is through the use of a form of structured English which provides the needed syntax

and semantics for computational operations for automation and is intended
to give an intuitive understanding for its users.

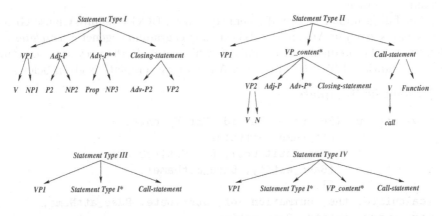

(* This construct can be used more than once, when connected by a comma)

(** This construct can be used more than once, when connected by the connective word "and")

Fig. 6.4. Grammar trees for BSDM attribute rules

Figure 6.4 shows the grammar for four types of statements which can be
used to describe BSDM attribute rules: each type is labelled with statement
type I, II, III or IV. The grammar trees adapts the convention used in the field
of natural language processing [74] [77]. The abbreviation *VP* stands for "Verb
Phrase", *NP* stands for "Noun Phrase", *Adj-P* for "Adjective Phrase" and *Adv-
P* for "Adverb Phrase"; wherever there is an ID attached to them, it indicates
the uniqueness of the corresponding phrases. For example, *VP1* and *VP2* are
different Verb Phrases, because each may deploy different key words for verbs,
or even with slightly different syntactic structure. There is a collection of words
and combinations of phrases (clauses) that are recognisable by this system. For
instance, there are two kinds of closing clauses that can terminate an attribute
rule: the "closing-statement" and the "call-statement", as they are shown in
the grammar tree. There is also a set of verbs which are acceptable by the
grammar, i.e. calculate, compute, use, search and find, where each verb is used
in a phrase where its meaning is the most appropriate for the context. The
set of recognisable vocabularies can be extended quite easily by extending the
system's dictionary; the grammar structure of the rules is predetermined.

The grammar design satisfies the requirements mentioned above for BSDM
attribute rules. Domain-specific (terminal) phrases have been introduced: *closing-
statement* and *call-statement*. Both statements indicate the enactment of the
specified evaluation function. *Call-statement* also specifies the input parameters and the obtained result(s). In order to support the complicated constraints
which can be applied when retrieving data and the diversity of calculation
methods, repetitive use of some phrase structures is possible: these are marked
by '*' or '**' in the figure. For instance, *Adv-P* can be used several times in

a sentence to define the multiple constraints applied when retrieving data. A statement type I may therefore has the syntactical structure of VPI, Adj-P, Adv-P and Closing-statement; or it may be VPI, Adj-P, two Adv-Ps and the Closing-statement.

The full grammar is formally defined using a DCG (Definite Clause Grammar) and is given in Appendix I. Based on this grammar, generic *templates* are derived for the predicate *derive_att_rule* which provide the necessary structure to be instantiated by attribute rules. An example template is given below.

(1) Example Template

```
derive_att_rule(Ent_name, Ent_id, Ent_Parents, }
                Att_name, AttValue,
                [Ref_EntityOcc1, Ref_EntityOcc2],
                [Base_entity, Base_attName],
                [],
      [calculate, the, summation, of, attribute, Base_attName,
      for, every, entity, Base_entity,
      with, condition,
      entity-ancestor, Ref_EntityOcc1,
      and, with, condition,
          entity-ancestor, Ref_EntityOcc2,
      when, finished, save, the, result, in, AttValue] ).
```

The predicate above can be understood as "To infer the derivable value *AttValue* for attribute *Att_name* of entity occurrence *Ent_id* with entity type *Ent_name*, one needs to sum up all of the values of attribute *Base_attName* of all entity occurrences with entity type *Base_entity*. However, not all of those entities occurrences with entity type *Base_entity* are valid for this calculation, but only those which have entity occurrence *Ref_EntityOcc1* and entity occurrence *Ref_EntityOcc2* as ancestor entities, which is specified using the key word 'entity-ancestor'. When all of the correct data items (attribute values) are collected and summed up, the result is stored in the variable *AttValue*."

The sentence *[calculate, the, summation,...]* follows the grammar structure for Statement Type I, which specifies the derivation method (summation) and the targeted attribute name (Base_attName) in VP1 (Verb Phrase type I) *'calculate, the, summation, of, attribute, Base_attName'*. It also specifies the searching method in the Adj-P, i.e. *'for, every, entity, Base_entity'*, which indicates that *every* entity occurrence with the entity name *Base_entity* which at the same time satisfied the conditions specified in the Adv-Ps should be collected. Two Adv-Ps are used to specify the additional identification method in the phrase *'with, condition, entity-ancestor, Ref_EntityOcc1'*, and *'with, condition, entity-ancestor, Ref_EntityOcc2'* connected by the key word *'and'*. Finally, the 'closing-statement' is *'when, finished, save, the, result, in, AttValue'* which indicates to store the result of the calculation in the variable AttValue.

The sentence is written in a predetermined syntax and is used in place of the argument *Attribute_rule_content* as shown in the *derive_att_rule* predicate above. When the key word *summation* is replaced by *average*, the derivation function is changed to average. To modify the "conditions" for collecting different data sources, the *List_of_index_entities* and *List_of_data_items* can either be shortened or extended.

It is also possible to give more constraints on searching for the data items by giving multiple "with condition..." phrases. This is denoted as a Adv-p (Adverb Phrase) and the possibility of the repetition of this phrase is marked with '**' in Figure 6.4. Each new Adv-p is connected with an "and" key word with the previous phrase (as it is shown in this example where two Adv-Ps have been used).

(2) Construction and Execution

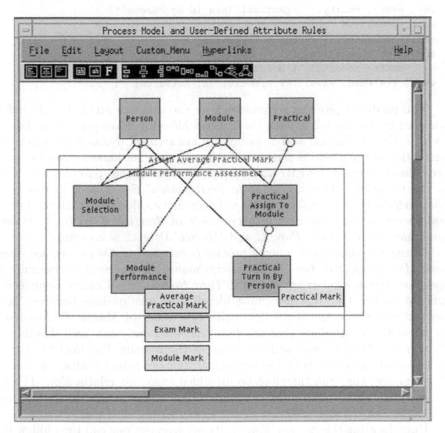

Fig. 6.5. Example process to illustrate attribute rule

Figure 6.5 shows a business model with process *Assign Average Practical Mark* and *Module Performance Assessment*. To illustrate the instantiation of a user-defined attribute rule, the relevant attributes of the corresponding entities are labelled: *Average Practical Mark, Exam Mark* and *Module Mark* are derivable attributes for entity *Module Performance*, and *Practical Mark* is a "normal" attribute for entity *Practical Turn In By Person*.

To specify the derivation method for calculating *Average Practical Mark* which will be used and carried out by process *Assign Average Practical Mark*, the template mentioned earlier is instantiated below.

```
derive_att_rule('Module Performance', Ent_id),
                [('Person', Parent1), ('Module', Parent2)],
                "'Average Practical Mark'", AttValue,
                [('Person', Parent1), ('Module', Parent2)],
                ["'Practical Turn In By Person'", "'Practical Mark'"],
                [],

    [calculate, the, average, of, attribute, "'Practical Mark'",
    for, every, entity, "'Practical Turn In By Person'",
    with, condition,
    entity-ancestor, ('Person', Parent1),
    and, with, condition,
        entity-ancestor, ('Module', Parent2),
    when, finished, save, the, result, in, AttValue]        ).
```

This predicate provides a framework for executing an attribute rule and is specified by the modeller when the Process Model is developed. Its variables, such as *Ent_id, Parent1* and *Parent2*, are instantiated dynamically when the simulation of the model is carried out, therefore are not known when the rules are defined. *'Person' Parent1* and *'Module' Parent2* are the parent occurrences of the targeting occurrence *'Module Performance' Ent_id* and, in this case, happen to be the indices for searching. There are two blocks of "with condition" statements, because the entities occurrences of *Practical Turn In By Person* must have both *'Person' Parent1* and *'Module' Parent2* as ancestors.

During the simulation, when a process occurrence of *Assign Average Practical Mark* is created, the *'Module Performance' Ent_id* entity occurrence is specified, but the referring *Practical Turn In By Person* entity occurrences are not known. One therefore must identify the relationships between these two entities. Given the particular entity occurrence of *Module Performance*, to calculate the attribute *Average Practical Mark* one must first identify the *Person* and *Module* concerned before all of the relevant *Practical Marks* can be collected. However, both *Person* and *Module* are parent entities of *Module Performance*, they can therefore be identified from this relationship. The located *Person* and *Module* entity occurrence IDs are instantiated in *Parent1* and *Parent2*.

Upon locating the two ancestor entity occurrences, one can then follow the dependency links downward to identify all of the descending *Practical Turned In By Person* entity occurrences. Once all of the *Practical Turned In By Person* entity occurrences are found, the relevant *Practical Marks* can be obtained and the average of the marks can be calculated using the system built-in function, *average*. The result is returned in *AttValue* which is stored in the attribute *Average Practical Mark* of the *Module Performance* entity occurrence.

In summary, when the process *Assign Average Practical Mark* was created, it only had the information of *Module Performance* and *Module Selection* entity occurrences. The needed data set (*Practical Marks*) for the derivation function was not known to the process and was only loosely connected to the targeting attribute. However, given the necessary indices and specifications in the predicate, the system is able to locate the missing information and generate the desirable value. It was based on the observation that most of the referring entity attributes and the target entity attributes share common characteristics, in this case the common ancestor entities. In the case when common ancestors cannot be identified, the specific indexing entity occurrences are provided at run-time.

This example demonstrated how a generic template is instantiated by a particular attribute rule, why the indexing and searching method are much needed and most importantly how the grammar provides syntax for attribute rules which gives a framework to instruct the gathering of dynamic information and producing of desirable result. The next example illustrates the construction of a user-defined attribute rule using a user-defined function.

(3) User-Defined Attribute Rule Using User-Defined Functions

Users can also define their own derivation functions using the above generic template with only minor modification. For example, the user-defined function given below (written in Prolog) uses again the example model of Figure 6.5. This rule states that the final *Module Mark* (*Res*) of a module is taken as 70% of the *Examination Mark* (*Exam*) and 30% of the *Average Practical Mark* (*AvePractical*).

```
derive_module_mark(Exam, AvePractical, Res) :-
          Res is (0.7 * Exam + 0.3 * AvePractical).
```

This user-defined derivation function can also be represented. The attribute rules description used here is of Statement Type II. Several places are modified: (1) the calculation function is specified to the full name of the Prolog rule, *derive_module_mark*, to specify the particular function to use and the sentence is started with the *use* description to improve the readability of the sentence; (2) two *VP_content* constructs are used, starting with key words, 'find attribute', which in themselves identify the referring entity occurrences (with the key word 'for entity') and attributes; (3) at the end of the rule description a *call-statement* is used instead of a *closing-statement*, which indicates that a user-defined function is called. The corresponding predicate and rule description is given below.

```
derive_att_rule("'Module Performance'", Ent_id,
            [ParentOcc1, ParentOcc2],
             "'Module Mark'" , AttValue,
            [ParentOcc1, ParentOcc2],
            ["'Module Performance'", "'Average Practical Mark'",
             "'Exam Mark'" ],
            [derive_module_mark(AttValue1, AttValue2, AttValue)],
```

```
[use, the, derive_module_mark(Exam, AvePractical, AttValue),
 for, calculation,

 find, attribute, "'Exam Mark'", for, entity, "'Module Performance'",
 with, condition,
 entity-ancestor, ParentOcc1,
 and, with, condition,
     entity-ancestor, ParentOcc2,
 when, finished, save, the, result, in, Exam,

 find, attribute, "'Average Practical Mark'",
 for, entity, "'Module Performance'",
 with, condition,
 entity-ancestor, ParentOcc1,
 and, with, condition,
     entity-ancestor, ParentOcc2,
 when, finished, save, the, result, in, AvePractical,

 call, derive_module_mark(Exam, AvePractical, AttValue)
]     ).
```

6.5 Representing Domain Knowledge

BSDM suggests standards of good practice. It also provides several check lists
of rules and guidelines which are designed to help the modellers to review
whether a developed model is correct and appropriate. Similar to the advice
given for Entity Models, the BSDM advice on process models concerns three
kinds of issues: general methodical issues, application domain related methodical issues and pure application related issues. We have captured the first two
types of advice in our formal language. Since the third type of advice is application domain dependent, there may not be a consensus regarding which advice
should be given, therefore we leave (most of) this issue to the modellers (some
such advice is embedded in generalised sector-specific BSDM models and therefore provided by the *Generic Model Adviser (GMA)*, a *Case-Based Reasoning*
component of *KBST-BM*, which will be described in detail in Chapter 8). We
have also added modelling guidelines which are not described in BSDM, but
a derivation from it, and thus also appropriate for guiding Process Modelling.
They give rise to the following four kinds of rules and guidelines.

1. Rules concerned with a single process and its entities: i.e. the checking of
   correctness and appropriateness within the process. This includes the checking of the appropriateness of the naming style of a process, the provision
   of the required trigger information for a process, and the appropriateness
   of the defined content of a process scope and entity functions. For example, according to BSDM, each process can only include one *focal* entity, i.e.
   there must be only one *originate focal* entity or one *change focal* entity in
   any process.

2. Rules concerned with several processes: i.e. to determine the appropriateness of process scopes by observing the relations between processes. For example, by comparing two process scopes, one can determine whether one process is subsumed by another and therefore decide whether these two processes should be merged. A further example is the detection of processes which may cause errors in their execution, such as leading to a *deadlock* between two or more processes. The latter example is given in BSDM but a derivation from BSDM and is illustrated as an example extended rule later in this section.

3. Rules concerned with several processes and entities: i.e. to determine whether all entities are handled properly and consistently by all processes. For example, according to BSDM, each entity must be covered by at least one process, and each process must include at least one entity.

4. Rules concerned with the definition of a process and the actual drawing of the Process Model and the life cycle diagram: i.e. the consistency checking between the process scopes (from KBST-BM definition form) and its graphical displays. For example, for any entity whose start life status is created by a particular process, this entity must be included in that process scope as either an *originate focal*, *originate normal* or an *originate in-flight* entity (function).

Example Process Model Rule (Type 1)

BSDM states that each process can only include one *focal* entity in its scope, i.e. there must only be one *originate focal* entity or only one *change focal* entity in any process. The rule below formalises the fact that if there is an *originate focal* entity in the process scope, then there should not be another *originate focal* or *change focal* entity in the scope.

$$
\begin{aligned}
& originate\_focal\_fun(Process\_name, Entity\_name1) \\
& \Rightarrow \\
& \neg \left(\begin{pmatrix} originate\_focal\_fun(Process\_name, Entity\_name2) \wedge \\ Entity\_name1 \neq Entity\_name2 \end{pmatrix} \vee \right. \\
& \left. \begin{pmatrix} change\_focal\_fun(Process\_name, Entity\_name2) \wedge \\ Entity\_name1 \neq Entity\_name2 \end{pmatrix} \right)
\end{aligned}
$$

Similarly, to formally represent the fact that if there is a *change focal* entity in the process scope, then there should not be another *originate focal* or *change focal* entity in the same process scope, one can write:

$$
\begin{aligned}
& change\_focal\_fun(Process\_name, Entity\_name1) \\
& \Rightarrow \\
& \neg \left(\begin{pmatrix} originate\_focal\_fun(Process\_name, Entity\_name2) \wedge \\ Entity\_name1 \neq Entity\_name2 \end{pmatrix} \vee \right. \\
& \left. \begin{pmatrix} change\_focal\_fun(Process\_name, Entity\_name2) \wedge \\ Entity\_name1 \neq Entity\_name2 \end{pmatrix} \right)
\end{aligned}
$$

Since this rule should be strictly followed, it is represented as a model rule which uses the strong inference symbol, $\Rightarrow$, in our formal language.

Example Extended Process Model Guideline (Type 2)

Deadlock, in the context of Process Modelling, occurs when two or more processes cannot be executed because the information which is needed to execute one process is generated by the other process(es), however, the execution of these process(es) can only take place after the initial process has already executed. Since these processes depend on each other's information for execution, no processes can be carried out.

In BSDM, *originate in-flight* entity occurrences in a process must be present or created before the occurrence of the *originate focal* entity can be originated. However, it is also possible that the demand for creation of the *originate in-flight* entity triggers another process. A *deadlock* will happen if this newly triggered process requires the presence (or creation) of the above-mentioned *originate focal* entity occurrence; or it will happen if it subsequently invokes other processes which require the presence (or creation) of the above-mentioned *originate focal* entity occurrence.

In general, a *deadlock* situation in BSDM may be found when a group of processes are inter-dependent through triggering a chain of *originate in-flight* entity functions. To specify the fact that the creation of an in-flight entity occurrence in a process invokes another process, the predicate *originate_if_invoke* is used. We can then present the chain of inter-dependency between processes in the formal expressions below.

$$\left(\begin{array}{l} originate\_focal\_fun(Process\_name, X) \land \\ originate\_if\_fun(Process\_name, Y) \land \\ originate\_if\_invoke(Process\_name) \end{array} \right) \Rightarrow inflight\_chain(X, Y)$$

$$\left(\begin{array}{l} originate\_focal\_fun(Process\_name, X) \land \\ originate\_if\_fun(Process\_name, Y) \land \\ originate\_if\_invoke(Process\_name) \land \\ inflight\_chain(Y, Z) \end{array} \right) \Rightarrow inflight\_chain(X, Z)$$

The first formula states that the creation of X is dependent on the creation of Y, whereas the second formula indicates that the creation of X depends on the creation of Z, because the creation of X depends on Y, and the creation of Y depends on Z. This chain of dependency is derivable from the definition of the *originate in-flight* entity function.

Given the definition of the predicate *inflight_chain*, the guideline which detects the possibility of *deadlock* between processes can be formally given as:

$$\left(\begin{array}{l} originate\_focal\_fun(Process\_name, X) \land \\ originate\_if\_fun(Process\_name, Y) \land \\ originate\_if\_invoke(Process\_name) \end{array} \right) \triangleright \neg(inflight\_chain(X, X))$$

This rule is not expressed in BSDM, but a logical deduction from it. It can also be understood in business terms. The existence of deadlock among business processes may very well indicate the contradictions existing in the policies for business operations. For instance, if a business always checks the credentials of a company before it opens a customer account for it (that is having a process including "customer order" as the *originate focal entity*, and "credential" as the *originate in-flight entity*) then there should normally not be another process which requires the creation of a current customer account in order to gain information as a basis for credential assessment. However, since this testing only takes place at a very high level, i.e. only looking at entities and their functions in a process, it does not take into account any of the details within the business environment. It therefore merely forms a guideline.

Example Process Model Guideline (Type 3)

As all entities included in an Entity Model are "fundamental" and "important" to a business,[4] it is reasonable to assume that the creation methods of all entities should be documented and included in processes. Therefore, BSDM has the check below:

Are all entities originated (created) by at least one process?

However, since the modeller may decide that the creation of a particular entity lies outside the scope of his/her model, this question forms a guideline, rather than a strict rule in our formal language. Since an entity can be created in either of the three entity functions, *originate focal*, *originate normal* or *originate in-flight* entity function, this guideline states that each entity *should* play the role of either *originate focal*, *originate normal* or *originate in-flight* entity function in at least one process.

$class(entity, Entity\_name)$

$\triangleright$

$$\exists Process\_name. \left(\begin{array}{l} originate\_focal\_fun(Process\_name, Entity\_name) \vee \\ originate\_normal\_fun(Process\_name, Entity\_name) \vee \\ originate\_if\_fun(Process\_name, Entity\_name) \end{array} \right)$$

Given the above guideline, we infer a less restrictive rule with a stronger recommendation which states that all entities in the model *must* be included in at least one process for some roles. For this, we use the following rule.

Both the rule and guideline above are example critiques regarding the appropriate inclusion of (or relationship between) entities in processes. Therefore they belong to the third kind of advice.

More Process Model rules and guidelines are given in detail in Appendix H. They all follow the same basic notation as the examples given above.

---

[4] The definition of a BSDM Entity Model.

$class(entity, Entity\_name)$
$\Rightarrow$

$$\exists Process\_name. \left(\begin{array}{l} originate\_focal\_fun(Process\_name, Entity\_name) \vee \\ originate\_normal\_fun(Process\_name, Entity\_name) \vee \\ originate\_if\_fun(Process\_name, Entity\_name) \vee \\ change\_focal\_fun(Process\_name, Entity\_name) \vee \\ change\_normal\_fun(Process\_name, Entity\_name) \vee \\ refer\_normal\_fun(Process\_name, Entity\_name) \vee \\ refer\_master\_fun(Process\_name, Entity\_name) \end{array} \right) \qquad [1]$$

6.6 Inference

The Process Model analysis detects errors which violate any of the four types of process-related model rules and guidelines (within a process, among processes, in the inter-relationships between entities and processes, and the usages of entities across the model) and provides advice on how to correct such errors.

Similar to the verification facilities for the Entity Model, processes rules and guidelines are grouped into sets for error detection and advice display. The Process Model rules and guidelines are also implemented modularly and operate independently. Therefore, they enjoy the same benefits that Entity Model verification facilities offer.

There are in total 19 sets of Process Model rules and 13 sets of Process Model guidelines. Inferencing techniques similar to the ones used for the entity model in Chapter 5 are also applied here. Several types of critiques are offered below.

- *Correctness* critiques cover structural, syntactic and semantic errors in a process.
- *Completeness* critiques alert the user to missing information in a process and potentially missing links between processes and entities.
- *Consistency* critiques highlight contradictions in process properties and entity-process relationships.
- *Appropriateness* critiques point out differences between the user model and standard practices.
- *Presentation* critiques identify discrepancies existing in process properties and drawings which have been defined in different places of the model.
- *Alternative* critiques find subsumed and over-specialised processes and suggest alternative processes (in contrast to entity models, this is not done by GMA,[5] but using guidelines).

Inference using the Process Model follows the same approach as described for the Entity Model. Model primitives and their properties are each represented formally by logical expressions. Rules and guidelines are negated and translated into CLIPS rules which make use of the given class hierarchy and the formalisation of the primitives and the derived information. Once a CLIPS

---

[5] Generic Model Advisor is a subsystem in *KBST-BM* which is described in Chapter 8.

goal has been proved to be true (detecting a violation), an explanation of the modelling problem and possible solutions are suggested.

6.6.1 Process Model Consultation Example

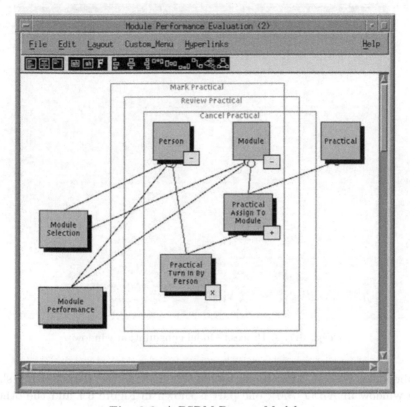

Fig. 6.6. A BSDM Process Model

An example Process Model consultation window is given in Figure 6.7[6] which is based on the Process Model given in Figure 6.6, extending the Process Model given in Figure 6.1 with three *change processes*. BSDM has deployed graphical symbols such as '*', 'o', '>', '+', 'x', '-' and '=' to denote the different entity functions. We have used them to label the commonly shared *change focal*, *change normal* and *refer normal* entities for these processes with '+', 'x' and '-'

---

[6] Due to the limited space available for the advice window, part of the advice is not shown in Figure 6.7. In practice, the user can scroll down the window bar to see the rest of the advice. The part of the advice which is not shown in this figure states: "Since entity 'Practical' is the parent entity, it may store the needed information for these process operations. In this context, we consider *Focal, Normal* and *In-Flight* entity functions to be important."

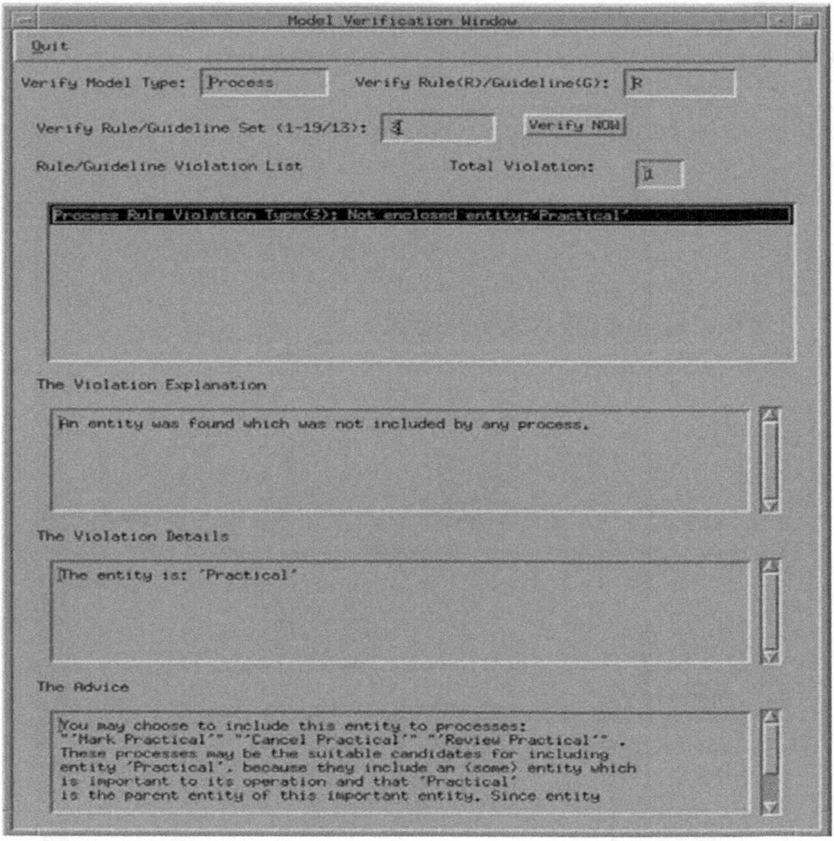

Fig. 6.7. A Process Model consultation window

symbols, accordingly. The process model now includes two parts (each is shown
in a window in *KBST-BM*): one part is shown in Figure 6.1 and the other in
Figure 6.6. The verification takes both parts into account.[7]

Figure 6.7 shows that the Process Model rule, set (3), has been applied.
One violated model rule was found "Process Rule Violation Type (3)"[8] which
was given as an example in the previous section. The layout and the usage of
the consultation window follows the same structure as the one used for Entity
Models. In this verification session, one error has been found: entity *Practical*
was found not to be included in any process and has been reported to the user.
It was also suggested that it may be included in the processes of *Mark Practical*, *Review Practical* and *Cancel Practical*. This advice was based on the fact
that *Practical* is a parent entity of *Practical Assign To Module*. Since *Practical
Assign To Module* somehow plays an important role to all of these processes,
entity *Practical* as a parent entity of this entity may carry information needed

---

[7] During the consultation, every part in the business model is taken into account.

[8] Each rule set may have its own numbering system.

for the execution of these processes. In this context, we consider the following entity functions to be important: *originate focal, originate normal, originate in-flight, change normal* and *change master*.

6.7 Conclusion

The second activity in BSDM business modelling is to build process models. All of the information specified during the building of Process Models is expanded upon the information given during the entity model building activities. This includes adding process information to *Life Cycle Diagrams* and *Entity Models*. In this chapter, the formal representation of a Process Model, including process information recorded in the *Life Cycle Diagram* and user-defined attribute rules, has been described. In addition, modelling advice given by BSDM for Process Models has been formalised into modelling rules and guidelines which use the above formal representation as a basis for detecting possible errors and generate advice to assist the user in aligning their model to standard practice.

BSDM's model-building process is incremental and iterative. Our formal framework fully supports this principle. Based on the *Inheritance Class Hierarchy* described in Chapter 5, the formal language *DefBM* extends this with process information, stating with diagrammatic annotations and adding process rules, therefore allowing the knowledge base to be enlarged incrementally. The added process knowledge can also be automatically verified, even when only partial information is available. This facility assists the user in going through the iterative *plan-build-test-refine* cycle which is a common way to build models.

The formal representation of processes also provides a basic foundation for model simulation which is described in detail in the next chapter.

6.8 Exercises

1. Discuss the potential use of an entity function in a BSDM Process Model. Refer back to the Inheritance Class Hierarchy (ICH) in Figure 5.1, explain the semantics (meaning) of an entity function and its relationship to the ICH.
2. Discuss the common and potential different life statuses of a process and whether it is useful to have such a facility. Can the life statuses of a process conflict with each other, e.g. via transition?
3. Compare the types of inference that may be carried out on a BSDM Process Model with those for an Entity Model, and discuss any similarities between them.
4. Are user-defined attribute rules useful? What are their main functions in a Process Model?
5. Compare BSDM's Process Model with another existing process modelling language, e.g. IDEF3, PSL, PIF, Petri-Nets, BPEL4WS, etc.

6.9 Advanced Exercises

1. Based on *DefBM*, implement the two Process Model rules of type 1, Section 6.5, using an appropriate programming language, e.g. Prolog, Lisp, Clips or JAVA.
2. Repeat the previous question, but implement the three process model guidelines of type 2 instead.
3. Repeat the previous question, but implement the two process model guidelines type 3 instead.

7

Reasoning on and Executing Processes

Conventional BSDM business models describe semi-formally what processes are, what they consist of and what can be done by them. The BSDM method, however, is not specific about how a process may be executed. In order to allow the execution of BSDM business processes, we introduced an additional modelling facility; the *Procedural Model*, which specifies the logical sequence and components of a process' execution. This is not the only possible form of execution consistent with the earlier stages of BSDM, but is characteristic of the sort of execution which fits well with the style of modelling. The notation used to describe this stage of modelling is not present in conventional BSDM manuals, so practitioners require training to use it.

7.1 Introducing the Procedural Model

The *Procedural Model* was inspired by modelling methods such as the organisational process modelling methods [70], process modelling methods IDEF3 [73], PIF [62], PSL [98], workflow modelling method [49] and planning theories [2]. These methods concentrate on specifying and managing tasks which are operational and have a close (if not direct) mapping to the actual practices in an organisation, e.g. the process of designing, building, testing and manufacturing a new product, or the procedure of a billing system.

The *Procedural Model*, on the other hand, has been designed to specify the *logical* and *internal* execution sequence of a business process which enables a conventional BSDM processes to be executable. The specified procedure is still independent of an organisation's current working practice and therefore can be implemented in several different ways depending on the organisation's goal and requirements. In other words, it specifies the data to be manipulated and conditions to be considered, but not how to do them in the real world. This is consistent with the declarative style of conventional BSDM which concerns itself with things which should be done, and does not give a deterministic order of execution or specify any implementation details in practice. However, some commitments to the sequence of execution are required at this stage of design

to enable process execution, and these are reflected in the successive layers of
Figure 7.1.

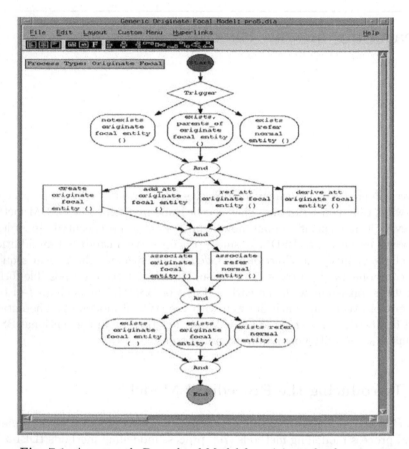

Fig. 7.1. An example Procedural Model for originate focal processes

The figure shows an "un-instantiated" generic Procedural Model for *originate focal* processes. It specifies the structures and components of an *originate
focal* Procedural Model but leaves their parameters un-instantiated. The structure of the successive layers of tasks can be used as a template to derive most
originate focal processes. An *originate focal* is the most basic kind of *originate*
process in our process classification which was shown in the inheritance hierarchy in Figure 5.1. BSDM only distinguishes between originate and change
processes. We classify them further depending on the purpose of a process,
because it is clearer and easier for us to distinguish between different types of
processes and inherit functions from them.

An *originate focal* process includes only one *originate* type of entity function
in its scope, i.e. an *originate focal* entity function. A combinational addition
of *originate normal* and/or *originate in-flight* entity functions makes it a more

specialised process, such as an *originate normal* or *originate normal if* process
which are shown as subclasses of *originate focal* process in the inheritance
hierarchy in Figure 5.1.

Process execution follows the arrows in a Procedural Model, as in Figure
7.1. It always begins with a 'start' node after which is a 'trigger' node which is
followed by preconditions and an 'and' node which leads to two layers of actions
connected by an 'and' node. After the actions come the postconditions and finally the 'end' node. In this generic procedural sequence, there is an empty
bracket "()" in each precondition, action and postcondition node. The empty
bracket will be filled with the corresponding entity name when this procedural
sequence is instantiated by a particular process. The instantiated procedural
model defines the dynamic behaviour for that process, i.e. requirements to be
fulfilled and activities to be carried out. This information provides a framework for the user to fill in the detailed occurrence information for entities and
processes at execution time.

BSDM provides text-based forms for the user to describe triggers and entity
functions in a process. A trigger represents a request to invoke a particular
process. It can be caused externally (by the user) or internally (by another
process). If a trigger is present, all preconditions specified in the procedure
must be satisfied before any actions can be carried out. All postconditions will
be confirmed after all actions are finished.

Each BSDM entity function designates particular actions for a process to be
carried out on the corresponding entity. These actions are represented as actions
in the *Procedural Model* and are specified in two layers: in the first layer are those
actions which represent the main purpose of the corresponding process (e.g.
the creation of entity occurrences, the changing of entity attributes); actions
in the second layer cover the inclusions of the newly created or manipulated
entity occurrences in the newly created (executed) process occurrence: this
case includes the *originate focal* and *refer normal* entity occurrences to the
process occurrence. Although *precondition* and *postcondition* statements are
not explicitly specified in BSDM, they are derivable from entity functions, as
shown in the figure. The user can also specify their own preconditions and
postconditions.

All of the model primitives in the *Procedural Model*, i.e. trigger, preconditions, actions and postconditions of a process, are specified by the user prior the
execution. At execution time, the entity occurrence information for all preconditions, postconditions and actions are specified interactively by the user and
automatically instantiated. If all preconditions of a process have been satisfied,
this process can be executed: a new process occurrence will be created which
may create new entity occurrences, and/or modify existing (entity occurrence)
attributes – those entity occurrence which have been manipulated are included
in the scope of the corresponding process occurrence. This form of interactive
process execution illustrates the corresponding possible dynamic states of a
business model. Before the formal description of a Procedural Model and its
instantiation are described, the next section illustrates the formal representation of a dynamic business model.

7.2 Representing Dynamic Business Models

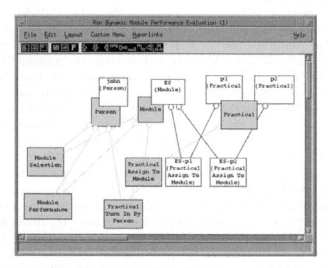

Fig. 7.2. Instantiation of a business model

Chapters 5 and 6 have described the static structure of a business model described in BSDM and our corresponding formal representation for them. We have also demonstrated how this formal representation can be used as a basis to represent the extracted "strongly recommended" model rules and "generally recommended" guidelines from the method. Such rules and guidelines give *KBST-BM* the needed knowledge to provide systematic and automatic help for model verification. *However, to demonstrate and thus evaluate the* **dynamic behaviour** *of the business model, one must be able to display and capture the* **dynamic state changes** *of a business model.* In our work, a graphical notation has been used to capture and display the dynamic aspects of a business model in a **Dynamic Business Model**. Formal representations have also been devised to capture the dynamic details which form the basis for the necessary reasoning for its behaviour.

Figure 7.2 shows an example *Dynamic Business Model* which is automatically generated by *KBST-BM* from the static business model given in Figure 6.1. In addition to the information initially displayed in Figure 6.1, the user fills in the individual information about a particular entity occurrence, known information about this occurrence would be inferred and filled-in automatically. Each entity occurrence is linked via the corresponding dependency occurrences to other relevant entity occurrences.

In this figure, six entity occurrences are specified: one person (John), one module (ES), two practicals (p1 and p2), and two practical assignments ('ES-p1', 'ES-p2'). These entity occurrences represent a snapshot at some point of time that this business model may describe. Our first aim is to represent these occurrences and any corresponding attributes using the formal language *DefBM* in a way which is consistent with what has been used for Entity and Process models. Based on those formal descriptions, inference methods can then be devised and dynamic behaviours of a business model can be derived.

Two predicates have been used to capture entity occurrences and their attributes. The predicate name *dyn* indicates the dynamic nature of an occurrence.

> *dyn(ent_occ(Ent_name, Ent_ID, Parents))*
> *dyn(ent_occ_att(Ent_name, Ent_ID, Att_name, Att_value))*

Following the convention used in BSDM that "entity name" and "entity ID" together identify a unique entity occurrence, the same principle is also applied in our formal language. In both predicates, *Ent_name* stores the name of the entity (e.g. Person), whereas *Ent_ID* stores the name of the entity ID (e.g. John). The argument *Parents* stores the corresponding parent entity occurrences of this entity occurrence. *Att_name* and *Att_value* store the name of the attribute and the value of the attribute. For instance, the representation of a person 'John' and the fact that he is male is given below:

> *dyn(ent_occ('Person', 'John', []))*
> *dyn(ent_occ_att('Person', 'John', 'gender', 'male'))*

Since the entity "Person" is at the top level of this business model, none of the occurrences of entity "Person" will have a parent entity. This is represented as an empty list '[ ]' in the *Parent* argument. The entity occurrence attributes have been identified by the modeller during the Entity Modelling exercise, and have been formally represented in the *attribute* predicates as previously described in Section 5.3.

A similar approach has been adapted for representing business processes. The representation of a process occurrence is given below:

> *dyn(pro_occ(Process_name, Process_ID))*
> *dyn(pro_occ_att(Process_name, Process_ID, Att_name, Att_value))*

The interpretation of these predicates is the same as those used for entity occurrences, only they are applicable to processes in this case. Building on the representation of the dynamic aspects discussed in this section, the next section introduces the representation of Procedural Models.

7.3 Representing the Procedural Model

Several important components have to be specified and instantiated before a process can be executed: the trigger, preconditions, postconditions and actions of a process. These components deal with the state changes of a model and must therefore in their formal description include the kind of dynamic information which will be referred to and used when generating new data.

A trigger needs to specify *which* (type of) process it invokes and *when* a process should start to act. Each process occurrence (instance) is unique and is invoked by a unique trigger occurrence which can be dynamically generated. A trigger occurrence must, therefore, also be able to distinguish itself from other trigger occurrences. This information together with the actions which are to be carried out by the process is represented in a *trigger_information* predicate, as shown below, for conciseness:

trigger_information(Begin_time, Process_name, Trigger_ID, Action_list)

More details about this predicate are given in a later paragraph when describing process *actions*. An example instance of this predicate is also given later in this section.

Preconditions for a process are requirements which make sure that process actions can be carried out successfully. Their existence is often linked to the actions to be carried out by a process. For instance, in Figure 7.1 the first precondition used is 'notexists originate focal entity', i.e. if a process is to generate its originate focal entity (occurrence), then this entity (occurrence) must not already exist. The generic precondition expression and this particular precondition are described formally below:

```
precondition(Process_name,
             Entity_function_name,
             Precondition_statement)
```

```
precondition('MODULE PERFORMANCE Assessment',
             originate_focal_entity,
             [notexists, originate_focal_entity(Ent, EntID)]).
```

This predicate specifically instructs the checking of the 'non-existence' for the *originate focal* entity occurrence with entity name *Ent* and entity ID *EntID* in the process *MODULE PERFORMANCE Assessment*. The users can also define their own precondition statements using the same form, where the argument *Entity_function_name* is still used to indicate which entity (function) it is referring to. Also, the *Precondition_statement* starts with the key word *exists* or *notexists* followed by a normal dynamic predicate. This format provides some flexibility for the modeller to specify simple business and attributes preconditions for any properties of an entity. The representation of a **postcondition** is similar to that of a precondition; the predicate name is replaced with 'postcondition'.

Actions that a process carries out are of two types: actions which realise the purposes of a process, and actions which link the relevant entity occurrences with the newly generated process occurrences. These actions are displayed in two consecutive layers in the *Procedural Model*.

Process actions described in the *Action_list* of the *trigger_information* predicate are the main actions and are described in the first layer. Each action node as shown in Figure 7.1 is represented as one single predicate in the *Action_list*. Example actions are the creation of the originate focal or the originate normal entities, the generation, modification and derivation of entity occurrence attributes, and the reference of entity occurrences and its attributes. An example of how these actions are represented in the *Action_list* is given at the end of this section.

Actions of the second type are also part of a process, because they link entity occurrences to the corresponding process occurrence. They are the "standard" actions of a process, therefore they are not specified in the *trigger* predicate. Standard action types which are currently handled by *KBST-BM* include all of the entity functions that are described in BSDM. Extensions of these actions can be easily made based on the existing formal structure, if desired.

7.3.1 Example Procedural Model and Representation

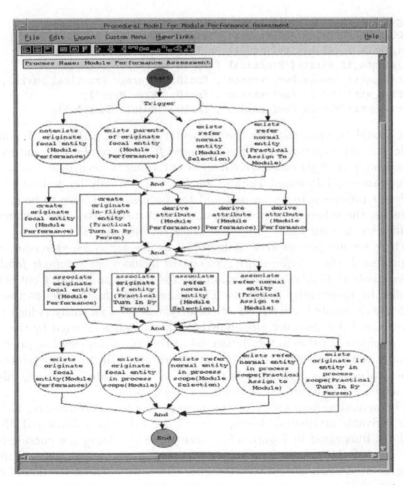

Fig. 7.3. The Procedural Model for 'Module Performance Assessment'

Figure 7.3 shows an example Procedural Model for the process *Module Performance Assessment* in Figure 6.1. Each node in the Procedural Model is labelled with the corresponding entity name. Since there are five action nodes specified in the model, there will be five corresponding actions specified in the *Action_list* of the corresponding *trigger_information* predicate: these actions are 'create originate focal entity', 'create originate in-flight entity', and three 'derive attribute' nodes.

This Procedural Model is an extension of the one described in Figure 7.1 which is a generic model for any *originate focal* process. Since this process also includes *originate in-flight* entities, it must fulfil requirements for this entity function, which are shown in all of the additional *originate in-flight* related precondition, action and postcondition nodes. A *trigger_information* predicate which invokes the process *Module Performance Assessment* can be described formally below:

```
trigger_information(Begin_time,
 'MODULE PERFORMANCE Assessment', Trigger_ID,
 [originate_focal_entity('Module Performance', EntID),
  originate_if_entity('Practical Turn In By Person', EntID2),
  derive_att('Module Performance', EntID, 'Average Practical Mark'),
  derive_att('Module Performance', EntID, 'Exam Mark'),
  derive_att('Module Performance', EntID, 'Module Mark') ])
```

It should be apparent that the particular *Begin_time, Trigger_ID* and the particular entity occurrence of the *originate focal* entity (*EntID*), and that of the *originate in-flight* entity (*EntID2*) (i.e. the entity occurrences of *Module Performance* and *Practical Turn In By Person*) can only be decided when a particular process is to be invoked and the process occurrence to be created. Therefore, the values of these arguments are not instantiated here, but will be specified when a particular process instance is to be created.

There are five process actions described in the *Action_list* argument. Since the process *Module Performance Assessment* includes one *originate focal* and one *originate in-flight* entity, the main process actions are to carry out actions specified by these entity functions. The process must firstly refer to the (dynamically designated) occurrence of the *originate in-flight* entity (which needs to be created if it does not already exist): this action is denoted by the predicate *originate_if_entity* in the *Action_list* in the *trigger_information* predicate. Secondly, the process needs to create an occurrence of the *originate focal* entity of the process. This is denoted in the predicate *originate_focal_entity*, also in the *Action_list* in the *trigger_information* predicate.

The *originate focal* entity of the process, *Module Performance*, includes three derivable attributes: *Average Practical Mark, Exam Mark* and *Module Mark* (as illustrated in Figure 6.5). Since these attributes are considered to be a part of the process, the values of these attributes are also calculated and generated when the entity occurrence is created.[1] The derivation of these

---

[1] The decision whether these derivable attributes or any attributes are to be generated by one process or another relies entirely on the modeller's judgement.

attributes is specified in the three *derive_att* predicates which indicate the entity occurrence involved and the derivable attributes. The actual derivation method is defined in the *derive_att_rule* predicate which was described in Section 6.4.

Given an 'instantiated' dynamic business model and Procedural Model for the processes with corresponding time references, the business model may now be simulated, given the appropriate simulation procedure. A simulation algorithm is described in Subsection 7.4.3. Before the simulation algorithm is introduced, we provide a way to predict the dynamic behaviours without any simulation.

7.4 Representing Domain Knowledge

7.4.1 Actions, Effects and Temporal Relations

As mentioned in Section 7.1, BSDM specifies trigger and entity functions in a process. Since the trigger and each of the entity function has a special meaning in BSDM, we are able to derive the corresponding preconditions, actions and postconditions for a process, and describe them in the procedural model.

BSDM also allows complex conditions to be specified within a trigger. These conditions can be described in complex decision trees and involve internal and/or external factors: internal factors are information that is derivable from the model, whereas external ones cover information which is not captured in the model. We simplify the meaning of a trigger as the prerequisite of its presence before a process execution in our system, and allow internal conditions to be specified as "preconditions" in our formal notation. The satisfaction of external conditions are assumed in our system when the trigger is present.

Although BSDM describes the sketch of a process without specifying any execution mechanism, the dynamic behaviours of its processes exhibit some similar characteristics compared with the actions or events described in a planning system. Therefore, issues which concern a planning system are also of interest to a BSDM process. Some key characteristics of BSDM processes are given below:

- Business processes take time. A business process is normally not instantaneous and must take a period of time to accomplish. Furthermore, the effect of a business process is normally not realised until the process is completed. This is due to the authority and/or commitment that bonds a business and all participants which is given only on completion of a process. This authority also allows the business to take further actions and execute other processes.

  For instance, a business will not fulfil a contract unless it is signed by all parties. This is because the contract is not legally binding unless the negotiation of drawing the contract is finished and it is signed by all parties involved – which is the completion state of a contract-drawing process. If it is necessary to indicate the intermediate state of the business during process execution, it is perhaps more appropriate to represent it in more than one processes to reflect these intermediate states. For example, the above contract-drawing process can be modelled in two separate processes: "draft contract" and "sign contract" to reflect the two different states in the contract-drawing process. In fact, it is also important to indicate whether a contract is closed or cancelled which may be represented in another two separate processes: "close contract" and "cancel contract":

- Business processes may be carried out concurrently. As a result, these processes may contradict each other or change effects of the other process while it has been executed. Interferences normally happen when more than one process tries to create or modify the same data item, or when one tries to create it while the other one tries to modify it. The error when one process tries to refer to a data item while others try to create it is prevented by the checking of preconditions.

- Business processes may or may not constrain each other: a business process sometimes can only be executed after a certain process has been executed, this constraint is imposed by the fact that for its execution a process may need information which is provided by another process. For instance, an entity occurrence cannot be modified unless it has already been created. Therefore, the process which modifies this entity can only be executed after the other process which creates this entity has been executed.

On the other hand, some processes may be prohibited from execution, if certain other processes have been executed. For instance, the entity occurrence "contract" cannot be signed and claimed to be valid by any process after it has been cancelled. This constrain is particularly captured in the *Life Cycle Diagram* (Figure 6.3). All of these constraints impose partial execution orders between processes and are explained in further details in Subsection 7.4.2.

- Business processes may be influenced by external events. In BSDM external events are shown as the presence of triggers. The presence of these newly created triggers will incur the execution of new processes. As a consequence, new processes are created which may create contradictions with the existing processes, thus changing the behaviour of the system.

Given these characteristics it is obvious that the notion of time must be represented in our formal language to indicate the duration that a process takes and also to recognise and handle any conflicts that may be incurred by processes that are carried out at the same time. Co-operation and communication between BSDM processes is done by passing information through entity occurrences which is only possible when a process has been committed (i.e. successfully executed). This suggests that a system which simulates processes concurrently and independently through time and which produces an aggregate effect for all of the processes while resolving the conflicts and constraints between processes will be suitable for our purpose. The system also needs to be interactive to accept any new arriving events which can be integrated into a commonly shared knowledge base which is referred to and updated by all processes.

The dynamic world of a BSDM business model has been represented in a state-based system where each state is a snapshot of the status of the dynamic world at a particular time. Processes are represented as functions which propagate between these states. Within each state a set of fluents are used to describe the property of the state. These fluents are without individual time stamps. The absence of a particular fluent indicates, by default, the negation of its property.

Time reference points have been used to indicate time points of the model. A period of time is marked by a begin and an end time stamp. The life span of any process or entity occurrence therefore is indicated by two time points, i.e. the creation and terminating time of the occurrence. Since at any point of time there is only one set of fluents available in the system, the changes of fluents between states are recorded. These recorded changes allow the system to restore any previous state of the world and, hence, allow the system to exploit a different route of expedition from the previous state.

Because the system is interactively accepting new events from users, these new external events are supplied to the system and subsequently change the course of action of the system.

7.4.2 Process Dependencies and Partial Execution Order

Although an automatic simulator can predict the future by running through several hypothetical business scenarios, often there are potentially an infinite number of combinations for process execution sequences which can be tested. It therefore would be useful if the system could suggest possible sequences for process execution based on the static description given in the Entity and Process models thus decreasing the testing space.

During close examination of the Process Model, we discovered ways to determine process relationships which can be automatically inferred from a Process Model. These relationships can be used to outline an overview of process relationships and operations and are helpful to get an insight into process executions without any actual simulations. These relationships are *process dependencies*, because they are one-directional and impose constraints on the execution of other corresponding processes.

Four types of process dependencies were found. The first two types of dependencies are drawn from information which describes the operations within a process and between processes. This information provides clues about (partial) process execution order. The latter two types of dependencies have been derived from the requirement for gaining information, which also places limitations on process executions. These dependencies are described below (in descending order of strength that each dependency imposes on process execution ordering).

Dependency Type I: Process execution order-1

This dependency is derived from the extended *Life Cycle Diagrams* for entities: one example is shown in Figure 6.3. In the extended *Life Cycle Diagram*, processes which can be used to create and transfer an entity's life status are described as directional arrows between the corresponding two transitional life statuses. This information also indicates the possible execution orders between the two specified processes. Two rules have been derived from *Life Cycle Diagrams* and represented in the following two formulae:

$$orgprocess(Process1, Entity, Life1) \wedge$$
$$chgprocess(Process2, Entity, Life1, Life2)$$
$$\Rightarrow$$
$$followed\_by(Process1, Process2)$$

$$chgprocess(Process1, Entity, Life0, Life1) \wedge$$
$$chgprocess(Process2, Entity, Life1, Life2)$$
$$\Rightarrow$$
$$followed\_by(Process1, Process2)$$

As previously described in Section 6.3, the predicate *orgprocess* indicates an originate process, and *chgprocess* indicates a change process. Both of these two rules state that **if** it is specified by the user that *Process2* can transfer a life status *Life1* of the entity *Entity* to another life status *Life2*, and that *Life1* was created by *Process1*, **then** we can conclude that *Process2* may be the next process candidate to be executed after *Process1* has worked on this entity. This dependency has been denoted by the predicate *followed_by* and is shown in blue colour in our system.[2]

This dependency places the strongest constraint and indicates the closest relationships between two processes. It states a rather close execution sequence between two processes, i.e. one process can normally be executed after the completion of the previous process without any additional processes being required to be executed.

Dependency Type II: Process execution order-2

This dependency was derived from the definitions of process scope. From the point of view of manipulating one single entity, an entity cannot be modified unless it has already been created. Therefore, it is derivable that the process which modifies it cannot be executed unless the process which creates it has already been carried out. This rule can be described formally below:

$$\left(\begin{array}{l} originate\_focal\_fun(Process1, Entity) \vee \\ originate\_normal\_fun(Process1, Entity) \end{array} \right) \wedge$$
$$\left(\begin{array}{l} change\_focal\_fun(Process2, Entity) \vee \\ change\_normal\_fun(Process2, Entity) \end{array} \right)$$
$$\Rightarrow$$
$$maybe\_followed\_by(Process1, Process2)$$

The predicates *originate_focal_fun* and *originate_normal_fun* indicate that Process1 creates the entity Entity as part of its process operations; whereas *change_focal_fun* and *change_normal_fun* indicate that Process2 modifies entity

---

[2] In fact, all dependencies are in this colour scheme.

Entity as part of its process operations – these predicates have been described in detail in Chapter 6. The rule above states that if there exists a process Process1 which includes an entity Entity as an *originate focal* or *originate normal* entity (function) and there exists another process Process2 which includes the same entity as a *change focal* or *change normal* entity (function) then Process2 may only be executed after Process1 has been executed.

This dependency constitutes the second strongest partial process execution ordering, because it is based on a broader relationship between processes: there could be many change processes which modify the same entity, but not all of them can be executed directly after the execution of the corresponding originate process – some other processes may also need to be executed. These missing processes are often described in the *Life Cycle Diagrams*. In reality due to the limited scope of a project, often not all *Life Cycle Diagrams* are captured in a business model. The above rule establishes additional vital relationships between processes in the situation when incomplete information has been supplied.

Dependency Type III: Prerequisite of information-1

Prerequisite of information (type 1): this dependency is derived from the prerequisites for process execution which requires the provision of certain information before a process can be executed. The process of concern includes at least one *refer normal* entity function, therefore by definition it needs to refer to the specific entity (occurrence) before it can be executed. If the required information is produced by another process, then this other process must have been executed and provided the needed information prior to its execution.

The rule below formally describes it:

$$refer\_normal\_fun(Process2, Entity) \wedge$$
$$\left(\begin{matrix} originate\_focal\_fun(Process1, Entity) \vee \\ originate\_normal\_fun(Process1, Entity) \end{matrix} \right)$$
$$\Rightarrow$$

$$prerequisite(Process1, Process2)$$

This rule states that if there exists a process Process2 which includes a *refer normal* entity Entity and there exists another process Process1 which originates this entity, then the execution of process Process1 is a prerequisite for the execution of process Process2.

This type of dependency imposes an even weaker dependency constraint compared with the previous two types of dependencies, because it only requires the existence of some information before process execution. It does not indicate the natural flow of process execution. In fact, it states a minimum prerequisite for a process execution – that it cannot be executed unless the other processes have already been executed earlier. In practice, more processes may need to be carried out before this process can be executed. This dependency relationship can point out relationships between processes which are not captured in all of the previous rules and therefore helps to provide a more complete picture for process inter-relations.

Dependency Type IV: Prerequisite of information-2

This type of dependency is also derived from the prerequisite for a process execution. In this case, the entity function involved *originate in-flight* entity (function). *Originate in-flight* entity function works, by definition, as a combination of *refer normal* and *originate* function: when used it imposes a prerequisite for the process to refer to the designated *originate in-flight* entity (occurrence) before its execution. However, it can also create this entity (occurrence) as a part of its process if it is not already created. This dependency is described formally below:

$$originate\_if\_fun(Process2, Entity) \wedge$$
$$\left(\begin{array}{l} originate\_focal\_fun(Process1, Entity) \vee \\ originate\_normal\_fun(Process1, Entity) \end{array} \right)$$
$$\Rightarrow$$
$$maybe\_prerequisite(Process1, Process2)$$

The rule above states that if there exists a process Process2 which includes an *originate in-flight* entity Entity and there exists another process Process1 which includes this entity as an *originate focal* entity (function), then the prior execution of process Process1 may be a prerequisite for the execution of process Process2.

Because of the definition of the *originate in-flight* entity, a process can create this entity when it is absent, this implies the weakest constraint compared with all of the previous dependencies. This type of dependency signifies that a process (Process2) can be executed when the other process (Process1) has been carried out at a previous time; however, the process (Process2) may also be carried out without this restriction. This dependency further points out additional process relationships that have previously not been captured.

Subsection 7.5.1 describes the use of the described dependencies.

7.4.3 Simulation Algorithm

Model rules derived from the Procedural Model are primarily concerned with the operational aspect of process execution. A process is normally carried out when its trigger is present and all of the precondition statements are satisfied. A process may not be applied if the user has chosen to explore a different route. The operation of the business model simulator can be described in the algorithm below:

1. If the required simulation time span is finished then stop the simulator and report the result of the simulation to the user; otherwise, go to 2.
2. Search for all of the triggers in the system. If all of the preconditions for any of the processes are satisfied and the designated **starting time** (for execution) for that process is due or has passed due time, then put them in the *Process Agenda*. Go to 3.
3. Check for all of the processes in the *Process Agenda* and collect into a set of those processes with an **ending time** which is due or past due time.

Perform a **process conflict check** on all of the processes in the set; if any contradictions are found between those processes, then go to 4, otherwise go to 5.

4. Report any contradictions found between processes, the detailed information which has caused this problem, and a brief suggestion for conflict resolution to the user. The user can decide if any of the processes should be removed from the *Process Agenda*, and thus from the system. After communicating with the user and performing the operations required by the user, go to 3.

5. The user can now select eligible processes to be executed. Each selected process is checked again to make sure that all of the process preconditions are still satisfied, and that the actions within each process are syntactically correct and the detailed requirements for executing each action are satisfied. The requirements for executing an action are different from a process precondition, because it concerns the details of the actual execution mechanism, e.g. the attribute of an entity occurrence must not be changed unless there is already an old attribute value present.

   These eligible processes are selected (by the user) and carried out (by the system) one by one. The user may also choose to ignore some (or indeed all of the) processes for execution in order to explore a specific execution route. When this happens, the ignored processes are left untouched in the *Process Agenda*. After each process execution, the postconditions are checked. Report to the user, if any irregularities have been found. Go to 6.

6. Advance the system to a new time. Advance the system to a new state if any changes have been made to the current state. Enquire whether the user wishes to "rollback" the system and specifically which state he/she wishes to restore. If the answer is yes, restore the system to the specified state. Go to 1.

As a result of a process execution, an occurrence of a process is created, its begin and end time are also specified as part of these actions. The begin and end time of a process are denoted by the *occ_begin_time* and *occ_end_time* predicates, as shown below:

occ_begin_time(*Process_name*, *Process_Id*, *Begin_time*)
occ_end_time(*Process_name*, *Process_Id*, *End_time*)

The same predicates are also used to denote the lifespan of entity occurrences, but the attributes *Process_name* and *Process_ID* with *Entity_name* and *Entity_ID* are also instantiated. The predicates which identify Entity and Process occurrences and those which describe the attributes of them, together with other system predicates which indicate the time and the state of the system, constitute a set of fluents which describe the state of the system.

The properties of a state of the system are recorded as a set of fluents, the changes made by processes to these fluents between states are recorded in a special *change* predicate. As described earlier, these recorded changes allow the system to rollback and restore any previous state of the world and allow the user to exploit a different route of expedition from the previous path.

Details about what kinds of conflicts can be detected during process execution and the use of the simulator are given in the following chapter. In this chapter, the use of process dependencies is demonstrated next.

7.5 Inference

7.5.1 Process Execution Sequence Constructor

Based on the inferencing rules for process dependencies given in Subsection 7.4.2, the **Process Execution Sequence Constructor** automatically generates **Process Dependency and Partial Execution Order Diagrams**. Figure 7.4 shows one such diagram which was automatically generated by *KBST-BM*. (This is automatically generated from the Process Model developed for the university (course) management domain which consists of 44 processes in more than 30 diagrams. Some of them are given in Appendix E.)

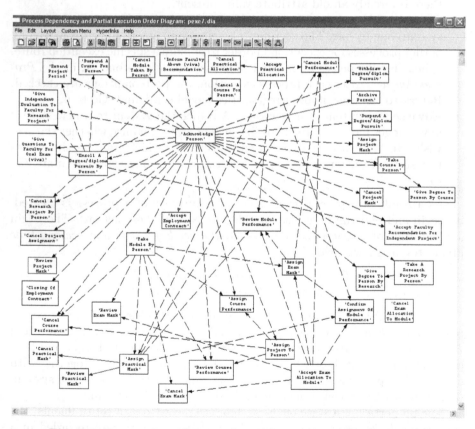

Fig. 7.4. Process dependency and partial execution order diagram (1)

Three types of process dependencies have been captured in this diagram. They are dependency type I, III and IV. Each of these dependency links is drawn as an arrow from a starting process to a depending process node. Each link indicates a type of dependency constraint on the depending process that is dominated by the starting process.

This diagram shows an overview of relationships between processes and at the same time the dependencies between them. For instance, the type I dependency arrow[3] leaving from "Acknowledge Person" to "Archive Person" states that (the information of) a person cannot be archived unless he/she has been acknowledged (i.e. known to the organisation) before. Because this dependency type was derived from a Life Cycle Diagram which describes the logical sequence of processes, it indicates a strong relationship between the two processes. It also means that it is possible to archive a person right after he/she has been acknowledged (despite the fact that it may not be useful to do that right away).

Dependency type IV is derivable from *originate in-flight* entity functions.[4] The one shown in the diagram connects "Acknowledge Person" to "Accept Employment Contract". This dependency type is relatively weaker compared with dependency type I, because it only imposes a "may be" constraint. According to this particular dependency, a person can draw an employment contract with the organisation (in this case the university) if he/she is already known to the university; otherwise, the university first needs to acknowledge this person before signing a contract with him/her. In other words, the process "Acknowledge Person" does not necessarily need to be carried out before the process "Accept Employment Contract" is executed.

Indication of this type of dependency is particularly useful for detecting any misuse of *originate in-flight* entities. For instance, the starting process may depend on other processes, which means that some other processes need to be executed before the designated entity can be originated (created). Consequently, the assignment of an *originate in-flight* entity may be too weak – if this is the case, the assignment of a *refer normal* entity may be an alternative choice.[5]

The most used links in this diagram are of the dependency type III.[6] The central node in the figure that leads to many other processes is "Acknowledge Person" which means that this process has the most freedom and least restriction to be carried out and it provides (generates) commonly shared information for many other processes. These arrows indicate how information flows between processes as well as prerequisites for process execution (this has been discussed previously in Subsection 7.4.2 in detail).

---

[3] Dependency type I is denoted as a blue dashed arrow in *KBST-BM*.

[4] Dependency type IV is denoted as a red dashed arrow in *KBST-BM*.

[5] It is also possible that instead of creating the *originate in-flight* entity by the process itself, it can be specified that the initial process which originates it is to be invoked. If this is the case, this particular type of error can be avoided.

[6] Dependency type III is denoted as a black dashed arrow in *KBST-BM*.

One interesting observation which can be made in this diagram is to look for any isolated (process) nodes. One such node "Cancel Exam Allocation To Module" has been identified in the diagram. An isolated node normally indicates the lack of integration with other processes, or that the needed information is not provided by other processes. In this particular case it indicates the boundary of the design, the process which supplies the needed information for this process, is outside the scope of the project (i.e. it was intentionally not included in the Process Model).

Figure 7.5 shows another example *process dependency and partial execution order diagram* which has also been automatically generated by KBST-BM from the same DAI process model. In addition to the previous three types of dependencies as shown in Figure 7.4, this diagram also includes dependency type II. Furthermore, wherever there is a dependency type II present, all of the corresponding dependencies of type III which link to the particular depending process node are removed. As a result, the weaker relations (referral dependency type III) are deleted from the diagram and replaced by the stronger relations (update dependency type II).

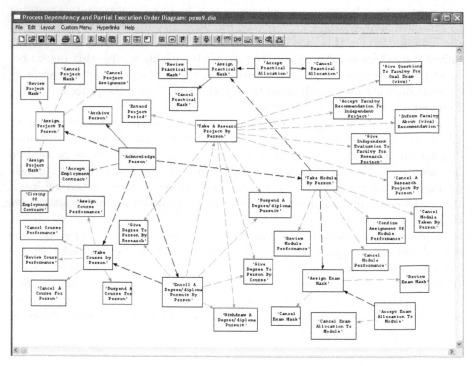

Fig. 7.5. Process dependency and partial execution order diagram (2)

This has simplified the diagram and clustered relevant processes in groups.[7] Each group of processes indicates operations which are carried out in some relevant business areas. This enables the user to examine relevant processes together and to identify relationships between these groups. One interesting observation in this diagram is that the isolated node, "Cancel Exam Allocation To Module", has now disappeared. Although the process which provides information for it is not captured in the Process Model, it has been identified as relating to a group of processes because it operates on the same entity as others work on. As a result, each of these two types of diagrams show some properties that the other one does not.

Several observations can be made from these diagrams and insights and warnings for errors can be further drawn from the business model. This is described below:

- *Isolated processes:* indicate "orphan" processes which do not use information produced by any other processes nor do they produce data useful for other processes. Such phenomena may indicate the incompleteness or error in the model. As described previously, an isolated process signifies the boundary of the model design. It can, however, also mean that more potential processes are yet to be captured in the Process Model.

- *Process nodes with few or no in-coming arrows but many out-going arrows:* this type of processes are carried out with relatively little restrictions, and provide commonly shared information to many other processes. It also indicates the boundary of the design.

- *Process nodes with many in-coming arrows:* this type of processes requires lots of information for its operations. It can be a process which produces analytical information or a process of decision making. Because the constraints imposed by a process dependency are transferable, processes at the other end of any leaving arrows from the node are also constrained by the constraints imposed by all of the incoming dependencies to the node. It is therefore important to ensure that a process is not over-constrained.

- *Process nodes with many in-coming and out-going arrows:* this type of processes capture the central actions in a business's operation.

- *Leaf processes:* this type of processes does not have any out-going arrows. It normally indicates the boundary of the model design, or that the actions it carried out are terminal for some of the dealing entity occurrences. This means that no other processes can work on those entity occurrences (other than just passively refer to them) after this process has been carried out.

- *Process nodes with similar relationship architecture:* when two processes have many common in-coming and out-going arrows, then it may be worth checking the overlap of these two processes.

- *Process nodes with in-coming originate in-flight arrows:* these arrows indicate *originate in-flight* entity functions in the process, which refers to the need of referring a piece of information, yet they also indicate the freedom to create this information when it is absent. It is, therefore, important that

---

[7] Dependency type II is denoted as a green dashed arrow in *KBST-BM*.

this freedom has not been misused. Whether this freedom has been given wrongly to a process is determined by the "source process" which is initially responsible for generating this piece of information. If there are any dependencies which have been imposed at the "source process", then this arrow should not be allowed but should be replaced by a more conservative referral dependency: i.e. a *refer normal* entity function should be used instead by that process.

Ideally, in a well established business model where life cycle transitions are well-defined, all process nodes are connected via dependency type I, since they indicate the direct relationships between processes and data. It also gives the strongest constraints on the order of process execution. However, it is often not possible to get a business model that has been modelled at this level of detail. When this is true, other types of dependencies are inferred to fill the gap. Advantages of using the *Process Execution Order Constructor* are given below:

- It provides an overview for inter-relationships between processes which was not obvious or given in the business model: it indicates how information is used, shared and passed between processes.
- It establishes a partial process execution order which is not previously known to the model, based on which the user can construct potential business scenarios which make use of a series of business processes.
- It provides another way to analyse the business model; more importantly, it gives the user another chance to examine the appropriateness of the context of process scopes and the sufficiency of the existing processes.
- It cuts down the search space for testing what-if business scenarios: the workflow which is suggested in the *process dependency and partial execution order* diagram is constrained; workflows or business scenarios which violate these constraints depicted in the diagram violate constraints that have been put on the business model and will not be acceptable by the simulator. This facility, therefore, not only helps to give the user an initial and integral view of potential business workflow and helps the user to construct useful testing scenarios, it also saves the user effort in testing fruitless business scenarios.
- This facility is relatively intuitive as it is visual-based and all operations are mouse–menu activated. No additional information is required from the user rather than the already developed Process Model: therefore it is a very simple and easy way to get a lot more insight into a developed business model. Furthermore, the method which has been used to derive this information entirely complies with BSDM which increases the acceptability of the tool by this group of users.[8]

---

[8] In *KBST-BM*, the *process dependency and partial execution order* diagram is color-coded, it therefore greatly enhances the readability.

7.5.2 Process Conflict Detector

It is often the case that several processes are proposed to be carried out concurrently in the system. It is, therefore, important to ensure that only coherent processes are carried out at the same time. Several error checking facilities on the Entity and Process Model are provided and have been described in Chapters 5 and 6. For instance, the potential for *deadlocks* between processes can be detected during the verification of the Process Model using the guideline *deadlock prevention among processes* which identifies possible deadlocks from the static structure of processes. A more detailed description of these rules is given in Appendix H.

In addition to the static checking of process conflicts, during the execution of a model, the *process conflict detector* looks for potential contradictory processes dynamically. It examines particular data items (entity occurrences and attributes) that are involved in a process' execution, checking for three types of errors:

- *Inconsistent handling of a data item* is reported to the user when two processes are found to be creating the same entity occurrence, or updating the same entity attribute, or one process refers to an entity and the other one modifies it at the same time. (The case where one process creates an entity occurrence while the other is updating it is actually prevented from happening in our system through the use of preconditions.)
- *Erroneous handling of a data item* occurs when a process tries to manipulate an entity occurrence which is already "terminated" in terms of its life status, since a "terminated" entity occurrence can only be used for archive purposes, i.e. only for reference but not for active data manipulation.
- *Suspended processes* are those processes which stay in the *Process Agenda* for a long time and cannot be executed. There are two ways of notifying/alerting the user of this type of error: a passive reminder and an active warning. The passive reminder is given to the user through viewing the content of the Process Agenda. With this the user can keep track of which processes are in the queue and for how long. An active warning is given to the user when a predetermined threshold of waiting time duration is expired. When the user finds a suspended process, he/she can ask for an explanation from the system for the delay of execution (i.e. to identify the failing preconditions of the process and type checking on the specified actions) and possible ways of fixing this problem.

Process conflict detector works as a part of the business model simulator and is carried out before process executions. The next subsection describes the use of the simulator.

7.5.3 Business Model Simulator

The inference engine, *Business Model Simulator*, generates the dynamic behaviour of the model, i.e. it simulates the execution of processes, according to

the instructions given by the user. The user can see how the model behaves
under the current design by exploring the model using potential business scenarios. More specifically, the user gives the length of time for simulation and
the set of triggers for processes to be enacted. The scheduler of the inference
engine selects a set of triggers which is appropriate for invoking processes which
are then added to a *Process Agenda*.

For those processes in the agenda which have all of their preconditions
fulfilled, the process occurrences are created and actions executed. This leads
to a new system state. The corresponding feedback is given to the user and the
system time advanced. The next cycle begins with the new system state and the
user decides whether or not to supply some new triggers. The model simulation
ends when the specified simulation time period is finished. The inference engine
is able to backtrack to any previous system state (going backwards in time),
thereby allowing the user to experiment with alternative paths of execution of
the model.

The transition from one state to another could be the result of more than
one process. We, therefore, must insure that processes which are carried out
at the same time are not in conflict with each other. To prevent conflicting
processes from executing at the same time, a *process conflict detector* is used
before any process execution. When a conflicting set of processes have been
found, the user is notified and one or more conflicting process(es) are selected
by the user and removed from the *Process Agenda*.

The execution history and the changes made in each state can be described
in a *state transition diagram*. An example use of the *business model simulator*
and the resulting *state transition diagram* is given next.

7.5.4 Example Inference and State Transition Diagram

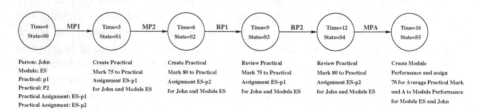

Fig. 7.6. A state transition diagram for originate focal process (1)

Figure 7.6 shows an example state transition diagram which demonstrates
a possible sequence of states generated by the system. It uses three processes
specified in the Process Model given in Figures 6.1 and 6.6. These are *Mark
Practical, Review Practical* and *Module Performance Assessment*.

The first oval denotes the initial state *S0* at time 0, which is also described
in the *Dynamic Business Model* in Figure 7.2. Assuming that in the initial
state we only have a few facts (occurrences): a person *John*, a module *ES*, two

practicals, *p1* and *p2*, and their assignments to module *ES*: *ES-p1* and *ES-p2*. We also assume that initially five triggers are given by the user: two invoke the 'Mark Practical' processes which assign the practical marks for *John* for *ES-p1* and *ES-p2*, two invoke the 'Review Practical' processes which confirm the practical marks assigned for *John* for *ES-p1* and *ES-p2*, and one trigger that invokes the process 'MODULE PERFORMANCE Assessment' which assigns the average practical mark and module performance for *John* and *ES*.[9] Notice that in this example we have assumed that all triggers are given up front at the initial state and all with the begin time zero for simplicity, although these triggers could alternatively be specified by the user at different times, since the reasoning engine is interactive.

The directed link *MP1* denotes that process *MP1* was executed. It transferred the initial state *S0* to state *S1*. Assuming that process *MP1* ends at time 3, the newly created state *S1* is generated at time 3. Process *MP1* has assigned a practical mark 75 to practical assignment *ES-p1* for *John* and module *ES*. Process *MP2* furthermore assigned practical mark 80 to practical assignment *ES-p2* for *John* and module *ES*. This process also transfers state *S1* to state *S2* denoted by a link labelled *MP2*. Since process *MP2* has ended at time 6, this has become the system time of the state. By the same reasoning, states *S3*, *S4* and *S5* are determined by processes *RP1*, *RP2* and *MPA* which review the above assigned practical marks and assigns 78 to *Average Practical Mark* and A to module performance for module *ES* for *John*, and the system time is 16 at state *S5*.

This demonstrates one possible way of executing a process. The process execution sequence is: *MP1*, *MP2*, *RP1*, *RP2* and *MPA*. The user can decide to backtrack this execution to find an alternative execution sequence, e.g. *MP1*, *RP1*, *MP2*, *RP2* and *MPA*. This alternative execution sequence is added to the previous diagram and shown in Figure 7.7. One other possible sequence is to execute multiple processes concurrently, e.g. *MP1+MP2*, *RP1+RP2*, *MPA* which is shown in Figure 7.8.

The processes involved are partially ordered: a practical mark must be given before it can be reviewed, and the average practical mark and module performance cannot be determined unless all practical marks are reviewed. This partially ordered sequence is determined by triggers and requirements of these processes (which are also influenced by entity functions). The possible execution sequence of processes obeys the process dependencies which have been described in Subsections 7.4.2 and 7.5.1.

Chapter 9 gives a comprehensive view of how *KBST-BM* can be used in assisting the development life cycle as a whole for building business models in BSDM.

---

[9] We assume that no exams have been set for this module, therefore the module performance is solely determined by the performance of the practicals.

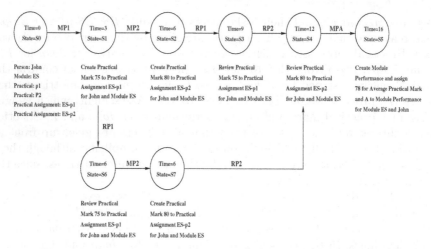

Fig. 7.7. A state transition diagram for originate focal process (2)

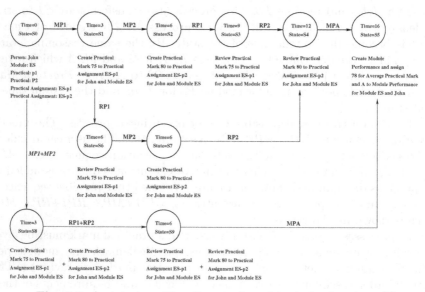

Fig. 7.8. A state transition diagram for originate focal process (3)

7.6 Conclusion

Conventional BSDM provides informally a structure and declarative method for capturing a complicated business environment in a business model. The fundamental and important "things" and processes are represented and described statically as entities and processes. These static structures have strong implications on the behaviour of the business model. When a business model describes a relatively complex and large organisation, it is very difficult to understand all these implications. Therefore, it is useful if this dynamic behaviour of a business model can be demonstrated in a way which reveals how the defined business rules, policies and arrangements will affect the business when it is actually in operation. There is, however, in general a lack of support in most business modelling methods, including BSDM, for such facilities.

To illustrate the dynamic behaviours of a business model, an additional layer, the *Procedural Model*, was devised. It specifies the requirements, actions, logical sequence and elements of a process' execution. Given this information in a *Procedural Model*, a business model can be enacted by the execution of its processes. Since there are potentially infinite ways to "run" a business model, it is impossible to obtain all of the different outcomes of a large and complex business model by execution. Our *Process Execution Sequence Constructor* makes use of the constraints imposed on the processes which limit how an entity can be manipulated. It identifies process dependencies and provides a high level and integral view of relationships between processes which was not previously described by the method. The generated *Process Dependency and Partial Execution Order Diagram* is intended to help the modellers to construct their own business scenarios more speedily. It also gives the user another way to analyse and verify the Process Model, in addition to the support which was given in Chapters 5 and 6.

Our *Process Conflict Detector* dynamically detects possible conflicting processes and informs the modeller about it, together with advice for conflict resolution. This is an attempt to free modellers from the technical details of process execution so that they can concentrate on fundamental flaws in the business model.

The aim of the *Business Model Simulator*, which has been built as a part of our tool *KBST-BM*, to provide a means to demonstrate the dynamic aspects of an initially statically described business model has been achieved through the use of the Procedural Model. The system helps the modeller validate the appropriateness of a business model, one of the most important issues in the business modelling community.

7.7 Exercises

1. Why is an additional layer needed for BSDM's Process Model? Discuss how the layer of Procedural Model integrates with BSDM's modelling method and its complimentary role.
2. Why is a representation for the dynamic aspects of business model needed? Can one carry out verification and validation (V&V) on a process model without this facility?
3. What are the relationships between triggers, actions, pre- and postconditions of a process with that of dependency between processes?
4. Based on the different verification and validation techniques carried out on BSDM's models, discuss the different **types** of V&V techniques that may be applied on a model.
5. Discuss whether these verification and validation techniques are generic and whether they may be adapted to be used on other modelling methods.

6. To help understanding a domain, different models/diagrams are often used to illustrate the different aspects of a domain. Identify the different types of models/diagrams that have been used in this book so far.

7. Explain the function of the Process Conflict Detector and its role in a business model simulation.

8. Based on the semantics given in a BSDM Process Model and its Entity Functions, can you identify any other types of dependencies, other than the ones already mentioned in the book, that will constrain the order of process execution?

7.8 Advanced Exercises

1. Provide a logical description for another modelling method, e.g. IDEF3 [72] or UML's activity diagram [94]. Explain model requirements and your design rationale.

2. Based on the above chosen modelling method, propose the types of V&V that may be carried out on it. Describe details of these V&V firstly in natural language (English) and then in logical formulae.

3. Design and provide automatic V&V support for the above chosen modelling method.

4. Not all process modelling method provides a facility to describe the data that is manipulated by its processes. Can you list some of those methods? Explain whether it is important to have such a facility and any (dis)advantages associated with it.

8

Knowledge Sharing and Reuse of Models

8.1 Introduction

As mentioned in the previous chapters, *KBST-BM* is integrated with *GMA*, the *Generic Model Advisor*. *GMA* is a *Case-Based Reasoning (CBR)* engine which facilitates the analysis of new BSDM business maps by comparing them with existing BSDM models. It also retains the newly developed business models in its library and uses them for future consultations. By gaining new knowledge, *GMA* is able to enhance its consultation capability over time [22].

This chapter investigates how human modellers work and the intelligent assistance that *GMA* may provide for the modellers as well as how *GMA* can assist in completing the life cycle of CBR. After a brief introduction to *Case-Based Reasoning* in general, a detailed account of the design and implementation of *GMA* is given and an example use of *GMA* described (a more comprehensive example consultation using *GMA* is given in Appendix L).

8.2 Intelligent Assistance for the Business Modeller

A BSDM entity model consists of two basic components: entities and dependencies. Entities are things that a business needs to manage and dependencies are the relationships between these things. Certain kinds of scenarios or relationships between entities are common to many businesses. Hence, one would expect the corresponding BSDM maps to reflect these commonalities. It would be an advantage if a library of these maps for such common cases could be provided. The modeller of a new business map could then reuse these generic models or use them as a reference for comparison with his/her own maps. We will firstly look at how these reusable knowledge components can be used in practice by BSDM practitioners. We will then suggest means to provide automatic support for the reuse of this knowledge.

In practice, IBM provides a catalogue of small-size generic entity models [50] [51] as well as more domain-oriented full-sized generic models for selected sectors. Provided with these models, BSDM practitioners help clients build their business model by using this information implicitly or explicitly. For BSDM consultancy, an experienced IBM consultant, Martin King, suggested three possible ways of reusing a generic model [57].

- *Back-Pocket Approach:* the clients are made aware of the existence of these generic models, but they are only used to support consultancy. The client will see little or none of the generic model. A consultant keeps these generic models at the back of his/her mind and tailors them to the clients' special requirements.
- *Reference Model Approach:* supply the client with a relevant complete generic model with a detailed description, together with a contractual consultancy service which provides help for the interpretation and use of the model.
- *Software System Solution:* provide developed software systems as packages which are based on generic industrial models. These software systems can then be used by the clients. The client may or may not see the generic business model which was used to develop the required software system.

The first two suggested approaches make direct use of the relevant generic models while developing new business models. In the first approach, since generic models are kept in the background, several relevant generic models may be deployed by a consultant. In the second approach, normally only one specific generic model is chosen and supplied to the client for reference.

A BSDM business model consists of several business areas, or *views*, where each view is a representation of some sub-domain knowledge of an organisation. There may be several different ways to represent a view. For the first two approaches, it seems appropriate to reuse generic models (presented in views) by developing a tool that provides a retrieval mechanism for relevant generic BSDM models, and making them available to the users (IBM consultants and the clients). It can also be used to analyse the user's model with respect to existing generic models. By providing this facility, the known generic models can be shared among users, and a structural method of reusing this knowledge is provided via the tool.

Although there are existing business modelling tools (as discussed in the literature review in Chapter 2 and later on in Chapter 10), most of them focus on the capturing and storing of a business model. The tool that we propose (*GMA*) takes a pro-active role which encourages good modelling practice and provides correction advice of models, if needed. The user can also systematically explore why a model is different from a generic one. Furthermore, when a new business model is correctly built, this newly built model can be generalised and retained by the tool in its memory, thereby enabling the reuse of this new model and enabling the tool to enrich its knowledge through time. The *GMA* tool uses a technique called *Case-Based Reasoning (CBR)*. Before *GMA* is described in more detail, a brief introduction to case-based reasoning is given.

8.3 Case-Based Reasoning (CBR)

Case-based reasoning was inspired by observing human reasoning. People perform CBR on a daily basis: they solve new problems based on their past experience in similar situations. They learn how to solve particular problems by remembering solutions successfully applied to similar problems in the past and hence becoming more competent in dealing with these problems over time.

In the same way, a CBR system solves new problems by comparing them with old problems and their solutions, which are stored in the system's memory. Old solutions are adapted for new problems, and new solutions are stored back into the system's memory for future reference; this is how a CBR system learns [61] [88]. General knowledge and heuristic judgment is sometimes used to guide the choice of old problems, to determine how well a new situation matches an old one, and to choose adaptation strategies from old to new solutions.

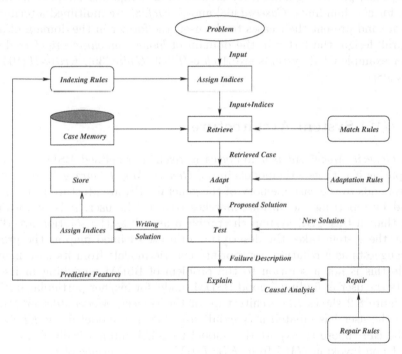

Fig. 8.1. General architecture of a case-based reasoning system

Figure 8.1 presents the general architecture of a case-based reasoning system. A past experience is called a *case* which consists of an old problem and its (successful) solutions. Cases are stored in a *case memory*. Different cases in the system are identified by their *indexes*. Indexes are significant features of cases that allow the system to distinguish between them. The first task of the system is to identify and assign indexes to the new problem, an activity which is governed by *indexing rules*. *Match rules* are used to compare the assigned indexes of a case with those in the case memory; a case with a similar problem as the new one can be identified and retrieved. *Adaptation rules* are applied to the solution of the previous case to adapt it to the new situation. If the proposed (adapted) solution is appropriate for the given problem and worthy of recording in the case memory then new indexes are assigned to it and it is stored in the case memory. If the proposed solution failed to solve the problem, an explanation of failure is produced and an attempt is made to repair the solution, i.e. the solution is modified according to *repair rules* and then tested again. If the failure is due to the inappropriate indexing of the current problem, new indexes are assigned and the mechanism starts again from the beginning. In many applications, modification and testing of solutions is carried out by the user.

In the past, several *CBR* systems have been built to support design: *Cadet* [78] [107] supports better conceptual design for electro-mechanical devices; *Cadsyn* [69] provides guidance for architectural design and adapts existing designs for new buildings; *Casecad* [68] and *AskJef* [8] use multimedia technology to store and present their cases to the user, the former in the domain of architectural design, the latter in the domain of *human–machine interface* design. Other example CBR systems are *Archie-II* [33], *Cadre* [36], *Kritik-II* [106] and *Julia* [48].

8.4 *GMA* System Architecture

The *Generic Model Advisor* analyses a given user-defined BSDM model by comparing it with generic models in the *Generic Model Library (GML)* – GML corresponds to the case memory of the general CBR architecture in Figure 8.1 – and by reporting the various matches back to the user. It is important to note that in this CBR system the problem as well as the solution are BSDM maps: the system takes the description of a user-defined map as the problem and suggests as a solution appropriate generic models from its case memory. While this is not a solution to the problem of BSDM modelling in itself, it assists the user in finding a good BSDM model for his/her particular business.

Figure 8.2 shows the architecture of the *Generic Model Advisor (GMA)*. After the user has created a (partial) user business model using *KBST-BM*, he/she can choose to export this model to *GMA* automatically from *KBST-BM*. Upon invoking *GMA* from *KBST-BM*, a user interface of *GMA* is shown to the user which gives instructions to the user and accepts user commands for further actions. Figure 8.3 gives a screen shot of *GMA* when it is started.

After the user has started *GMA* (typed 'run.'), *GMA* firstly identifies and assigns indexes to the problem, i.e. the user-defined BSDM model. These indexes, together with background contextual information, in our case the *Entity Conceptual Hierarchy*, are passed to the pattern-matching algorithm. Equipped with this background knowledge, the pattern-matching algorithm compares the indexes of the user's model with those of the generic models in the case mem-

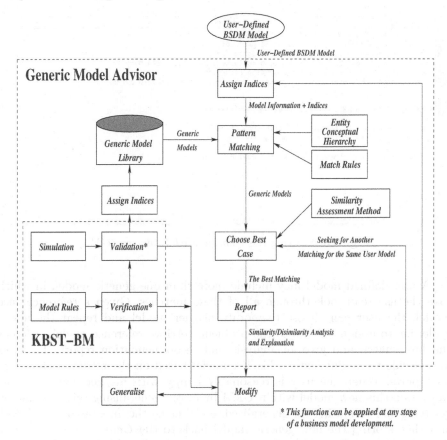

Fig. 8.2. Architecture of *Generic Model Advisor (GMA)*

ory, in our case the *Generic Model Library*, to retrieve a set of models which exhibit similar characteristics to the input model.

The retrieved models are past cases relevant to the current problem. After they have been retrieved they are examined for their relative degree of similarity with the user's model. For such a comparison, *GMA* provides a heuristic method for assessing which is a better match for the current problem. Alternatively, the user can dynamically define his/her own similarity assessment function by alternating the weights of designated measuring features during a consultation session. (More details on similarity assessment below.)

The best matching case according to the similarity assessment method is chosen and an analysis report of similarities and differences between the user model and the retrieved model, together with some explanations, are given to the user. The user can then either read the report or ask the system to present a different matching result for another retrieved model, if there are any. Matches are shown in descending order of their scores in the chosen similarity assessment method.

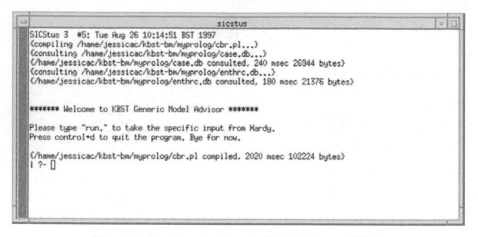

Fig. 8.3. Starting the *Generic Model Advisor (GMA)*

A user-defined model may include more than one generic model, in which case the user can look through all of these matches. Given a reference case model, the user can choose to modify his/her model and repeat the above cycle, i.e. to assign indexes to the problem, retrieve reference models, present the best match and give an analysis and recommendation report. The user may decide to modify/extend his/her model based on the retrieved cases and its reports. When the user is reasonably happy with his/her model, he/she can retain this new model within *GMA* by firstly generalising this new model, verifying and validating the generalised model using the integrated *KBST-BM*, and then storing the new generic model back to the *Generic Model Library*. The Case-Based Reasoning Cycle is now completed, and *GMA's* knowledge can be enriched and evolved through time via the inclusion of newly acquired knowledge during operations.

The smaller *KBST-BM* system box in Figure 8.2 illustrates how *KBST-BM* can assist in completing the CBR cycle. It is equivalent to the "Test" activity in the standard CBR process shown in Figure 8.1. Since verification and validation can be carried out at any stage of model development, it is also appropriate during the "Modify" activity in Figure 8.2.

The following sections describe the various components of *GMA* in more detail.

8.5 Indexing and Domain Knowledge Representation

As mentioned in Section 8.3, *indexes* are features which can be used to distinguish cases in the case memory and to find appropriate matches between a given problem and previous cases. In the context of *GMA*, these indexes must describe the characteristics of a BSDM business model and, at the same time, the differences and commonalities between models.

As was mentioned above, a business model is presented in several views. A view is a building block of a business model, and is also the way that a business model is read. Although each view of a model has a *view name* associated with it, these names alone are not always useful when trying to identify common features of BSDM maps. It is, therefore, necessary to look at the actual BSDM maps. Simply looking at the graphical representation of maps, however, is not sufficient.

For example, drawing an existing map upside-down does not make it a different map, the semantics of the inter-relationships (dependencies) between entities must be taken into account. Furthermore, the business contextual similarities may be disguised. For instance, if a business model is a more elaborated or specialised version of another one (or vice versa), then these two models normally will not have the same architecture (e.g. one may expand parts of the model in some areas), and often they do not share the same entities (e.g. using domain-specific vocabularies instead). However, because they are essentially describing the similar business operations, it will be useful to refer one to the other.

To be able to make meaningful comparisons between BSDM models, one must have an integral understanding of the business context which is described in both the architecture of a model as well as the business context that each entity represents. The dependence (link) which connects two entities and denotes the relationship between entities embeds this information. Therefore, these dependencies are used as indexes for BSDM models in *GMA*. To enable a concise and explicit representation of information needed for matching, new predicates are introduced in addition to those already introduced in Chapter 5. The *data_arc* predicate represents an Arc, the dependency relationship, from parent entity *Ent* to the dependent entity *Dependent_ent*:

$$data\_arc(Arc,\ Ent,\ Dependent\_ent)$$

To capture a more comprehensive understanding of a business map, we include entities as another index. This enables the system to select a model based on the similarities of both, entity architecture as well as the covered business domain. This information is captured in a *data_ent* predicate:

$$data\_ent(Entity)$$

where *Entity* is the name of an entity. At the beginning of a *GMA* consultation session, this information is automatically derived by *KBST-BM* and exported to *GMA*.

A dependency is described by the parent and child entities, and an entity is described by words which are appropriate in the corresponding domain. To match two models, one needs to match dependencies and entities between them. The difficulty that arises is to map entities representing similar but not the same concepts: while a more generic model may be referring to more general things, e.g. "party", a more specialised model is likely to use two separated entities to express this, e.g. "business" and "person"; or one may be using similar but different names but at the same level of abstraction, e.g. "trade agreement" and "business arrangement".

Differences at the same level of abstraction may also be caused by business-dependent vocabularies (e.g. a "customer order request" to a store is similar to a "reservation" for a restaurant). Although they make commitments to different things, one for the product to be ordered, the other for a space to sit, they really are expressing a similar concept: to express an informal request for a purchase which must be dealt with by a business accordingly. To handle such different levels of abstraction and to recognise the analogy of two similar entity concepts, the concept of an *entity conceptual hierarchy* is introduced (Section 8.7).

Since a *view name* is normally given by the user when a model is built and is conveniently available, we therefore also make it an index and provide a simple substring matching mechanism. However, this index is only useful if the user is very familiar with the internal naming scheme of the *Generic Model Library*. As in our own assessment (Chapter 10), we found that the provision of *view name* is not crucial for a successful retrieval.

Sections 8.7, 8.8 and 8.9 describe in detail how these indexes are used to retrieve the relevant generic models for a user model. However, before more details are given, an introduction to the *Generic Model Library* is described.

8.6 Generic Model Library (GML)

A *Generic Model Library (GML)* stores a set of *Generic Models*. A *Generic Model* may be a standardised, generalised or example BSDM business model. Four different sources have provided models for the *Generic Model Library* used for experimentation with the prototype implementation of *GMA*:

- the standard and example business models provided by the method, i.e. business models given in the BSDM manuals and its teaching materials;
- an industrial business model that was developed by IBM for its client in the sector of automobile parts distribution (which is sometimes referred to as the *automobile model* for short in the book);
- a generic business model that has been developed for small and medium sized restaurants;
- a business model that has been developed for course management and evaluation for the Department of Artificial Intelligence (DAI), The University of Edinburgh.[1]

BSDM provides a catalogue of standard models that describe business contexts that are commonly exhibited within different organisations. It also provides stereotypical example business models to illustrate the selected business operations. Together they naturally form the foundation of the content of *GML*.

---

[1] The Department of Artificial Intelligence is now a part of the University's newly formed Informatics Division.

These models are interesting to us, because they are generic and therefore may be used as references for many businesses and in various sectors. A set of such standard models are given in Appendix A for readers' interest, other example business models can be found in Appendix B.

Obtaining business models which are developed and used by industry is difficult. This is mainly due to the large cost for industry in building them and, for those that have been built, their content is usually confidential (as it often conveys a business' trade secrets). However, we were fortunate to get permission from one company, which operates in the sector of automobile parts distribution,[2] and obtained a small portion of their model. This model is valuable because it is a realistic model which was independently built and used by a commercial company. It is intriguing because it gives insights into business operations in a specialised context, i.e. in the domain of automobile parts distribution. As a result, it contributes to both the realism and "specialisation" properties of *GML*. A model similar to this industrial model is given in Appendix C for readers' interest.

To further enrich *GML*, another industrial model was developed by me by talking to the industry directly. As a result, a generic model for small and medium-sized restaurants has been built. The business areas covered include such issues as customer inquiring, ordering, invoicing and stock control. This domain is representative, because the above business areas are commonly shared by Small and Medium-sized Enterprises (SMEs) in other sectors. Since SMEs are organisations of smaller size, we imagine there are similarities in their business structures, implying commonalities in their business models. The business model of an SME is also useful for larger organisations, because although small and medium-sized enterprises are smaller in scale compared with international trading companies, such a model covers most of the typical *core* business operations, but describes them in a much more concise way. It is therefore interesting to see whether the built business model can be used to help build business models on a much larger scale and describe more complex operations in similar business areas. This issue will be explored in Chapter 10. The generic restaurant model is given in Appendix D.

To further extend the *GML*, a business model was built by me for the Department of Artificial Intelligence (DAI), The University of Edinburgh. It consists of 35 individual diagrams and covers the areas of Module Evaluation, Course Structure, Personnel Management, Course Evaluation and Degree Evaluation.[3] The model was built to demonstrate the generality of the BSDM business modelling method and that it is able to describe a variety of organisations. It was also built for testing the automatic *Verification and Validation (V&V)* abilities of *KBST-BM*. Since this model is also realistic, it may be used for reference if another similar model were to be built for another university in the future. The model is given in Appendix E.

---

[2] The company wishes to keep their name confidential.

[3] A small part and a much simplified version of the "module evaluation" part of the model have been used as a self-contained model in the previous chapters to illustrate the formal aspects of the work.

All of the above-mentioned business models form the current content of *GML*. Since a business model is presented in views, this is also the form that is stored in the *GML*.

8.6.1 Presentation and Representation Issues

A *Generic Model* is essentially a BSDM business model. However, since it plays a different role (an advisory role) in our system, a different but similar notation should be deployed for its presentation to the user. It is important to use a similar notation because then the user can easily recognise the notation without additional training. It is important to use a different notation so that the advisory role of the generic model is explicit for the system and for the user. The underlying development platform of *KBST-BM*, *Hardy* [101], a hypertext diagramming tool, provides *diagram card* facilities that allow its system developers to design and define new types of modelling notation. In this case a BSDM diagram card has been designed and used to capture a BSDM business model and a *Generic Model Library* diagram card has been designed and used to capture a *BSDM Generic Model* stored in the *Generic Model Library*. More details about the implementation of *KBST-BM* will be given in Chapter 9. Figure 8.4 shows an example generic model present in a *GML* diagram card in *KBST-BM*.[4]

For the same reason, the formal representation of model primitives in a generic model are also different from a normal business model. We report two main predicates: *gml_link* and *gml_ent*. A dependency relationship in a generic model is formally represented in a *gml_link* predicate:

$$gml\_link(Card\_id,\ Link\_id,\ Ent,\ Dependent\_ent).$$

where *Card_id* is the *GML* diagram card[5] ID and *Link_id* is the link ID of the dependency that connects *Ent*, that is the parent entity, and *Dependent_ent*, that is the child entity. Since there may be many diagram cards (distinguished by their IDs) representing the same business area differently in views, all of the above information is needed to identify a particular link. An entity in a generic model is represented in a *gml_ent* predicate:

$$gml\_ent(Card\_id,\ Entity)$$

where *Card_id* is the GML diagram card ID and *Entity* is the described entity. These two predicates above will be used to compare with *data_arc* and *data_ent* predicates mentioned earlier to provide a basis to determine the similarities between two models.

In the next section, the link which enables the mapping from a user model to a generic model is described.

---

[4] In *KBST-BM*, entities in a generic model diagram are shown in orange to distinguish them from the light-blue coloured entities in a BSDM diagram.

[5] A Hardy card type determines the subset of the notation that is allowed to be used for this card.

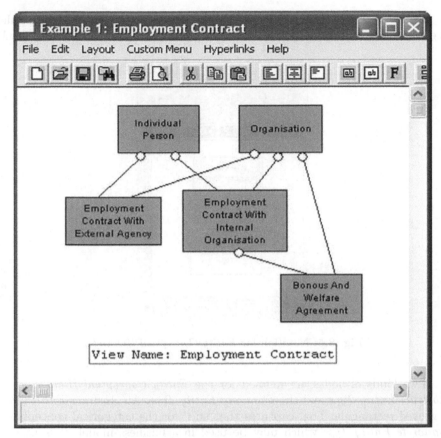

Fig. 8.4. An example generic model

8.7 Entity Conceptual Hierarchy (ECH)

BSDM recommends that four or fewer layers (or levels) of entities are normally built in a business model, i.e. each entity in a business model normally does not have more than three dependent entities (child entities). BSDM further exemplifies the "sorts" of entities and actual entities that are frequently used in an entity layer that are named *Entity Families* [51]. Since there are four recommended entity layers, we adapt those examples and group them in a hierarchical structure of *Entity Families* in the four categories corresponding to the recommended layers: layer One, Two, Three and Four.

The *Entity Family* hierarchy records the commonly used entities in a structural way and may be referenced during a model-building session. This information is highly reusable and bears important contextual information about entities. We capture these *Entity Families* in our devised *Entity Conceptual Hierarchy (ECH)* which gives entity families a hierarchical and graphical representation. In addition, it allows subclass relationships to be described between entities using directional subtype links that are not included in BSDM.

Figure 8.5 shows the notation used in an *Entity Conceptual Hierarchy* which is captured in an *Entity Conceptual Hierarchy* diagram (card) using *KBST-BM*.

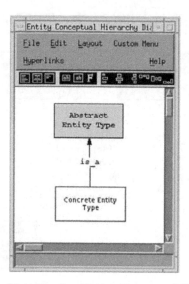

Fig. 8.5. Notation for *Entity Conceptual Hierarchy*

Two kinds of nodes are defined for the *Entity Conceptual Hierarchy*: the *Abstract Entity Type* and the *Concrete Entity Type*. An *Abstract Entity Type*, a greyed rectangular box, captures the "sort" or the categorical concept of a *Concrete Entity Type* which may be used in a business model. It is used to identify and distinguish the different concepts that are represented by entities. There can be several levels of *Abstract Entity Types* at a particular path which allows the exploration of the more specialised areas of interest. Since an abstract entity type describes the categorical and contextual information of an entity type, it is at a higher level of abstraction, which means it is represented at a higher level in the *Entity Conceptual Hierarchy*. A *Concrete Entity Type*, a clear rectangular box, is the actual entity that may be included in a business model. A *Concrete Entity Type* is always at a lower level of an abstract entity type or another concrete entity type.

The *Entity Conceptual Hierarchy* serves a similar purpose to that of a context tree which describes the hierarchical structure in an *is-a* relationship. An *is-a* link may describe the relationship between two concrete entity types, between a concrete and an abstract entity type, or between two abstract entity types. For example, an *employment contract* (concrete entity type) *is a* special kind of *contract* (concrete entity type) which *is a* special kind of *trade binding* (abstract entity type).

At the highest level of abstraction for all BSDM entities is the abstract entity type *Things*. All (other) concepts are grouped into four subclasses at the next level of abstraction, the four layers of the entity family. We represent each of them as an abstract entity type: "Layer 1 Entity", "Layer 2 Entity", "Layer 3 Entity", and "Layer 4 Entity". For example, in the branch of "Layer 1 Entity" (Figure 8.6), at the next level of abstraction, things are classified into: "External Item", "Agent", "Physical Thing", "Abstract Thing", "Category" and "Group of Things".[6]

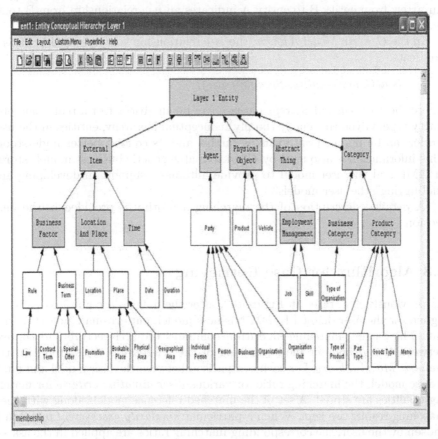

Fig. 8.6. The *Entity Conceptual Hierarchy (ECH)* at Layer 1

These categories are then further subdivided at the next lower level of abstraction. The Entity Conceptual Hierarchies do not have to be "strict" tree structures: an entity at one level of abstraction may have an *is-a* relationship with more than one entity at a higher level. This design is to allow automatic reasoning for the approximate meaning of an entity without the burden of having to produce an "absolute" taxonomy to suit all cases – as this is extremely difficult, since not everything in the real world is a clear-cut case; also doing so

---

[6] "Group of Things" and its sub-hierarchy are not shown in the figure, because it is only a partial diagram of the *entity families* in layer one.

may not be necessary, since the main purpose is to identify the analogy between entities but not to classify them.

Figure 8.6 shows a part of the entity hierarchy diagram card containing the suggested entities for the top layer (layer 1) of a BSDM entity model using *KBST-BM*. The shaded rectangular boxes represent the *Abstract Entity Types*, and the clear rectangular boxes represent real entities, *Concrete Entity Types*. An arrow from entity B to entity A indicates an *is-a* relationship from B to A, i.e. B *is-a* A.

In the *Generic Model Advisor*, the *is-a* relationship is represented in an *is_a* predicate:

$$is\_a(Generic\text{-}entity, \ Specific\text{-}entity)$$

where the *Generic* and *Specific* entities can be an abstract or a real (concrete) entity type. Given this entity (family) conceptual hierarchy, entities in the user model can be mapped onto this hierarchy, and its context better understood. This information is also used by *GMA* to match generic business models stored in GML and the user model to provide automatic support in developing and "debugging" the user models.

A detailed description of the matching algorithm is provided in the next section.

8.8 Algorithm for Case Retrieving

As previously illustrated in Figure 8.2, after the indexes are automatically assigned for the user-defined BSDM business model, pattern-matching is carried out. The pattern-matching algorithm compares the architecture and context between the given user model and all of the reference models stored in the *Generic Model Library*. For each comparison between the user model and a reference model, the matching ratio for various *discriminating criteria* for matching qualities are stored. A set of the matched reference models along with their matching results are kept. When a particular *similarity assessment* function is chosen by the user, the corresponding matching ratios are applied in the assessment function to determine which is a better match, therefore determining the recommendation/selection order of the matches to the user. More information about the discriminating criteria and the similarity assessment function will be given in Subsections 8.9.2 and 8.9.3.

As explained in Section 8.5, view names, dependencies and entities are the indexes used for matching two entity models. For a modeller familiar with the naming scheme used by *GML*, a view name may bear important discriminating information when it is given correctly for the user model and appropriately to the *GML*. A simple approach is therefore taken to matching between view names: a user view name is matched to the view name of a reference model, if it is a substring of the latter.

Two dependencies match if their child and parent entities match. In other words, a dependence in the user model is matched to a dependence in the generic model, if the parent entity of the dependence in the user model can be mapped to the parent entity of the dependence in the generic model, and if the child entity of the dependence in the user model can be mapped to the child entity of the dependence in the generic model. The declarative nature of this matching of two dependencies is well-suited for the declarative programming style of *Prolog*. Furthermore, for each user model it is possible to find more than one matching generic model. The additional matching models can be automatically found when making use of *Prolog's* built-in back-tracking facility. It was, therefore, decided to use *Prolog* as the implementation language for *GMA*.

The above matching algorithm of dependencies can thus be illustrated with the following *Prolog* predicate *match-dependency*:[7]

```
match-dependence(Generic-model-id,
    Data-model-id,
    Dependence-in-user-model(parent-entity-1, child-entity-1),
    Dependence-in-generic-model(parent-entity-2, child-entity-2) )
    :-
    map-entity(parent-entity-1, parent-entity-2),
    map-entity(child-entity-1,  child-entity-2).
```

The question that remains is how an entity in one model can be mapped to an entity in a different model. This mapping must take account of the *Entity Conceptual Hierarchy (ECH)* which means that all entities used in the user models and the generic models must be recorded in the entity conceptual hierarchies. In summary, using the entity conceptual hierarchy, two entities are matched if (1) one entity is at a higher level of abstraction of the other, or (2) both entities are at the same level of abstraction and are grouped under similar conceptual classes in the ECH. Without the entity conceptual hierarchy only identical entities can be matched.

The following Prolog predicates are used to map entities between models:[8]

```
(1) Identical entities
map-entity(Entity-1, Entity-2) :-
    Entity-1 = Entity-2.

(2) Subsumed entity I
map-entity(Entity-1, Entity-2) :-
    is_a(Entity-1, Entity-2).

(3) Subsumed entity II
map-entity(Entity-1, Entity-2) :-
    is_a(Entity-2, Entity-1).
```

---

[7] The actual implementation is more complicated; unnecessary details are left out for clarity.

[8] Again, a more complicated version of the predicates is used in *GMA*, but details are omitted here for clarity.

```
(4) Sibling relationship
map-entity(Entity-1, Entity-2) :-
   is_a(Shared-class, Entity-1),
   is_a(Shared-class, Entity-2).
```

```
(5) Distant subsumed entity I
map-entity(Entity-1, Entity-2) :-
   is_a(Intermediate-class, Entity-2),
   map-entity(Entity-1, Intermediate-class).
```

```
(6) Distant subsumed entity II
map-entity(Entity-1, Entity-2) :-
   is_a(Intermediate-class, Entity-1),
   map-entity(Entity-2, Intermediate-class).
```

The first clause of *map-entity* maps two entities at the same level of abstraction; the entities are identical. The second and third clauses map an entity to another entity at the level of abstraction immediately above. The fourth clause maps two entities at the same level of abstraction; these entities have similar or identical semantics that share one common entity at one immediate higher level of abstraction. The fifth and sixth clauses extend all of the above mappings to one additional level of abstraction, i.e. similar entity types located at two levels of abstraction away can also be matched. The closer the relationship is between two entities in the ECH, the higher the quality of the match is rated.

The aggregative quality of matching from one model to another is evaluated by the similarity evaluation function which is given in the next section.

8.9 Similarity Assessment

8.9.1 Matching Models

As mentioned in the previous section, a user model may include several generic models. On the other hand, a generic model may include or partially overlap with the user model. Therefore, there are four possible kinds of matches between a user model and a generic model, as described below:[9]

- Case 1: the generic model is entirely included in the user model;
- Case 2: only parts of both models are matched;
- Case 3: the user model and the generic model are fully matched;
- Case 4: the user model is entirely included in the generic model.

---

[9] The no-match case is not discussed here, since the corresponding generic model is not relevant to the user model and therefore will not provide useful advice to the user; it will not be presented to the user.

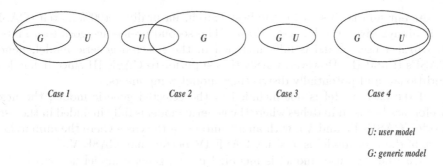

Case 1   *Case 2*   *Case 3*   *Case 4*

U: user model

G: generic model

Fig. 8.7. Possible matching between user models and generic models

Figure 8.7 uses an ellipse marked "G" to represent a generic model and one marked "U" to represent a user model to further illustrates the above matching cases. We use the same type of diagram to describe which match types are preferred; Figure 8.8 elaborates the above four general matching results into eight different matching outcomes and lists them in the order of preference.

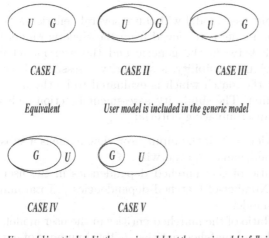

CASE I   *CASE II*   *CASE III*

Equivalent   *User model is included in the generic model*

CASE IV   *CASE V*

User model is not included in the generic model, but the generic model is fully included in the User Model

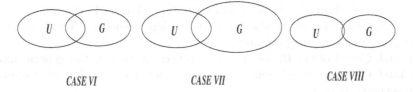

CASE VI   *CASE VII*   *CASE VIII*

User model is partially overlapping with the generic model

Fig. 8.8. The preference of matching results

As our aim is to seek for the best match, naturally a 100% match (CASE I) is always given the highest priority. The second preference goes to a match in which a user model is fully included in the selected generic model, hence CASEs II and III. However, CASE II is superior to CASE III since it has less additional, and potentially distracting, model components.

If the user model is not included in the selected generic model, the next preference lies with matches where the generic model is fully included in the user model (CASEs IV and V), with an advantage in the case where the unmatched part of the user model is less, i.e. CASE IV better than CASE V.

If neither the user model is included in the generic model nor vice versa, we opt for the match where the overlap is greatest (CASEs VI and VII) and if there is no difference in the overlap, prefer the case where the unmatched part of the generic model is less (CASE VI better than CASE VII).

These preferences bear various implications; when the details of the matching algorithm are given below, these implications are explained. Based on our preferences, discriminating criteria are identified and the selection mechanism formed, as discussed next.

8.9.2 Discriminating Criteria

It is common that an input user model will cause several generic models to be retrieved. When a generic model is retrieved from the Generic Model Library, the quality of the match between the generic and the user model must be evaluated. For each matching possibility, a similarity assessment between the two models is computed; the match which is evaluated to be the most similar is presented to the user first. The similarity assessment function embedded in *GMA* uses the following discriminating criteria:

- Match-View: Match-view = 1, if the input user view name is a substring of the generic model's view name; 0, otherwise.
- Match-Data-Link: Ratio of the matched dependencies in the user model. Match-Data-Link = Number-of-matched-dependencies / Total-number-of-dependencies-in-user-model.
- Match-Data-Entity: Ratio of the matched entities in the user model. Match-Data-Entity = Number-of-matched-entities / Total-number-of-entities-in-user-model.
- Match-Case-Link: Ratio of the matched dependencies in the generic model. Match-Case-Link = Number-of-matched-dependencies / Total-number-of-dependencies-in-generic-model.
- Match-Case-Entity: Ratio of the matched entities in the generic model. Match-Case-Entity = Number-of-matched-entities / Total-number-of-entities-in-generic-model.

8.9.3 Heuristic Similarity Assessment

GMA provides a heuristic similarity assessment function which makes use of the above five criteria to determine the quality of matches. In this heuristic function, we assume that the user will provide a view name for matching only when they are sufficiently familiar with the view naming-scheme of the case library. If this is the case, then this index will provide good discrimination.

When comparing two matches, the heuristic method prefers the one with a matched view name, i.e. Match-View = 1. When the matching results of the view names are the same, i.e. either both found a matching view name or both didn't, *GMA* will rate higher the model which matches the most of the dependencies in the user model with dependencies in the generic model (i.e. the match with the maximum ratio of Match-Data-Link). This is desirable, since dependencies embed the architectural information of a model. The higher ratio of Match-Data-Link indicates more aspects of the user model are also represented in the corresponding generic model.

Although the ratio Match-Data-Link covers most of the architectural similarity between two models, it does not include the case when an architecture is a specialisation of another. In this situation, the more specialised architecture will have more entities and dependencies to describe a situation where the more general one will use less entities and dependencies. As a consequence, although similar concepts have been captured in the two models, the relevant links can no longer be matched because the corresponding parent–child entity set doesn't exist in the representation of a link. To take this into account, an independent entity-matching algorithm is carried out and the ratio, Match-Data-Entity, is made the third discriminating criterion. In the case when two matches have the same values for Match-View and Match-Data-Link, the one with the higher Match-Data-Entity rate is designated the better fit.

If both matches have equal ratios for Match-View, Match-Data-Link and Match-Data-Entity, then they are probably equally good matches for the user model. Therefore further discrimination may not be as crucial. However, in the case when many generic models are retrieved, it is time-consuming to review all of these matches, thus it is important that all of the retrieved cases are classified and presented in a meaningful order. To further classify these matches, *GMA* looks at how well the generic model has been matched to the user model, i.e. it chooses the match with the higher Match-Case-Link, i.e. the match which has a higher ratio of matching dependencies. This heuristic has a hidden consequence, i.e. when two generic models have the same number of matching dependencies, *GMA* prefers the generic model which is smaller in size. This is desirable, since smaller models are normally simpler and therefore easier to understand. If they are presented first, the user can use them for confirming the correctness of their own models, before they continue to examine larger and more complicated models.

If all of the above-mentioned discriminating criteria have not been able to distinguish two matches, then the match which has a higher Match-Case-Entity is preferred. Figure 8.9 summarises the selection of a better match.

HEURISTIC SIMILARITY ASSESSMENT FUNCTION

Given two matches, X and Y
if match−view(X) > match−view(Y) then SELECT X
else if match−view(X) = match−view(Y) and
      match−data−link(X) > match−data−link(Y) then SELECT X
else if match−view(X) = match−view(Y) and
      match−data−link(X) = match−data−link(Y) and
      match−data−entity(X) > match−data−entity(Y) then SELECT X
else if match−view(X) = match−view(Y) and
      match−data−link(X) = match−data−link(Y) and
      match−data−entity(X) = match−data−entity(Y) and
      match−case−link(X) > match−case−link(Y) then SELECT X
else if match−view(X) = match−view(Y) and
      match−data−link(X) = match−data−link(Y) and
      match−data−entity(X) = match−data−entity(Y) and
      match−case−link(X) = match−case−link(Y) and
      match−case−entity(X) > match−case−entity(Y) then SELECT X
else SELECT Y

Fig. 8.9. The heuristic similarity evaluation function

8.9.4 User-Definable Similarity Assessment

The heuristic function has been designed in such a way that the most suitable matches are presented to the user first. In our experiments (reported in Chapter 10), the test results were favourable. What exactly constitutes the best match in reality is not entirely clear. It depends on the nature of the input user model as well as which general models are currently in the library, not to mention the intention of the user.

One solution to solve this problem is to supply a more generic and dynamic selection method, i.e. to use a *Weighted City-Block Function* [3] (also called Nearest-Neighbour Ranking [61]) for similarity assessment. There are several possible implementations. We have chosen to use the five identified discriminating criteria above as key features of the function and allow weights to be put on them. The matching results of these key features can either be strengthen or weaken and therefore influence the summarised comparison result. This allows the user to dynamically define their own similarity assessment function by changing the weights of the above five measure criteria.

The user-definable evaluation function, SA(U, G), is given below, where U represents the user model ID, and G is the generic model ID; and W1 to W5 are the corresponding user-definable weights (between 0 and 1) for the five discriminating criteria presented earlier.

```
SA(U, G) = W1 * Match-View(U,G)          + W2 * Match-Data-Link(U,G) +
           W3 * Match-Data-Entity(U,G) + W4 * Match-Case-Link(U,G) +
           W5 * Match-Case-Entity(U,G)
```

Using this evaluation function, the match with a higher value of SA(U, G) is preferred by *GMA*, and therefore is presented to the user first. Since the weights of the function can be dynamically defined, *GMA* is very flexible in retrieving and presenting generic models. It also provides a means for the user to explore the generic models stored in the Generic Model Library in different dimensions. Because of the nature of the similarity assessment functions that we have chosen, *GMA*'s presentation operation is independent from the storage method of the Generic Model Library. This is advantageous compared with a case base reasoner which employs a deductive approach for retrieving a reference case.

8.10 Report Generation and Retaining New Cases

GMA produces a two-stage report for its matching results. The first part of this report is a summary about how well the retrieved generic model is matched with the user model. It informs the user about which generic model has been retrieved and the matching ratios of the five discriminating criteria mentioned in Subsection 8.9.2. It tells the user the number of dependencies and entities in the user model which could and could not be mapped to the generic model. It also gives the number of dependencies and entities in the generic model which could and could not be mapped to the user model. This overview gives the user a good idea how well the user model and the generic model match each other as well as the size of the retrieved generic model. Figure 8.10 shows an example of the first part of the report. A full dialogue of an example use of *GMA* and its reports are given in Appendix L.

The second part of the report provides the user with the matching details. It gives the name of the selected generic model and describes which dependence in the user model was mapped to which dependence in the generic model, and which entity in the user model was mapped to which entity in the generic model. Furthermore, it describes which dependencies in both models could not be mapped. In addition, simple explanations are given why the models could not be matched. For example, it may be the case that no corresponding entities existed; or even though matching entities were found, no corresponding dependencies were found. This could be a hint to the user that they may have left out an important aspect in the user model.

Based on the comparison between the user model and the retrieved generic model, the user may wish to modify or extend their model, or view the next matched generic model. A separate statistical summary report is produced in a file format which records the mapping results for all of the matches that have been viewed by the user. This summary report is useful for the user to

```
*********      Stage Report No. 1      **********

**********  Fitness Measure of Matching **********

(A) The matched CASE model is: Restaurant: Customer Order
    The similar assessment ratio is: 0.5027777777777778

* Matching View Name: yes
* The link matching ratio of the retrieved CASE model: 0.2916666666666667
  The entity matching ratio of the retrieved CASE model: 0.3888888888888889

  There are 7 links matched,
  and there are 17 links not matched.
  There are in total 24 links in the CASE model.

  There are 7 entities matched,
  and there are 11 entities not matched.
  There are in total 18 entities in the CASE model.

(B) The input USER model is: Order

* The link matching ratio of the USER model: 0.3333333333333333
* The entity matching ratio of the USER model: 0.5

  There are 7 links matched,
  and there are 14 links not matched.
  There are in total 21 links in the USER model.

  There are 7 entities matched,
  and there are 7 entities not matched.
  There are in total 14 entities in the USER model.

luc1.shell line 44/1668 4%
```

Fig. 8.10. An example consultation session (part I)

gain an even greater overview over all of the relevant generic models. It also provides the user with a convenient means to refer back to a particular match. One example of such a report is given in the following section. A more detailed example is given in Appendix L.4.

When the user finished their new model, the user may wish to retain this newly developed model for future reference. The user can generalise this new model and use *KBST-BM's* verification and validation facility to help ensure the correctness and appropriateness of the model, and use *GMA* to automatically store this newly developed model back to the Generic Model Library. Once the new model is added to the Generic Model Library, it is ready to be reused for the next consultation. This final step also completes the life cycle of CBR.

8.11 Example Use of *GMA*

This section gives an example of how *GMA* can be used to help the modeller design a new model from scratch and how to provide a head-start by providing relevant generic models and modelling guidance for the user in the problem domain. In the chosen example, the user wants to build a model in the business area of customer order handling. Initially, the user identified only two fundamental concepts in the domain: the individual customers who place customer orders with the company and those customer orders placed by them. Based on a certain amount of training and experience with BSDM, one recognises that these two concepts may be represented as entities "Person" and "Customer

Order", respectively. The two entities, therefore, which form the initial model (as shown in Figure 8.11) will be used as the input (user) model to the *GMA* for consultation.

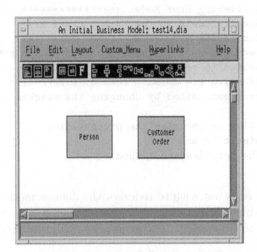

Fig. 8.11. The initial business model

Before the consultation of *GMA* can begin, the background knowledge of *GMA*, i.e. the most recent *Generic Case Library* and *Entity Conceptual Hierarchy*, must be made available to *GMA*. The user can do so by selecting menu-items *"Custom Menu/Export Case Library to CBR"* and *"Custom Menu/Export Entity Conceptual Hierarchy"* from any of the *Generic Model Library* or *Entity Hierarchy* diagram cards in *KBST-BM*.

The user exports the initial model to *GMA* in a similar fashion, i.e. selects the menu-item *"Custom Menu/Export User Model to GMA"* on the (BSDM) diagram card which captures the initial model. The user can then activate *GMA* by selecting the menu-item *"Custom Menu/ Run Generic Model Adviser"* from the same BSDM diagram card. This will trigger the creation of a separate window which automatically loads the *GMA* inference engine and the necessary background knowledge. The activated *GMA* is shown in a Prolog window: the welcome messages and instructions generated by *GMA* are given below:

```
******* Welcome to KBST-BM Generic Model Advisor *******
Please type "run." to take the specific input from KBST-BM.
Press control+d to quit the program. Bye for now.
| ?-
```

Since the user wants to use their own model as input, they type "run." to take the newly exported user model as input. *GMA* then compares the user model with generic models in the case library and collects all of the models that match. After the collection process is finished, *GMA* comes back to the user and asks for the selection method for presenting those generic models. This part of the *GMA* dialogue is given below.

```
| ?- run.
************** Retrieving User Model ****************
**** Matching Generic Models in the Case Library ****
******* Choose Similarity Assessment Method *********
All of the relevant cases to the user model have been retrieved
and will be presented to you one at a time. The sequence of display
may be determined using the default method. Alternatively, if you wish,
you can design your own method by changing the weights on selected
features.
  How would you like to optimise the presentation:
  (1) Use The Default Method
  (2) Redefine The Optimisation Method
|: 1.
```

Since the user does not wish to redesign the default method, the option "1" has been taken which leads to the first recommended case: the generic model "Deliver Product to Customer". The generated analysing report is given below.

```
*********** Finished Optimising Solution *********
**********       Stage Report No. 1      **********
**********   Fitness Measure of Matching **********

(A) The matched CASE model is:
    BSDM: Deliver Product to Customer.
    The overall similar assessment ratio is: 0.23

* Matching View Name: no
* The link matching ratio of the retrieved CASE model: 0
  The entity matching ratio of the retrieved CASE model: 0.14

  There are 2 entities matched,
  and there are 12 entities not matched.
  There are in total 14 entities in the CASE model.

* The link matching ratio of the USER model: 0
* The entity matching ratio of the USER model: 1.0

  There are 2 entities matched,
  and there are 0 entities not matched.
  There are in total 2 entities in the USER model.

********        Stage Report No. 2       *********
********   Result Analysis & Suggestion  *********

(1) The selected matching case model is:
    BSDM: Deliver Product to Customer.

(2) Matching of entities:
```

```
- There are 2 sets of entities found matched:

- The Entity "Customer Order" in the USER model.
  was found to be matching with
  the Entity "Order" in the CASE model.

- The Entity "Person" in the USER model.
  was found to be matching with
  the Entity "Organisation" in the CASE model.

(3) An independent match from User to Case Model:

- No dependency was found to be matched.

============== End of Report ==============
```

In this report, a summary of the overall matching is given in the first stage of the report followed by detailed supporting evidences in the second stage of the report. If the user wishes to see the above selected generic model, they can use *KBST-BM* to view it and modify/extend their own model accordingly. The above recommended generic model is shown in full in Figure 8.12.

Alternatively, the user may wish to see another matching model for the same user model. In that case, they may type "y." at the end of the first *GMA* consultation session to ask *GMA* to present the next best matching. This part of the dialogue is given below.

```
============== End of Report ==============
Do you want to see an alternative matching ? (y. or n.)
|: y.
```

GMA will repeatedly ask whether the user wish to see an alternative match until the user answers "n.", or until all of the appropriate options have been displayed. In this fashion, all of the matching generic models may be displayed to the user in the order based on the chosen selection method. If the user decides to make direct use of any of the selected generic model, the user can export that model out of the *Generic Model Library* using *KBST-BM* by choosing the menu-item "Custom Menu/ Export *GML* to BSDM" on that generic model. This will cause *KBST-BM* to automatically generate a new BSDM (user) model from that generic model.

A more comprehensive consultation example of *GMA* including the corresponding underlying formal representation of the user model is given in Appendix L.

8.12 Conclusion

Since common business scenarios exist in different business environments, it is an obvious advantage if one can reuse already existing generic business models.

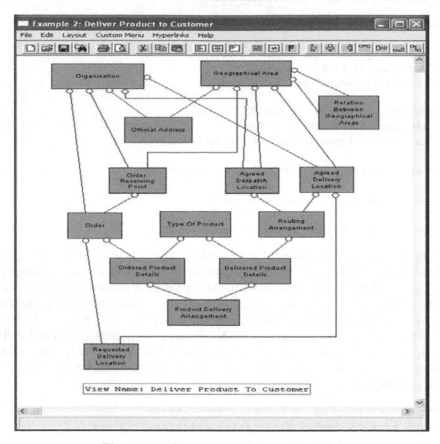

Fig. 8.12. The recommended generic model

As observed earlier in this book, not all human reasoning about how to build an appropriate business model can be formalised as rules. In responding to both of these two issues, Case-Based Reasoning was used to provide supplemental support to the user in addition to the support which is already provided by *KBST-BM*.

A Case-Based Reasoning Engine, *Generic Model Advisor (GMA)*, has been developed and was described in this chapter. Also, a brief introduction to the standard CBR life cycle was given, followed by the system architecture of *GMA*. Integrated with *KBST-BM*, *GMA* is able to store business models which are provided by the method as well as newly developed generic models. It can retrieve and recommend relevant business models to the user when only given a partial model.

A concept similar to that of the *context tree* has been deployed by *GMA*, namely the building of an *Entity Conceptual Hierarchy (ECH)*. The *Entity Conceptual Hierarchy* provides a framework to express the entity concepts which are captured in a business model as well as the inter-relations between them. This knowledge was used to match two business models (it is also used to determine if a business model has been over- or under-specialised as described in Chapter 5).

A heuristic similarity assessment function has been provided by the tool. This heuristic was found to be successful in our tests (as reported in Chapter 10). To provide more flexibility towards the retrieval of generic models, *GMA* allows the user to dynamically alter the similarity assessment function. Both of these two similarity assessment methods allow an independent operation of the case presentation to the user from the storage method of generic models in the *GML*.

Combined with *KBST-BM's* verification and validation facilities, a business model's correctness can be verified and its appropriateness examined, new models can be retained to the Generic Model Library and subsequently the retained models can be used for future *GMA* consultation sessions, thereby completing the life cycle of *GMA*.

8.13 Exercises

1. Explain why reusing past models is useful. How does it compare with normal BSDM practice?
2. What is CBR? How is it related to reusing past models?
3. What is *GML*? What kind of models are worth of storing in it?
4. What is *ECH*? What is its role in a CBR cycle? Can one carry out a CBR without it?
5. Explain how new cases are matched with past cases in this chapter. Explain the rationale behind this method. Can you propose a matching method for another modelling method, e.g. UML's Class Diagram?
6. New cases may be overlapped with past cases in various different ways. List those and provide possible explanations for their outcomes.
7. Explain the heuristic similarity assessment function used in this chapter. Describe the rationale behind this method. Can you propose an assessment function for another modelling method, e.g. UML's Class Diagram?
8. Explain the analysis report given in this chapter and its design rationale. Can you propose a report design using an alternative modelling method, e.g. UML's Class Diagram?

8.14 Advanced Exercises

1. Based on the above self-proposed matching algorithm and heuristic similarity assessment function, implement a CBR engine.
2. Based on the above self-proposed analysis report style, implement a report generation facility for the CBR engine described above.

9

Use of *KBST-BM*

The *Knowledge Based Support Tool for Business Models (KBST-BM)* is built upon a diagramming and hypertext development tool *Hardy* [101] which was developed and provided by the *Artificial Intelligence Application Institute (AIAI)* at *The University of Edinburgh.* Since *Hardy* has embedded within it the expert system shell *CLIPS* [79], we are able to enrich the built tool with method and application domain knowledge. *KBST-BM* is a design tool which uses our formal method to provide the user with intelligent support throughout the development life cycle of building business models using the Business System Development Method (BSDM).

KBST-BM has the following characteristics:

- it is event-driven;
- it is diagram and hypertext-based;
- it is knowledge-rich;
- it provides an automatic verification facility for business models;
- it extends BSDM's business modelling method with the *Procedural Model* and provides means to enable the simulation for the business model;
- it provides a notation to display a dynamic BSDM business model;
- it discovers *process dependencies* in business models and infers process execution order that was not previously known to BSDM;
- it accumulates model-building knowledge through time using the built-in system, Generic Model Advisor;
- it supports the full model development cycle and can be used to record design rationale.

This chapter describes an example user-scenario that deploys *KBST-BM* to build a business model in BSDM, thereby demonstrating the use of *KBST-BM* in the context of actual model-building.

9.1 Description of DAI Case

As mentioned in Section 8.6, a business model has been developed for the *Department Artificial Intelligence (DAI), The University of Edinburgh* during this research project which will be referred to as the *DAI* model for short here. A much simplified and partial view of the area of module evaluation at the same department was used in the previous chapters to provide example business models when explaining concepts and support of the tool. We will be referring back to some of the example models which have been shown in those chapters to keep our description more concise. We will, however, also use a more complete model to show aspects of the tool that have not already been shown.

In the more complete model, five interesting business areas have been identified for the AI department and they are categorised as *views* in the business model: "Module Evaluation", "Course Structure", "Personnel Management", "Course Evaluation" and "Degree Evaluation". The view "Module Evaluation" specifies the (business) context that is related to the assessment of student performance for a module that mainly involves the assessment for undergraduate and MSc students in the department. The evaluation of module performance for a student depends on two criteria: the performance of examination and practicals for that module which are illustrated as business processes in the view. We will use the development for the view "Module Evaluation" as a case study example.

9.2 Developing a Business Model

9.2.1 Overview of using *KBST-BM*

Once an organisation has decided to build a business model, the first consideration is to divide the business operations into several business areas. Each business area is built as a part of the business model: they sometimes form a *view* or several *views* in the model.

KBST-BM provides a tree hierarchy of *cards* to capture the business model.[1] Figure 9.1 shows the top-level control window which displays one possible organisation of a business model. Each text node indicates the name of a "card" which is a window of either the type of a *Text Card, Hypertext Card, BSDM Card* (which captures the BSDM business model), *Life Cycle Diagram, Dynamic Business Model* card, *Procedural Model* card, *Generic Model Library* card, *Entity Hierarchy* card, *Workflow Management* card, *Process Sequence Diagram* card, *Entity Relational Diagram* or a *State Transition Diagram*.[2] *Hardy* provides two text card types: *Text Card* and *Hypertext Card*, the rest of the

---

[1] This mechanism is provided by the underlying development tool *Hardy*.

[2] All of these card types have been introduced and shown in previous chapters; the *Workflow Management* card will be described here.

cards were devised based on BSDM and other appropriate notations using
drawing facilities provided by *Hardy*.

Figure 9.1 shows the tree hierarchy of the title of the cards stored in *KBST-BM*.

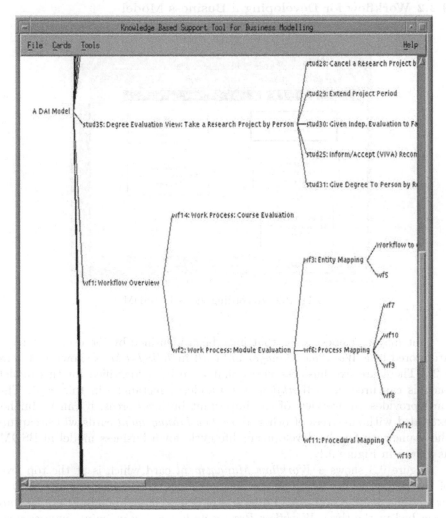

Fig. 9.1. Overview of *KBST-BM*

When modellers start to build a model, they create a "top card" in *KBST-BM*. The top card "A DAI Model" has been created as a root node for the hierarchy. There can only be one root node in *KBST-BM*. A *text card*, a card that only contains text, has been used in this case which gives a brief description (in natural language) about the captured model. Cards that share common interests are grouped together as sub-trees and expanded from the top card. For instance, the card *stud35: Degree Evaluation View: Take a Re-*

search Project by Person and its sub-tree describe the context of handling a student's research project. Other example *BSDM Cards* that have been used to capture the business model are shown in Appendix E.

9.2.2 Workflow for Developing a Business Model

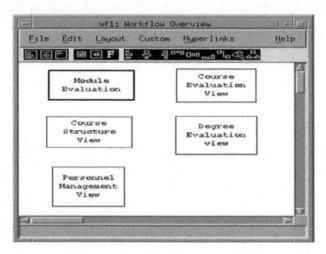

Fig. 9.2. Recording views in BSDM

The major business areas that have been identified by the user as "views" are stored in a *Workflow Management* card in *KBST-BM* as shown in Figure 9.2.[3] There are five business views that have been identified for this model, each is captured as a *Workflow View* node, a rectangle, in this card. This card provides an overview of the important business areas; it can be further extended with sub-trees of other *Workflow Management* cards which capture the framework for the development life cycle for a business model in BSDM, as shown in Figure 9.1.

Figure 9.3 shows a *Workflow Management* card which is at the top level of the framework for developing a business model in the business area *Module Evaluation* using *KBST-BM*. Three sets of BSDM model-building activities are described in the three *Workflow Process* nodes: *entity mapping, process mapping* and *procedural mapping*. Although modelling activities captured in this figure include only one business area, they can be used to cover several business areas. The *Workflow* arrows which connect two *Workflow Process* nodes suggest the developing sequence and iterative process.

The above development framework is compliant with BSDM [52]. An example development workflow for building a *Business Model* in BSDM is shown

---

[3] The notion of Workflow Management is a KBST-BM device.

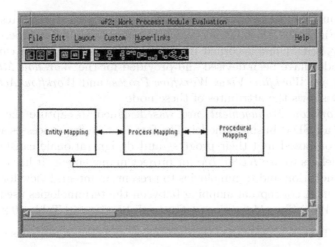

Fig. 9.3. Development framework for a business model

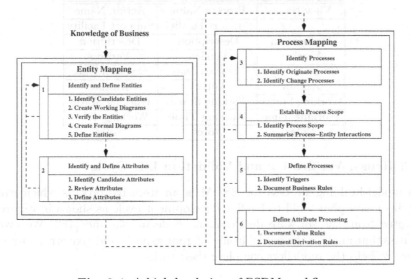

Fig. 9.4. A high-level view of BSDM workflow

in Figure 9.4.[4] The *procedural mapping*, on the other hand, is an extension to BSDM that is the model-building process for the *procedural model*. It is a new component added to BSDM and is similar to those described above for process mapping.

Each *Workflow Process* node can be further divided into more detailed activities and described as *Workflow Action* nodes in other *Workflow Management* cards which are shown at a lower level in the hierarchy.

---

[4] BSDM does not have a notion of workflow. We use it here for illustration and to provide assistance for modelling activities.

When business *views* have been identified and recorded in figures similar to the one in Figure 9.2, the modellers can now follow the building procedure which is given by BSDM and recorded in the *Workflow Management* cards. Three kinds of nodes have been devised and provided for the *Workflow Management* cards: they are *Workflow View*, *Workflow Process* and *Workflow Action*. Table (9.1) below shows the attributes of these node.

The *Workflow Management* card was designed to capture the process of developing a BSDM business model. The fact that design processes and actions can be decomposed and their progress and design rationale can be recorded allows modellers to use *KBST-BM* for project management. It has deployed its own set of notation and terminologies to present an integral view for modelling management. A conceptual mapping between the terminologies used in BSDM and in the *WorkFlow Management Card* will be given in Table 10.2.

Table 9.1: Nodes and their attributes in workflow diagrams

Workflow View	Workflow Process	Workflow Action
View Name	Process Name	Action Name
	Support Facility	Support Facility
Description	Description	Description
Version	Version	Version
Creation Date	Creation Date	Creation Date
Author	Author	Author
Working Status	Working Status	Working Status
Working Time	Working Time	Working Time
Notes	Notes	Notes

9.2.3 Reuse, Verification and Validation Life Cycle

The model-building process for BSDM is an iterative process which can be described as a plan-build-test-refine development cycle as shown in Figure 9.5 (adapted from the software development cycle in [83] and [41]). We provide facilities that analyse the model from different aspects and give error correction advice to help the modellers complete their tasks.

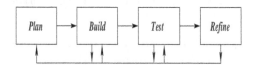

Fig. 9.5. The plan-build-test-refine development cycle

9.3 Developing an Entity Model

An example *Entity Model* has been described in Chapter 5 and a part of the model is shown in Figure 5.2. To begin with, the user can decide on a particular

business area to work with. The user can identify the key entities in this area
and the dependencies between them. The user can then use this partial model
as input to the *Generic Model Advisor*, which retrieves parts of (reference)
models from the *Generic Model Library* which are in the similar business circumstances, together with a comparison and analysis report between the user
and the retrieved models. The user can choose some of these retrieved models
and have them automatically exported to the user's own model. The user can
now adapt the newly retrieved model as his/her own model.

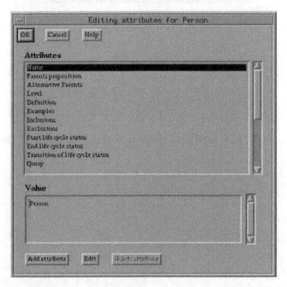

Fig. 9.6. The (property) definition form for entity "Person"

The creation of entities and dependencies on these cards is done using
mouse–menu interactions. After an entity is created, *property* values of this
entity can be entered through the definition form provided for in *KBST-BM*.
Figure 9.6 shows the definition form for entity "Person". The *attributes* for the
entity occurrences can also be specified at this time. Recall that entity *properties* are the commonly shared properties for every occurrence of an entity;
whereas the values of entity *attributes* are only applicable to the particular entity occurrence (a concept that has been described in Chapter 5). Figure 9.7
shows the *Attribute List Menu* through which the user can create and define
entity attributes for entity "Person".

Several entity attributes have been identified for a person: to name a few,
"First Name", "Last Name", "Other Name", "Birthday" and so on. Each entity
attribute can be further specified. Figures 9.8 and 9.9 show the definition forms
for the attribute "Nationality" for entity "Person". The actual instantiation
of values for these entity attributes can only be done when the corresponding
entity occurrence has been created; this is done in the *Dynamic Business Model*
which has been described in Chapter 6 and will be briefly shown again later.

Fig. 9.7. The attribute definition form for entity 'Person'

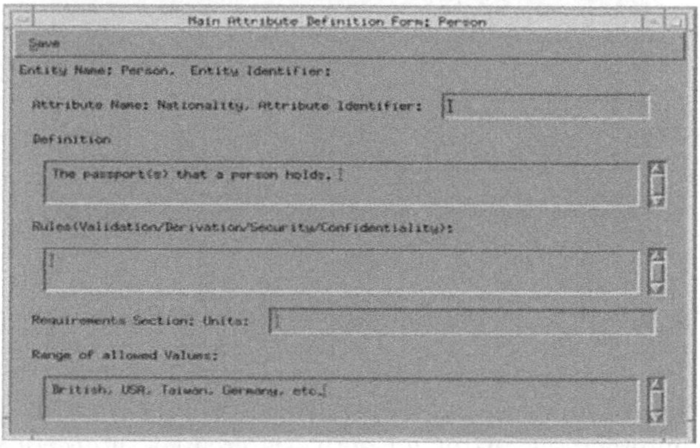

Fig. 9.8. Detailed definition form for attribute "Nationality" (1)

To help the user navigate around the model, several convenient facilities using mouse–menu activations have been provided: e.g. the facility to automatically browse/close/iconise/save all cards, to show the name of the file that physically stores the card, to see the type of the card, to get a summary information for all entities and processes in a particular card or in the whole model, to generate a summary report for all entities and processes in the model, to browse and search for all cards/processes which include a particular entity, to locate the *Life Cycle Diagram* for an entity anywhere in the model, to automatically infer the parents for all entities (because not all entity parents are included in all cards), and to infer the correct *level* for each entity in the model.

As the *Entity Model* is developing, the user may identify important entities for which the transition of life states needs to be specified. This information

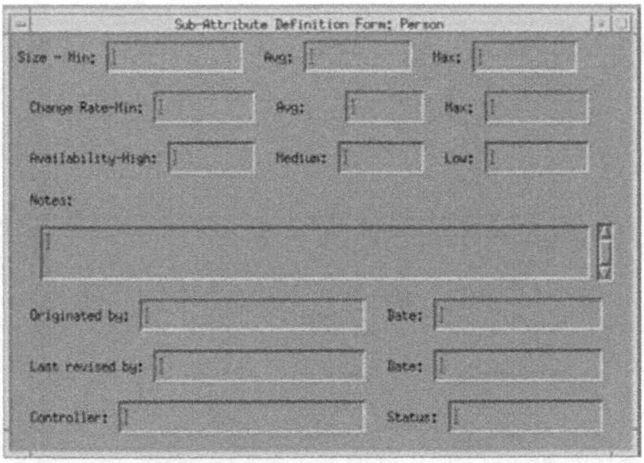

Fig. 9.9. Detailed definition form for attribute "Nationality" (2)

is recorded in *Life Cycle Diagrams*: one such example was given in Figure 5.3. At any stage of building the *Entity Model*, the user can decide to use the *Generic Model Advisor* again to gather further comparison results using the newly developed model. The user can also use the model verification facility in the *KBST-BM* at any stage of model development.

To carry out model verification, the user first needs to enact the representation of the model followed by the activation of a consultation window for entity model verification, both using a mouse–menu interaction. One such consultation window was shown in Figure 5.5. Verification of entity and process models is done by the application of sets of model rules and guidelines. The user can use all of the rules and guidelines to verify the model by specifying each set systematically in the consultation window and to adjust the model according to the automatically generated analysis and advice.

Since the process of the model development is iterative, the user may choose to review, verify, validate and modify the model using the appropriate support facilities provided by *KBST-BM* at any appropriate time. When the developed *Entity Model* is correct and adequate, the newly built *Entity Model* can be automatically imported into the *Generic Model Library* enabling future reuse of the model and increasing the knowledge of the *Generic Model Advisor* over time. Having finished building the *Entity Model* to a certain extent, the user is now ready to extend the model with processes.

9.4 Developing a Process Model

Based on the *BSDM Entity Model*, the modellers can now identify processes that manipulate those entities. Figure 6.1 shows an example process model using *KBST-BM*. Once a process is created, the user can define the process using definition forms in *KBST-BM*. Figures 9.10 and 9.11 show the definition forms for process *"Assign Practical Mark"* with which the user can define properties for the process and specify the corresponding process scope.

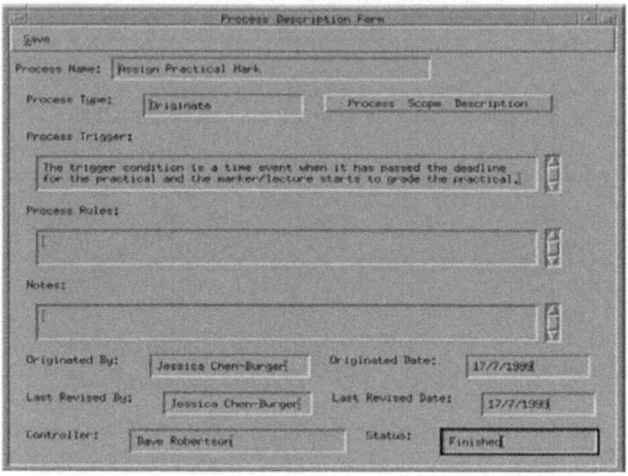

Fig. 9.10. Definition form for process *Assign Practical Mark* (1)

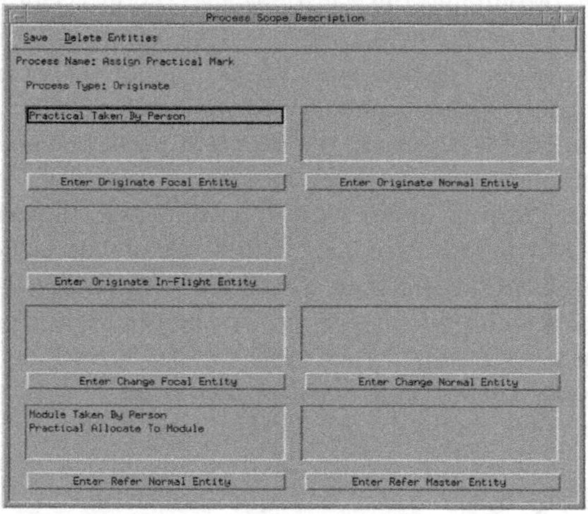

Fig. 9.11. Definition form for process *Assign Practical Mark* (2)

The user can also decide to extend existing entity *Life Cycle Diagrams (LCD)* with processes or create new entity LCDs, and relate them to the identified processes in the model. To help the user cross-check the correctness, completeness and appropriateness of the process model, the user can use the automatic model verification facilities at any stage. The way of using this facility is the same as the one applied for entity model verification. Having the errors (if any) identified and potential inadequacies pointed out by the tool, the user can modify the model accordingly. The user can also use the navigation facilities which are provided for in *KBST-BM* at any stage to assist the process model development.

When the process model is completed to a sufficient stage, the user can decide to use the *Process Execution Constructor* to infer the dependencies and constraints for process execution (Subsections 7.4.2 and 7.5.1). Two types of *Process Dependencies and Partial Execution Order* diagrams can be generated, one shows dependency types I, III and VI, and the other shows types I, II, III and IV. In the second diagram the type III dependencies are replaced by type II wherever type II dependencies are present since type II and III dependencies indicate similar (but not the same) relationships. Each of these two types of diagram shows some properties that other ones do not. An example of each type of diagrams was given in Figures 7.4 and 7.5. Both of these diagrams were generated using the *DAI* model given in Appendix E.

Given these diagrams, the users are provided with another independent way to evaluate the adequacy of processes and the relationships between them, and can determine if any overlapped processes should be merged or missing processes created. Possible conclusions that the user can infer from the *Process Dependencies and Partial Execution Order* and actions the user can take were described in detail in Subsection 7.5.1. Since those process dependencies also indicate the constraints for process execution orders the user can gain an insight into the dynamic behaviours of a business model even before the simulation begins.

9.5 Developing a Procedural Model

If the user wishes to perform simulations based on the business model, then he/she will need to learn our extension to BSDM, the *Procedural Model*, which captures the operational details of a process. The building of a procedural model is supported with standard procedural models. The user can select for adaptation the standard procedural model which has the same process type as the desired process (the process types are described in the *Inheritance Hierarchy*). The procedural model will then be instantiated with entity types and actions, which will be used to provide a framework for executing the process. Examples of standard and instantiated *Procedural Models* were given in Figures 7.1 and 7.3.

Having specified the *Procedural Model* the user can now design business scenarios that will be used to test the adequacy of the business model. To gain an overview and short cut in doing so, the *Process Dependencies and Partial Execution Order* diagrams can be used to help prune the "search space" by avoiding business scenarios that violate the constraints that have been stated in these diagrams. In fact, the system will not allow the user to simulate many of the scenarios in which the process execution contradicts the partial orders that have been derived and displayed in the *Process Dependencies and Partial Execution Order* diagrams. For example, the business model simulator make sure that an entity occurrence is already created before it allows a process to create an attribute for it. After the testing business scenarios have been decided, the user may invoke *KBST-BM* to automatically create a *Dynamic Business Model* from the *Process Model* using simple mouse–menu actions.

The user can instantiate the entity and process *types* in the *Dynamic Business Model* with the corresponding *occurrences*. An instantiated diagram was given in Figure 7.2. These occurrences constitute the initial state for the business model simulation. The user also needs to create process trigger occurrences[5] in the *Dynamic Business Model*. The content of a trigger occurrence follows the information specified in the *Procedural Model* for that process and will invoke the corresponding process occurrence to be created and executed, when all required constraints are satisfied.

After this is done, the user can export the business model including the dynamic information to the *business model simulator* and activate the simulator. During export, fundamental errors such as missing of information may be found by the tool and messages shown to the user. These errors should be corrected before using the simulator.

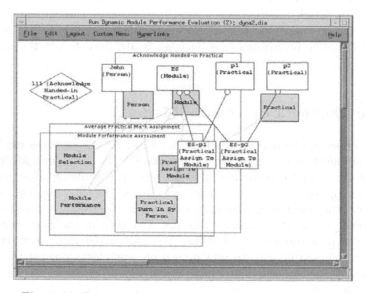

Fig. 9.12. Dynamic business model with trigger occurrence

Entity, process and trigger occurrences are normally scattered across several *Dynamic Business Model* cards, but can be exported as a whole to the simulator. A trigger occurrence includes all of the information that is needed to invoke the corresponding process: i.e. the actions, preconditions, postconditions and IDs of the entity occurrences involved. Figure 9.12 shows one trigger occurrence (in diamond shape): the trigger ID is 111, the process name is "Acknowledge Handed-In Practical", the time cost is 2 (units) and the process is to be activated at time 0.

---

[5] The trigger occurrence actually includes all information needed to execute a process, therefore it is not only a trigger occurrence, but also a trigger information pack. An example is given later in this chapter.

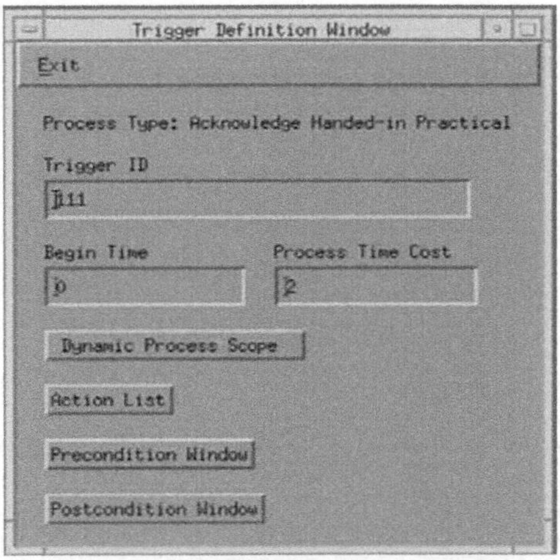

Fig. 9.13. Definition window for a trigger occurrence

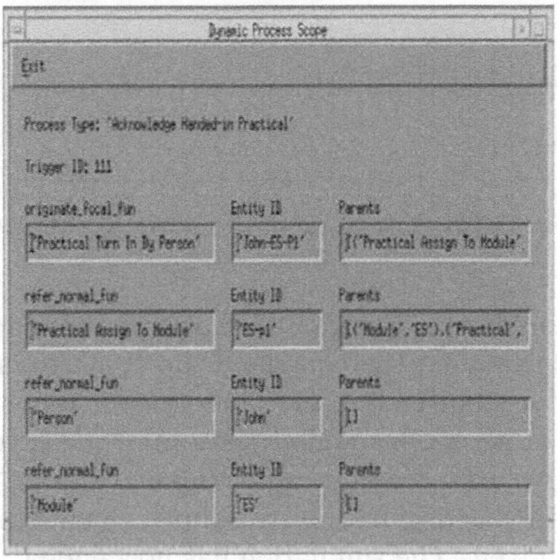

Fig. 9.14. Process scope described in a trigger occurrence

Figure 9.13 shows the definition window for the trigger occurrence which includes all of the information described above and control buttons which lead to other definition windows for additional details. Figure 9.14 shows the additional definition window *Dynamic Process Scope* which describes the entity occurrences that are included in the process *Acknowledge Handed-In Practical*, in which entity types are automatically generated based on the information specified in the corresponding procedural model. Since entity occurrence information is changed every time a new trigger occurrence is created, it is gathered by the user dynamically either through mouse or keyboard interactions.

The business model simulator can be activated from the *Dynamic Business Model* or from any *BSDM Cards*. Upon activation, a window that runs the simulator is opened and the user can give instructions for how many simulation

Fig. 9.15. Activation of the business simulator

steps the system should take. Figure 9.15 shows the simulator window.[6] In this example, the user has issued the command top "(1)" to enable the system to infer one step (one system time unit). The system reports back to the user about the progress of its actions and at the end of the execution asks the user for any new trigger occurrences that can be imported from a *Dynamic Business Model*. Since the user has decided not to supply a new trigger occurrence, the command "n." was given. The simulation has now ended.

The initial state consists of a system state ID "0", time 0 and all of the dynamic information that was imported from the model. To see which state the system is currently in, the "look." command is issued in the simulator. This command can be used at any stage when the simulator is not executing. Figure 9.16 shows the results of the simulator. As mentioned in Chapter 7, trigger occurrences are represented in a *trigger_information* predicate:

trigger_information(Begin_time, Process_name, Trigger_ID, Action_list).

Since the above trigger occurrence suits the time requirement at time "0" and all corresponding preconditions were satisfied at that time, this trigger occurrence is put inside the process agenda. The *trigger_information* predicate is

---

[6] The simulator is written in *Prolog*.

Fig. 9.16. Simulation result (1)

therefore deleted and an *agenda* predicate inserted (shown in Figure 9.16):[7]

agenda(process(Process_name, Trigger_ID,Action_list, (Begin_time, End_time))).

At this stage, since no processes have been executed yet, no changes are made to the dynamic state of the system. The system therefore still stays at "state 0" (the initial state)[8] and has used up one time unit and stops before the entering of time 1.

The user has now decided to advance the system for another 2 time steps, hence gives the command "top(2)". The process trigger is now matured (time-wise) and its effects are realised. Figure 9.17 shows how the system operates and reports to the user. The user may decide to execute several processes at any time point, if there are more than one matured processes. The user may also decide not to execute a process and postpone the execution until later. However, if a matured process has been postponed for too long (a pre-determined time span), a warning/reminder will be given to the user. Note that before a process can be executed, various aspects must be checked: the detection of any potential conflicts between any competing processes (described in Subsection 7.5.2), the correct syntax of the triggers and its actions, the satisfaction of the process preconditions (stated by the user in the procedural

---

[7] *End_time* is the dynamic *Begin_time* when a process is in the agenda plus the necessary time cost to execute the process.

[8] A system state can only be changed if a process has been executed.

```
| ?- top(2).
>>>>> Searching for Processes
>>>>> Searching for Triggers
End Time: 1
Step left: 1
Would you like to add new occurrences to the system? (y./n.)
|: n.
>>>>> Searching for Processes
**************************************
All processes in the Agenda are given below:

Acknowledge Handed-in Practical,111

**************************************
* Searching for contradictory processes...
  No contradictory processes found.

**********************************
Would you like to execute process:

Acknowledge Handed-in Practical
Trigger ID: 111
**********************************
Execution? (y/n) y.

**********************************
        Process Execution Phase
**********************************
* Checking the triggers....
  checking triggers succeed.
* Checking then preconditions....
  checking precond succeed.
* Checking the referred attributes...
  checking referred attributes succeed.
* Checking the adding attributes...
  checking adding attributes succeed.
* Checking for the changing attributes...
  checking changing attributes succeed.
* Executing the process ...
  Process execution succeed.
* Verifying the postconditions...
  Verifying postconditions succeed.
>>>>> Searching for Processes
>>>>> Searching for Triggers
End Time: 2
Step left: 0
Would you like to add new occurrences to the system? (y./n.)
|: n.
End of simulation. Simulation stops at time: 3
****** export_data_to_archive ******
System States are saved in sim.out

yes
| ?- look.
------- report dynamic system state -------
Shown State: 1  State Time: 2. It is now time: 2
```

Fig. 9.17. Simulation result (2)

model) and any other prerequisites for process actions (system built-in). If any of the above checks fails, the execution is aborted and the user will be prompted with error messages and advice. The aborted process execution can be continued in the next time step if the error has been corrected.

After executing the process, the user may decide to issue another "look." command to the simulator to see the changes made to the system state. He/she will find that the process has been executed and effects realised: the corresponding entity and process occurrences and attributes have been created, and the state is now advanced to "state 1", because of the process execution. A full dialogue of this operation is given in Appendix M.

In the above case, no conflicts between processes have been found. However, in a case when a potential conflict is present the tool is able to detect that and report it to the user. As mentioned in Chapter 7, the execution of processes and changes made to the dynamic states of the business model can be described in a *State Transition Diagram*. The user can use the business model simulator to help predict if the design of the business model will allow the business organisation to behave in certain ways.

9.6 Conclusion

The process of developing BSDM's business model is an iterative one. Parallel to the development framework, which was summarised in Figure 9.3, is the plan-built-test-refine development cycle as shown in Figure 9.5. The development process of a business model is captured and represented in a workflow diagram, which enables the user to keep track of the current status of model development and the design rationale. As the model is extended, the user can decide to carry out verification and validation checks. If the user feeds the relevant process and procedural information into a model, further validation checking can be carried out. Based on the checking results, the user can modify the model to eliminate errors and repeat the plan-build-test-refine cycle until the model is complete. The tool also helps the user to reuse and retain model-building knowledge.

In summary, *KBST-BM* provides a knowledge-rich system which enables the reuse, verification and validation of business models. Its capabilities can be improved over time due to its *GMA* component. As a result, it can be used to improve the quality of business models and speed up the model-building process. *KBST-BM* complies with the method (BSDM) and can demonstrate the dynamic behaviours of a business model. It can, therefore, be used as a communicator (especially for those who are not BSDM professionals) and increase user confidence in the model.

9.7 Exercises

1. What are the characteristics of *KBST-BM*? What are the main purposes of *KBST-BM*?
2. Describe a typical workflow for using *KBST-BM* to build a business model.
3. *KBST-BM* supports several different graphical methods. List them and discuss how they complement each other to support the user.
4. Discuss how logical methods play a part in *KBST-BM*.
5. How does *KBST-BM* help as a part of the business modelling life cycle? Is this approach generic? Can you discuss how this approach may be applied to developing other modelling methods?

9.8 Advanced Exercises

1. *KBST-BM* is a graph-based tool that support various graph-based methods, but not all modelling methods are graph-based. Discuss how a graph-based (sometimes called a visual-based) method may (or may not) be useful compared with one that is not graph based.
2. You may have heard of black- and white-box testing from your experiences of Software Engineering. How would you compare those techniques with those V&V and critiquing techniques used in *KBST-BM* to test models?

Evaluation of System

10.1 Introduction

The functionality of *KBST-BM* was evaluated and improved as a consequence of using it to build the different business models described in this book. The usefulness of the tool was also demonstrated when it was successfully used for a large *Multi-Perspective Enterprise Modelling* project, *AOEM*, for (military) Air Operations [56] [19]. There, using *KBST-BM*, a *BSDM Business Model* has been built, including 41 BSDM diagrams, describing 162 different types of entities and 28 different types of processes.

This chapter describes an evaluation of *KBST-BM* based on work carried out during PhD research, i.e. not including many further details on AOEM. The main part of this analysis focuses on the level of support the tool provides for the method (BSDM), although a brief comparison with other similar modelling tools and a discussion of our experiences in using a logic-based method to provide such support are also included.

KBST-BM was built to test the idea proposed in the book: following a logic-based approach, it is possible to provide automatic support for informal methods. As mentioned in Section 8.6, business models in five different areas have been built using *KBST-BM* as a part of the research. They are the standard and example business models provided by the method, an industrial business model that was developed by IBM for its client in the sector of automobile parts distribution, a generic business model that was developed for small and medium-sized restaurants, a business model developed for course management and evaluation for the *The Department of Artificial Intelligence (DAI), The University of Edinburgh.*[1]

The actual use and evaluation of the tool has shown that it facilitates a level of automation of modelling tasks and support of the method that was previously not available. The tool previously used by IBM BSDM experts, FlowMark [65], has none of the sophisticated automation tools and only provides various

---

[1] The department of Artificial Intelligence has now been merged and forms part of the School of Informatics.

documentation facilities for BSDM. The aim of this chapter is to evaluate how well AI techniques can be used to help business modelling activities; but not to assess the usability or user-friendliness of *KBST-BM* or *GMA*. Once the conceptual experimental work is proved successful, building industrial strength graphical user interfaces is better left to interested commercial vendors.

The evaluation of how well *KBST-BM* supports the method uses the following criteria:

- **Completeness:** how well the tool covers the user requirements which are needed to apply the BSDM method.
- **Model Verification Support:** how well the modelling rules and guidelines that BSDM specifies and which are used to check syntactic and semantic correctness of a model are included in the tool. The evaluation assesses to what extent these model rules are incorporated into the tool and used for verification and validation purposes and why certain rules were not included.
- **BSDM Development Process Support:** how well the tool supports the BSDM model development process. Does the tool support every model development stage? Do the practitioners and modellers need to change their modelling practices in order to use the tool?
- **Knowledge Integration and Sharing:** while it is useful to share model-building knowledge, it is generally difficult to do so because the knowledge is normally scattered around different documents to which not everyone has access and unique model experiences can be possessed by several individuals. How well the tool can help to integrate these forms of modelling knowledge and make good use of it to provide modelling guidance is the key question here. This test is particularly carried out on *GMA*.

A comparison of *KBST-BM* with other similar tools, the *Rose Business Process Link* (from Ensemble Systems Inc.) and *AIOWIN* (Knowledge Based Systems, Inc.), is given in Section 10.3.

10.2 Evaluation of Support for Method

10.2.1 Completeness Assessment

In this section, *KBST-BM* was evaluated against the user requirements of a typical BSDM modeller and the standard BSDM method. It does not include any BSDM extensions proposed as part of this book. The newly-added procedural model, the simulation ability of the tool and the workflow diagrams provided in the tool are discussed in later sections.

Business models are normally built during workshop sessions by business managers and a BSDM facilitator (business model expert), who makes use of flip charts and post-it notes for communication and documentation purposes. A diagramming and an editing tool are used after the workshop to record this information. It was suggested that the current tool in use (FlowMark [65]) is not satisfactory due to two main reasons: it does not support the method, i.e.

the tool does not provide direct support for the BSDM notation or its documentation, and the current tool lacks automatic facilities such as communication and error checking – the tool offers process execution abilities, but these are not applicable for BSDM processes. Therefore, a more suitable electronic support tool is much needed.

At an early stage of this research, several meetings were held to talk to an experienced BSDM business modeller (who later became the user of the tool) together with two AI scientists to draw up initial requirements for potential modelling support. These initial requirements formed the foundation of the tool design. To gain early feedback the tool was regularly demonstrated to and evaluated by the IBM expert (the intended user) while the tool was under development. Each feedback was taken into account during subsequent development work. The tool was given to the modeller for further evaluation when it was finished.

Table 10.1: Requirements and their priorities for tool

Requirements	Functions	Priority		Provision
		IBM	AI	
Entity:				
Entity Definition	1	h	l	yes
Attribute Definition	1	h	l	yes
Attribute List	1	m	l	part
Entity Family Specification	2	m	m	yes
Show Entity Dependence	2	m	m	yes
Entity Dependence Check	3	l	m	yes
Entity Occurrence Example	2	m	l	yes
Entity Life States	1,2	m	m	yes
Process:				
Process Scope Description	1,2	h	l	yes
Process Display	1,2	m	l	yes
Process Definition	1,2	h	m	yes
Process Generation	4	l	m	yes
Process Definition Check	4	l	m	yes
Others:				
Search Ability	2	h	l	yes
Diagram Repositioning	2	m	m	yes*
Generic Model Library	1,2	m	m	yes
Generic Model Advisor	4	l	h	yes
Report Generation	2	h	l	yes
Process/Entity Matrix	2	m	l	no
Model Browser	1,2	h	h	yes

- Functions:
    1. Capture abilities: capture BSDM notation and descriptions,
    2. Analytical and Communication abilities: automatic support for analysing and information deriving, searching, model traversing, summarising of information, diagram repositioning/layout and report generation.

3. Syntactic checking ability,
4. Semantic checking ability.

- Priority: indicates the priority for development from the user's, the modeller's, and AI's (or research's) point of view. The user and the modeller's view is given in the column "IBM", AI experts' view is given in the column "AI": h = high priority, m = medium priority, l = low priority.
- Provision: Whether the function has been provided by *KBST-BM*: yes = provided, no = not provided, part = partially provided.
- '*': indicates that the automatic diagramming layout facility is provided by the development platform, *Hardy*.

Table 10.1 is an extension of a similar table originally described in [26] that gives a list of initial coarse-grained user requirements for the tool obtained from several user requirement meetings. In this table, requirements are partitioned in terms of which activities they support during model development: support provided for entity and process modelling activities are grouped into 'Entity' and 'Process' categories; support which is applicable to all areas is grouped into the 'Others' category. There are roughly four different types of support functions (specified as 1–4) that these requirements specify. Detailed documentation about the held user requirement sessions is available in [26]. The initial built tool is described in [26] and [23].

Firstly, it is essential that the tool can accurately capture the correct shape of the notations and forms used in the method. Having to borrow notations from other methods would not only be confusing to the user, but might lead to misunderstandings of the model itself. This type of requirement is described as function (1). Secondly, the provision of analytical information, including the automatic generation of derivable information, and communication facilities are important in assisting the modeller to make sound design decisions and convey a clearer vision described in the model to the user. These are described as function (2). Functions (3) and (4) describe the automatic syntactic and semantic (error) checking of the model as described in the method.

Among the four specified functions, function (1) has been overall rated as the highest priority by the user, and lowest priority by AI experts since less AI techniques are required to fulfil these requirements. These facilities allow the user to draw proper entity and process models and record their properties in the corresponding (definition) forms. Being built on top of *Hardy*, *KBST-BM* is able to utilise the diagramming facilities provided by *Hardy* to capture the *exact* notations, i.e. the exact shape of drawing and the correct way of using entity, process and dependence, in the method. The definition forms in BSDM are also *accurately* captured in *KBST-BM* (implemented in *CLIPS* which is the language supplied by *Hardy*): some with added functions, and some with automatically generated derivable properties, but all are built in accordance with the method. A 'yes' is given in the "Provision" column to indicate that these requirements are accurately fulfilled in the tool; this could simply be checked by comparing existing BSDM model diagrams and forms with those provided by the tool. Although it wasn't initially specified as a requirement for the tool and is therefore not included in the table, some support for the BSDM concept of a "Life Cycle Diagram" has been provided, partly because it stores information that can be used by some of the advanced features of the tool, such as automatic model properties inferencing and simulation. Evaluation of these features will be discussed later.

Function (2) includes communication facilities that enable the user to browse, traverse and examine the model and therefore provide a "communication" channel to the user, as well as facilities which generate analytical (derived) information from the model. The communication facilities are provided by *KBST-BM*. For example, the user can browse through diagrams, entities and processes using the diagram and entity/process browsers, the user can also traverse the diagrams following the hierarchical tree structure which is presented at the top level of the tool. The user can also browse diagrams and processes which include a particular selected entity. Together, these facilities enable the user to examine the model from different perspectives, therefore providing adequate communication support.

Analytical information about architecture and properties of the model is also provided by the tool and described in function (2). It is derived using axioms and the knowledge stored in the tool. One such example of inferred information is the content of a process scope, which is determined from the actual drawing of a process and can be used by the automatic modelling checker to decide if it is consistent with the scope portrayed by the set of entity-functions. Other examples are the automatically generated *Process Dependencies and Partial Execution Order* diagrams and the summarised information of all the entities and processes in the model.

Details of functions (3) and (4) will be discussed in more detail in the next subsection.

Evaluation Summary

After the user requirements were drawn, an initial tool was developed and was brought back to the original user for evaluation. The result of the evaluation was satisfactory since the tool met a majority of the necessary requirements.

Since then the tool has been extended and refined to reach its current form, *KBST-BM*, and has provided all of the "Capture" facilities needed to describe and store the fundamental information of a business model, except for one, the "attribute list" which is only partially supported due to time limitations – although the recording of this information is not provided by a specific facility, but it can be done using a conventional *Hardy hypertext* or *text* card.

The majority of the required "Analytical and Communication" facilities are provided, except for the "Entity/Process Matrix" of BSDM, which was left out also due to time limitations. The inter-relationships between entities and processes described in the matrix can be gained using the "search by entity" facility which lists all of the processes and diagram cards that involved the particular entity in question. These inter-relationships have also been extracted automatically to derive *Process Dependency and Partial Execution Order Diagrams*, which provide an aggregate and an useful overview of entity-process relationships, as mentioned in Subsection 7.4.2.

Overall, all important user requirements have been fulfilled. The end-product has been successfully used to build experimental as well as industrial business models during PhD research. Further evaluation of the "Syntactic" and "Semantic Checking" capabilities of *KBST-BM* will be discussed in more detail in the next subsection.

10.2.2 Model Verification Support Assessment

In this subsection, the model verification abilities which are specified as functions (3) and (4) in the requirements table are examined in terms of the extent to which they support the method.

Automatic syntactic and semantic model checking functionalities in the tool are derived from the model rules in BSDM. They are formalised as model rules or guidelines in the system; the formal representation and explanation of them is detailed in Appendices G and H, which also give the original references from the manual.

To test the tool, it is impossible to find realistic and detailed models which are in use by industry and which exhibit all of the described errors in the method, as designers work hard to avoid these. Consequently, real models will not be sufficient for our testing purposes, as they do not possess all of the error examples. For this reason, an example model was built (the *DAI* example) as our testing case, given in Appendix E. *Error-injection* techniques [115] were also used to confirm the tool's error testing capability, i.e. to inject errors into the testing model and then test the performance of the system.

Case Study

A realistic business model was developed for the *Department of Artificial Intelligence (DAI)* in the *University of Edinburgh*[2] which was used to evaluate the tool's automatic model error detection and advice providing abilities. This model, referred to as the *DAI* model in this book, captures fundamental information and operations which are essential to the AI department to manage data about its students, evaluate their performance and award earned credits.

There are in total 55 entities and 41 processes captured in this model. Application domain knowledge is divided into five sub-areas which each forms a *view*: course structure, personnel management, course evaluation, module evaluation and degree evaluation. The entity model gives a relatively more complete skeleton of the overall structure of DAI, where processes captured in the model are mostly related to the assessment of student performance and awarding of credits.

The *KBST-BM* example window shown in Figure 10.1 describes an overview of the course structure in DAI. Each of the type degree/diploma, certificate/credit, course, theme and module which are known and offered by DAI

---

[2] The Department of Artificial Intelligence is now called the School of Artificial Intelligence, but since DAI is used throughout this book when referring to the model, the original name is used here.

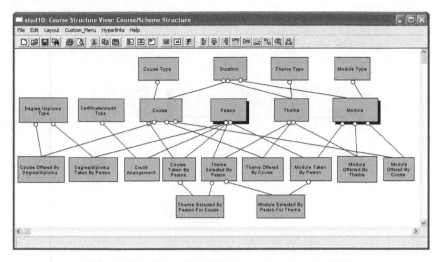

Fig. 10.1. Overview of course structure in DAI

are recorded as entity types (class): "Degree/diploma", "Certificate/credit", "Course", "Theme" and "Module". The actual courses, themes and modules which are offered each term are recorded as occurrences of these entity types, "Course", "Theme" and "Module", where each of them is associated with a particular "Duration", e.g. a course that is offered during autumn term 1998. Entities which are placed at the second or third layers are contracts, relationships and associations of their parents, e.g. an entity occurrence of "Degree/diploma Taken by Person" is created when a person officially follows a degree/diploma with the department; and an occurrence of "Course offered by Degree/diploma" is created when a particular course is offered by a selected degree/diploma.

Figure 10.2 gives an example process "Take Course by Person". This process states that for a person to take a course, (s)he must also decide the theme that (s)he will be taking for the course (if not already done so), that the selected course must conform with the requirements of the degree/diploma that (s)he is pursuing, and that the chosen theme must also confirm with the selected course. When a person has taken a course and the according theme, the relationship between them is linked (with "Theme Selected By Person For Course").

The whole model is described in 34 separate cards (presented in windows) using *KBST-BM*. To evaluate the model verification facilities, 465 errors were injected into the testing model. After errors had been injected into the model, the tool was used to formalise the erroneous model, and a model verification was carried out. Appendix K describes these errors in more detail and the model rules/guidelines which are responsible for detecting them. We found that all of the errors known to the system, i.e. error detections which are formalisable and have been formalised and implemented in the tool, were detected by the system, but that an error can sometimes cause violations of more than one rule/guideline. For example, a circular dependency error can add extra layers to the model due to the newly introduced dependencies, which may as a result

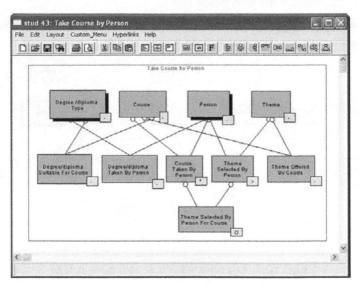

Fig. 10.2. Assign/change/cancel course performance processes

add too many layers and introduce a violation of the 4-entity-layer rule. On the other hand, as one would expect therefore, the removal of one error can sometimes remove more than one violation.

As a consequence, the usefulness of advice given to the user depends on the execution order of the rules/guidelines. For instance, for the above error, the more appropriate advice for the user is the "circular dependency error" rule and not the "4-entity-layers" guideline, since the former is the real cause of the problem. For an experienced modeller this kind of error can be relatively easily corrected once it is identified. For a naive user, this may not be so obvious. Fortunately, the system has classified BSDM rules into model rules and guidelines, where model rules deal with more fundamental modelling errors. Since it is normal practice to check on rule violations before dealing with guideline violations, many of the above situations can be resolved. For example, in the above case the user would have been given advice on the violation of the circular dependency error, rather than the 4-entity-layers problem. When the problem is not resolved in this way, the responsibility lies with the user to make a rational decision. The following paragraphs elaborate on model verification ability assessment in more detail.

Results

Model rules and guidelines which are formalised and provided in the tool can be distinguished into the three categories below.

- *Exact Match:* These model rules/guidelines are given in the method explicitly and all errors described by such rules are detectable by the tool and *correct* advice can be given.

- *Partial Match:* These model rules/guidelines are given in the method explicitly, but only part of the specified errors are detectable by the tool with *correct* advice given.
- *No Match:* These types of model rules in the method are completely unformalisable.

Exact Match

For this type of rule, all of the errors described in the method can be *correctly* detected by the tool and *accurate* advice given whenever an error is detected. Consider the following statement for *dependence*:

> As a general rule, entities have either two parents or none. This, however, is NOT an absolute rule, and you must treat it with caution.(page 43 [51])

This description is formalised as a **Null or two parents only** guideline in the formalism and is implemented accordingly in the tool. The actual formalisation is given below. A detailed explanation can be found in appendix G. Since it has been *explicitly* described as a *general* rule, but not an absolute rule in the BSDM manual, it was formalised as a guideline in our system, i.e. it is only provided as a reference, but not as a rule to be followed strictly.

As discussed in the previous chapters, to indicate this weaker enforcement of the rule, a triangle symbol, ▷, is used. The logic expression below can therefore be read as "**if** there exists a dependency (relationship) between a *dependent entity* (denoted as Entity) and its parent entities (denoted as Parents), **then** the *dependent entity* **should** have either *no* parents or *two* parents in this dependence."[3]

$parent\_type(Entity, Parents)$
$\triangleright$
$member\_no(Parents) = 0 \lor$
$member\_no(Parents) = 2$ *(entity guideline 20)*

Since the tool explicitly distinguishes between rules and guidelines, the activation of guideline detection is separate from that of the model rules, and the advice that is given to the user is less forceful. The explanation and advice given by the tool for the above guideline is shown below.

> *Explanation: under normal circumstances, an entity normally has either none or two parents, i.e. a binary entity-relationship between the two parents, since it is normally the most clear way to describe a relationship and therefore the best way for modelling.*

> *Advice: under special circumstances you can assign one parent to an entity; if you have more than two dependencies linked to this entity,*

---

[3] A dependent entity is also called a child entity in BSDM.

*then you either need to delete the spurious links, or create new entities
which can then be used to describe this missing relationship between this
entity and its parents, or only between its parents.*

Since the dependent entity can be seen as a "relationship" between its
parent entities, in the case when more than two parent entities are involved,
it is possible that either a spurious link is involved, or new entities should be
introduced to capture the missing relationship between them (pages 18 and
43 in [51]). Other example rules of this type are that each entity should be
originated by at least one process, and each process should have at least one
trigger identified (page 74 in [51] and page 62 in [52]).

Partial Match

Rules and guidelines that fall into this category are error cases which may
not all be detectable by the system. The inability of detecting all of them
is caused by the fact that it is impossible to record all knowledge which is
necessary to detect all kinds of modelling errors and for all kinds of business
organisations. Particularly, since business circumstances differ between companies and contradicting practices may exist between them, it is not possible to
generalise rules such that they apply to all companies.

For example, a rule which judges the appropriateness of the identified entities in a model is to inspect the name of an entity, and by doing so some
conceptual errors may be revealed. For instance, things that are a representation of (the real) things are unlikely to be modelled as an entity. For example,
Purchase Order Form is merely a means to capture and describe purchase order information, but not the information itself. It is therefore unlikely to be
included in a BSDM business model (page 25 in [51]). Based on this understanding, we derive that words such as *form, documentation* and *note* should
generally not be included and used as part of an entity name, unless that is
genuinely what the business is managing (page 39 in [51]).

To approximate this sort of modelling rule, we have devised a predicate
form_name(Name) which stores all of the known terms generally regarded as
"representation" of real things, rather than the "real things" that need to be
captured in the model. Given this knowledge, we can then use pattern-matching
techniques to search for their usage in any user-defined entities. If any of these
form names have been used in any entity, we can then suggest that this entity
name is not appropriate. This rule is formalised as an entity model rule, *"An
entity is a representation of real things"*, and its formal representation is given
below.

$class(entity, Entity)$
$\Rightarrow$
$\neg\exists Name. \left(form\_name(Name) \wedge sub\_string(Name, Entity) \right)$
(entity model rule 10)

The effectiveness of such a type of rule relies on accurate and sufficient
generic business knowledge being embedded in the system as well as business-

specific input from the user. When such knowledge is not available in the system, some common sense must be applied by the user. It is not likely that the tool can provide a high coverage of detection of such errors.

A further typical example is to determine whether an entity has been defined at an appropriate level, i.e. if it has been over-specialised and could be generalised and/or merged with other entities into a new entity. This type of error may be spotted by a comparison to an automatically retrieved standard model from the case library, or by a comparison with similar entity types included in the *Entity Conceptual Hierarchy*, but the final decision must rely on the modeller's judgement. More details about the use of case-based reasoning will be given in Subsection 10.2.4.

No Match

These types of modelling rules are un-formalisable due to the difficulty in gaining a complete and comprehensive understanding of the application domain knowledge, the common business knowledge, and/or the natural language involved. Examples of this type of model rules are evaluation criteria applied to business models such as: "Is each entity interesting enough to be managed (and described in the model)?" (page 74 in [51]) and "Does the business model cover the scope of the study?" (page 63 in [52]). To answer these two questions correctly, one must have both an insight into the specific business itself as well as some general business knowledge. The acquisition and formalisation of such knowledge is outside the scope of our research.

Summary

There are in total 60 rules/guidelines (Appendices G and H) derived from the method which are implemented in 46 sets of CLIPS rules in the tool (Appendix J). Around 70% of all BSDM model rules have been implemented.

Out of the 465 system-known errors which have been injected into the model, a majority of model rules/guidelines (85%) detect all of the specified errors, and are therefore classified as *Exact Match*. A smaller portion (15%) of these rules detect only some of the corresponding errors and therefore are categorised as *Partial Match*. More detailed information is given in Appendix J.[4]

10.2.3 BSDM Development Process Support Assessment

BSDM Business Model Building Process

The approach of BSDM and its practitioners towards building a business model is firstly to divide the whole of the application domain knowledge (the business knowledge) into sub-domains. The sub-domain knowledge is then captured and recorded in *views* or *local maps* of a business map. The summation

---

[4] Out of these formalised model rules, some (17%) of them are classified as *folklore rules*; and some (28%) are classified as *enhanced rules*.

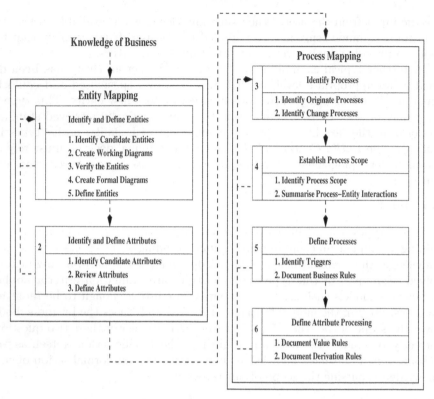

Fig. 10.3. Workflow for building a business model

of these *views* and *local maps* is called a *master map* which is also called a *Business Model*. The developers can build a master map by starting with the construction of a chosen view or local map. BSDM provides a detailed incremental step-by-step model-building procedure for the practitioners. Figure 10.3 is taken from a BSDM manual and summarises the necessary stages in producing a business model.

Within each view, one firstly builds an entity model (Entity Mapping), then based on this entity model, one can build a process model (Process Mapping). This working process is sequential, incremental, iterative and flexible. It is sequential, because activities are carried out in a sequential order. It is incremental because the activities carried out at later stages are based on data provided at earlier stages. It is iterative, because the modeller will go through several modelling cycles of adding new data to the model and regularly reviewing the model to identify possible improvements. It is flexible, because designers have the freedom to choose the order of the subject area (view) to work on and can decide to omit the specification of some knowledge for pragmatic reasons.

Evaluation of Representing BSDM Development Processes

Since we have seen that the BSDM development process is *incremental, sequential, iterative* and *flexible*, we shall examine if the support tool has similar characteristics. The workflow diagram is an integral part of *KBST-BM* and is used as electronic paper to capture the above development process and assist the user in using the tool in modelling development.

The workflow diagram captures and represents the BSDM development process in a hierarchical structure. It provides notation to capture all domain-specific concepts. For instance, the representation of sub-domain knowledge in *views*, the *activities* carried out to produce maps, and the *stages* involved in each activity. Table 10.2 shows the conceptual mapping between BSDM's terminology and that of the tool's workflow diagram. Figure 10.4 shows a hierarchical view of how these concepts are linked in the tool [51] [52].

Table 10.2: Mapping between BSDM and *KBST-BM* workflow concepts

BSDM	WorkFlow Diagram	Content	Example Instance
view	view	sub-domain business knowledge	order view
activity	process	a list of actions	entity mapping
stage	action	actions to be carried out	identify entities

At the highest level of a workflow diagram is a "Business Domain Knowledge Overview" where each *view* in the domain is represented and recorded. Each view leads to a sequential three-step work process: entity mapping, process mapping and procedural mapping (the procedural mapping is not included in the method, but is provided with the tool, therefore it is also included in the workflow diagram). The tasks which are to be carried out for each mapping process are specified as actions. Since each BSDM model-building stage may be further decomposed, the tool also provides the facility to break down actions into a more detailed granularity. As shown in the figure, the business action "Identify and Define Entities" has been decomposed and represented at a more detailed level of business actions.

The workflow diagram gives a framework for using the tool which is consistent with the working procedures specified in the method. Furthermore, since each view, process and activity is represented as model concepts in the tool, the usually more intangible factors such as working status and design decision rationale can now be recorded via their attributes as a part of model development, and therefore support the BSDM development method.

As an integrated part of *KBST-BM*, the use of the tool was found to be compliant with the principles of the BSDM development method. The designer can *sequentially* follow the workflow diagrams and use the tool to *iteratively* build a business model. The built knowledge can be *incrementally* added to using the tool. It gives the designer the *flexibility* to choose which part of the business area to work on. If a part of the model is left unfinished, errors may be found by the tool. However the designer may choose to "ignore" the recommendations and decide to come back to correct the model later – the

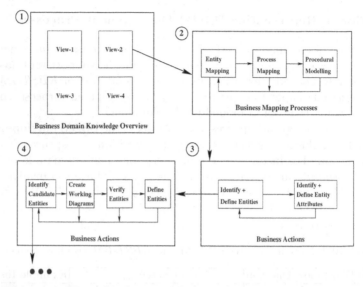

Fig. 10.4. Hierarchical view of development process in *KBST-BM*

tool merely points out the errors with possible corrections, it does not force the designer to comply.

Two essential aspects of *KBST-BM* support for BSDM its *iterative* and *incremental* model-building style which will be discussed further below.

Evaluation of Support for Iterative Development Cycle

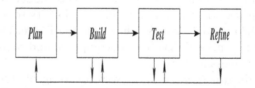

Fig. 10.5. The plan-build-test-refine development cycle

Model-building is an iterative process, following the "plan-build-test-refine" development cycle shown in Figure 10.5. In the context of BSDM, this iterative building cycle is indicated by the directions of the arrows as shown in Figure 10.5.

One key activity carried out in this process is "test", i.e. the detection of errors (model verification) and inappropriateness (model validation) that exists in the model. Because of the complexity and variety of knowledge required to make a good judgement in testing a model, this review process is conventionally done by hand. The automatic model verification ability enables *KBST-BM* to support the development cycle, in part because this facility can be used given only partial knowledge. It is suitable for error detection at all stages throughout entity mapping and process mapping. As mentioned earlier in this book, all of the verification model rules and guidelines can be applied independently of each other. The user can select "focus" areas to work on to avoid too many errors/inconsistencies being report by the tool. At early stages of model-building, it can also be used as a reminder for adding missing information.

The model validation facility can be used for process mapping. It is accomplished through information provided in procedural models. This newly added model type has been kept compliant with the method, because its content is based on the BSDM concept of entity functions and their relationships with processes. BSDM processes, which originally could only be modelled in a declarative way without definition of any actions that can be carried out by them, can now be simulated through the use of the procedural model. Automatic model validation is only available when a process model has been built and an appropriate procedural model has been derived. It can reveal errors in both the entity and the process model, since it captures the dynamic aspects of the entity as well as the process models. In summary, *KBST-BM* supports the iterative development cycle because it supports the planning of the model (by using workflow diagrams), building of the model (by using *KBST-BM* BSDM cards), testing of the model (by using the verification and validation facilities of the tool), and refinement of the model (using all of the above facilities).

Evaluation of Information Passing

In BSDM's business modelling method, all information that is entered into entity models is later used as a basis for process modelling. This is the incremental aspect of the model development. For instance, the life cycle status of an entity is closely linked to the life status of a process which is responsible for manipulating this entity. Another example are the significant attributes of an entity which may determine the validation of a process execution. In BSDM, processes retrieve data from and store data in entities, though they manipulate only the data of entities which are in their process scope. User-defined attribute rules, which constrain what manipulations are permitted on the attributes, and business rules which may involve more than a single entity are also used for process operations, because these rules control process execution.

A closer look at how *KBST-BM* incorporates this close relationship between BSDM's entities and processes shows that the system is able to capture the exact definition of entities and processes as they are described in the BSDM manuals, and is therefore able to capture the corresponding boundary between entities and processes as well as the subtle relationship between them. In the tool, entities are the constituent body of a process and are related to a process through entity functions. The attributes and business rules are captured within an entity and are accessible to any process which needs to use them. Furthermore, trigger and entity function information which is specified in a process model is extracted and used to derive a standard procedural model. Overall, *KBST-BM* information passing closely follows that of BSDM itself.

Summary

BSDM is an incremental, sequential, iterative and flexible method. These properties are also reflected in *KBST-BM*. The important facilities in the tool which provide this support for BSDM Business Model development are the workflow diagrams, the automatic model verification and the validation functions.

10.2.4 Knowledge Integration and Sharing: An Evaluation of *GMA*

The capturing of modelling knowledge and formalising it in rules and guidelines allows repeated reuse and knowledge sharing for new models/modellers. One of the main knowledge sharing components of *KBST-BM* is the *Generic Model Advisor (GMA)*, a *Case-Based Reasoning (CBR)* engine. This section therefore focuses on the evaluation of the *Generic Model Advisor*. In *GMA*, the sharing and reusing of knowledge is done through an iterative process of matching, ranking, retrieving and comparing of new and past models stored in the *Generic Model Library*. As in the discipline of CBR, imperial testing is often carried out. This section therefore uses one of the existing empirical testing methods.

Various types of knowledge and capabilities are used to help build a sound and appropriate business model. These are normally found in the following sources: (1) the standard and example business models provided by the method; (2) real and generic business models from industry; (3) the standard entities that are normally used in a business model which are captured in the *entity families* and from the method; (4) the conceptual relationships between entities from the method and from experience; (5) the ability to detect model errors and adhere to standard design practice; (6) the ability to retain and reuse knowledge from model-building experiences.

It is the case that the stake holders of this knowledge are scattered around different places and that only very experienced modellers will have full access and the ability to use them. Since the possession of such knowledge is essential for good-quality model building, it would be advantageous if this knowledge could be integrated in a tool and shared between modellers.

In this subsection, we will evaluate how the *Generic Model Adviser (GMA)* component of *KBST-BM* integrates the above knowledge to help the user develop models. As mentioned in Chapter 8, *GMA* is a *Case-Based Reasoner*. Its main task is to provide a framework for organising and storing past modelling experiences, and to provide a mechanism to produce references and guidance for new model-building projects.

The evaluation is concerned with the following issues: (1) to what extent can the tool provide a starting point to help build a new model; (2) how capable is the tool in helping to detect model errors by retrieving the appropriate reference models; (3) how well can the system help to retain new knowledge and store it for future reuse? In short, it will be interesting to determine how well the tool can help to speed-start model-building, encourage good modelling practice and accumulate model-building knowledge.

Althoff et al. [3] proposed an evaluation framework to test both the theoretical and practical aspects of *Case-Based Reasoning* systems. They have also carried out comprehensive tests and reviews on several *CBR* systems. Since some of their evaluation methods are appropriate to *GMA*, their testing methods were adopted and used in this book – the testing results are given below.

Types of Business Models

As previously mentioned in Section 8.6, five types of *business models* which have been developed based on four different resources are included in the *Generic Model Library*. They are the standard and example models from the BSDM method, the industrial models in the automobile and restaurant domain, and a business model built for the education domain (the *DAI* model).

The standard and example models from the BSDM method are included because they capture the typical way of describing common business scenarios for most industries, which makes them a useful resource to provide advice. They are also useful in the sense that they provide a standard for model-building exercises.

The argument for including the automobile example is three-fold: a) it provides a real, industrial example of a large multi-national company, b) it is an independently developed model, and c) it is very useful in determining whether the Case-Based Reasoning techniques used are helpful in giving advice in a very specialised domain given only generic knowledge, or knowledge in a similar but different domain.

Although the business model built for small and medium-sized restaurants is relatively small, it covers most of the common and important operations in the business domain, such as customer enquiring, billing and invoicing. The model is, therefore, relatively generic and can be used as a test case for this very important modelling domain. Furthermore, it can be reused to provide concise advice and an overview of the important concepts for other different business examples.

The *DAI* business model describes an education domain example and was built to help the development, testing and improvement of *KBST-BM*. Although it covers a different domain from most of the models stored in the library, it is nevertheless a legitimate business model and, therefore, serves as further evidence that *KBST-BM* is a generic modelling tool. The model did, however, not play an essential role in the evaluation of *GMA* in this book, due to the lack of sufficient similar models. Due to its importance as an external, industrial model, the automobile case study is explained in further detail next.

Case Study: the Automobile Model

We were able to obtain part of a real industrial model which was developed by an international automobile parts company.[5] A part of the model has been used for testing the capability of *GMA*: these parts are the business areas of "order", "parts", "rules" and "marketing information". There are in total five *views* involved, where each view describes a particular business area. The reason why we have chosen these business areas is that they are more commonly seen

---

[5] The company wishes to keep their identity confidential.

across industries. Although, as an international automobile parts company it follows a specialised business logic which fits its requirements, we nevertheless would expect to find some common features between these models and our generic models.

The model is described in two parts: a graphical model which is presented in several views and a separate supporting textual document for the model which is written in English. Both notational and textual information has been successfully captured using *KBST-BM*. The relevant textual information of corresponding notation is associated with the notation using its definition forms in the tool. Since *GMA* focuses on the semantics and architectural information described in the graphic model, the textual information is not used by *GMA*.

An example textual information of an entity, Customer Order, is given below:

```
Entity Name: Customer Order

Description: a request to supply one or part types and
services that WE* are prepared to offer, which once confirmed,
becomes a contract. It may not be a recognised part number. It
must be a recognised customer to take order.

Inclusion: Forward Orders, Advanced Orders.

Life Cycle: Received, Accepted, Rejected, Cancelled.

Note: the rules by which a received order is validated prior
to acceptance can vary significantly according to the type
of order.
```

In addition, BSDM models are normally organised in *views*. This is reflected in *KBST-BM*, *GML* and *GMA*. Example models are displayed in the Appendix of this book. In the following subsections, the above model as well as models mentioned in Chapter 8 and Subsection 10.2.4 will be used to test the ability of *GMA*. Appendix C gives a similar industrial model which is captured and produced by *KBST-BM*; Appendix A lists generic models similar to those stored in the generic model library. All of the test results below were obtained using the built-in similarity assessment heuristic in *GMA* as described in Subsection 8.9.3. An example *GMA* consultation output is given in Appendix L.

Test I

In this first test, the ability of *GMA* to help the user to have a head start building new models was checked. It was assumed that the user provides only very little information for the *GMA* to look for the appropriate cases, but expects *GMA* to provide some relevant examples. Those tests were carried out by providing the input data model with (1) only short view names, (2) view name and few key entities and, (3) view name and some key entities and their dependencies.

I have chosen to use view names, entities and dependencies of different degrees of sufficiency in order to test the capability of *GMA*, since when a modeller decides to build a model, the first things he/she must decide is which business area to work on (view), the fundamental concepts (e.g. actors, products, legal binding and things) involved (entities) and the relationships between them (dependencies). The test was designed to determine how well the system behaves when given only partial information.

Working with the *Generic Model Library* described in Appendices A, B, C, D and E, three sets of partial models in the business area of "customer order", "rule" and "purchase invoice" (represented in view names) were used as input to test the ability of *GMA* to retrieve the correct, relevant models.

Test I Results:

1. Given only view names, does the system retrieve ANY relevant model
   (where there is one available) ?

   customer order: yes
   rule: no (the current implementation performs partial
                       matching; since ''rule'' is not part of any
                       known view name, no model is retrieved. Skip
                       question 2 for this set of data)
   purchase invoice: yes

2. Given only view name, does the system include ALL relevant matches
   in its retrieval ?

   customer order: yes (retrieved 2 good matching cases)
   purchase invoice: yes (retrieved 2 good matching cases)

3. Given view name and partial model, i.e. two to three key entities,
   does the system retrieve any good matching models (i.e. where there
   is one available)? What is the recommendation order (in 1st place,
   2nd place, etc.)?

   customer order: yes, 1 and 2 (given 2 entities retrieved 13 cases)
   rule: yes, 6   (given 2 entities retrieved 12 cases,
                                  p.s. GMA was able to retrieve
                                  relevant models without any
                                  matching view names.)
   purchase invoice: yes, 1 and 2 (given 3 entities retrieved 12 cases)

4. Given view name, three key entities and two dependencies, does
   the system recommend good matches? What is the recommendation order?

   customer order: yes, 1 and 2
   rule: yes, 6
   purchase invoice: yes, 1 and 2

The experiments show that even when given only partial data, the system was able to retrieve relevant reference cases, if any existed in the library. The matching result is influenced by the view name of the data model, e.g. the view name "rule" fails to match any generic model in experiment 1. However, in the absence of a matching view name, *GMA* can still retrieve good matching cases from the library as long as some entities and dependencies are provided. This is desirable, since the system should not rely on the user's knowledge about *GML* for matching, but should provide relevant models through similarity analysis based on the modelled context.

During our experiments, we found that case models which have greater matching numbers (i.e. the number of matching dependencies) with the test model are given higher priority. However, when there are equal numbers of matching, the smaller-sized cases are presented first. For example, say 2 reference models called cases A and B, have been found to have 2 pairs of matching dependencies with the user model. However, since case A includes 4 dependencies and case B has 8, case A is presented first because it has a greater matching ratio $(2/4 > 2/8)$.

This result is beneficial for the user, because smaller reference models are normally easier to understand and can provide confirmation for a portion of the user model. Moreover, in the current library, most of the small-sized models are standard models extracted from the method itself. They give a good introduction to the user before more complicated and specialised models are introduced.

Test II

This experiment tested the correctness and robustness of the matching mechanism of *GMA*.

GMA uses *indexing features* to distinguish one business model diagram from another. Its successful application, therefore, heavily relies on the appropriateness of the chosen *indexing features*. To achieve high-quality performance, it is equally important that the *similarity assessment function* of *GMA* is suitable for the domain since it decides what is a better match. Therefore, this test determines whether the *indexing features* chosen for BSDM's Business Model and the *similarity assessment function* chosen for *GMA* has been appropriate.

To evaluate the correctness and robustness of the system, noisy models are used as input to test the capability of the system. Initially some reference models from the case library have been chosen as input data with some fixed portion of information randomly deleted from them, i.e. having 0%, 10%, 30% and 50% of their entities, with the corresponding dependencies and view names deleted. We then observed if the system can still fetch the correct case models and recommend them in a reasonable preference order.

To enlarge the test base, we included the automobile (parts) company's model (a similar model is included in Appendix C) in the case library, and chosen three representative case models from each of the three main sources: i.e. "Customer Order and Delivery" (from the BSDM method), "Employee Management" (from the restaurant example), and "Rule" (from the automobile

company example). (Although only three test examples are reported here, we
tested the tool with more examples during the development of the system.)

Test II Results:

1. Delete 0% of information from the initial model and its view
   name, does the system recommend the initial model? If so,
   what is the recommendation order?

   ```
   Customer Order and Delivery: yes, 1
   Employee Management:         yes, 1
   Rule:                        yes, 1
   ```

2. Delete at least 10% of information from the initial model and
   its view name, does the system recommend the initial model?
   If so, what is the recommendation order?

   ```
   Customer Order and Delivery: yes, 1 (delete a level 3 entity)
   Employee Management:         yes, 1 (delete a level 1 entity)
   Rule:                        yes, 1 (delete a level 2 entity)
   ```

   (p.s. when an entity is deleted, the associated dependencies
         are also deleted.)

3. Delete at least 30% of information from the initial model and
   its view name, does the system recommend the initial model?
   If so, what is the recommendation order?

   ```
   Customer Order and Delivery: yes, 1 (delete 5 out of 14 entit-
                                        ies, the deletion are
                                        evenly distributed in the
                                        model)
   Employee Management:         yes, 1 (delete 4 out of 12 entit-
                                        ies, the deletion are
                                        evenly distributed in the
                                        model)
   Rule:                        yes, 1 (delete 3 out of 7 entit-
                                        ies, the deletion is on
                                        the same path.)
   ```

4. Delete at least 50% information of the initial model and
   its view name, does the system recommend the initial model?
   If so, what is the recommendation order?

   ```
   Customer Order and Delivery: yes, 1 (delete 7 entities)
   Employee Management:         yes, 1 (delete 6 entities)
   ```

```
Rule:                              yes, 1 (delete 4 entities)
```

5. Delete at least 70% information of the initial model and its
   view name, does the system recommend the initial model? If so,
   what is the recommendation order?

   ```
   Customer Order and Delivery: yes, 1 (delete 10 entities)
   Employee Management:         yes, 1 (delete 9 entities)
   Rule:                        yes, 1 (delete 5 entities)
   ```

6. Randomly choose another view ''Customer Order'' from the
   restaurant example. Have its view name and 70% of the model
   deleted. We check if it confirms the above result.

   ```
   test 1: delete the entities from left to right, top to bottom.
   Result: the intended model is retrieved and at the first
           place.

   test 2: delete the entities from right to left, bottom to top.
   Result: the intended model is retrieved and at the first
           place.
   ```

Our test results consistently show that although a lot of information was
lost in the testing model, the intended reference model was always retrieved and
given in a highly favourable order (in our test examples, they are in the first
place which is the most favourable position). This test raises our confidence in
the correctness and robustness of the system.

Although the above tests have been proved to be successful, we can imagine
circumstances where the system may not produce similarly successful results,
i.e. instead of using a correct partial model, it gives an erroneous model with
vital mistakes. For example, a business model which uses an entirely wrong
view name or a partial business model which is grossly mis-represented. When
the input model is given in such a way, it will misguide the system to believe
that it is more similar to another reference model, hence the retrieval case will
be less likely to be successful. We, however, believe that the modellers normally
have sufficient judgement not to make such vital mistakes.

Test III

In this test, the automobile business model has been taken out of the case
library and used as input data, which leaves standard and example BSDM
models, and restaurant models in the case library. Since the automobile model
has been independently developed by and for a real business, it is a good testing
vehicle to demonstrate if *CBR* techniques can be used to contribute to general
business model-building exercises. I have chosen two business areas from the
model, views "Order" and "Rule", because some of the case models in the

library cover such areas. The test was to determine if *GMA* can retrieve similar cases from the library, given sufficiently different model architecture and entity names.

Test III Results:

1. Was any case retrieved, if there is a similar case existing in the library?

   Order: yes
   Rule: yes

2. Are similar cases retrieved? If so, are they recommended in a favourable order?

   Order: the best and good matched cases were present in the
          first and second place.
   Rule: the best match was presented in the first place.

3. Are there any favourable cases which are given a much lower priority?

   Order: one relevant but not the best matching case could be
          given a more favourable order.
   Rule: no, since there are not many relevant cases in the
          library.

For each of the above chosen views, *GMA* was able to retrieve some similar reference models for it, and present them in a reasonable order of preference with similarity analysis. The quality of the matching obviously is closely linked to the cases stored in the library. In our situation, we do not have full access to all the industrial models. Therefore, we could not have a well-balanced library. The testing result, however, shows that although some of our cases in the library are much less complicated and smaller in scale and most of them are indeed in a different domain of business, useful similarities (in the same business areas across sectors) have still been identified using *GMA*. We also found that cases highly recommended by the system cover the best or good matching models, although sometimes relevant (not the best) matching cases are given a lower priority than deserved.

Interestingly, the system also identified case models which describe different business areas exhibiting significant similarities in their architecture to the test model that was not clear before running these tests. Such matching cases bring to people's attention how business practices are similar to each other. This result also provides useful indications to help software engineers to understand and decide the business function boundaries when designing their systems.

Discussion

One vital step for a *Case-Based Reasoner* is its ability of retaining new knowledge for future reference. Given the above newly acquired industrial automobile model we were able to retain all of this model into our case library and integrate it with the rest of the knowledge base using *KBST-BM*. The correctness of the newly built model relies on a joint effort of the human and the automatic verification and validation abilities provided by *KBST-BM*.

The fact that *KBST-BM* integrates with *GMA* provides a more complete framework for *CBR*, including automatic indexing of input data, retrieving relevant cases from the library, comparing and analysing input with selected cases, revising cases for current problems, verifying and validating input, and retaining new input for future reference. We claim that with this support we are able to enhance the level of knowledge sharing and problem solving ability. Indeed, not only can new business models be automatically exported from the case library, the newly built business model can also be integrated into the library. This **bi-directional** knowledge flow provides a fuller support towards completing the development life cycle of building business models.

Summary

In our experiments, we found that *GMA* can provide relevant reference models given incomplete information. Its matching ability is sound and consistent throughout multiple tests, and appears robust against noisy data. All similarities and differences between the new model and the retrieved reference models are listed, each with reasons and remedy explained. One real industrial model was obtained for testing our case library. It showed that although its scale and domain is much different from our cases in the library, similarities have been identified which demonstrated the value of reusing knowledge and the usefulness of *GMA*.

A part of the vital cycle of *CBR* is the retention and reuse of newly acquired knowledge. We were able to retain all parts of the industrial model using *KBST-BM* and integrate them in the case library, thus making them available in the full modelling system *KBST-BM*. Verification and validation of the correctness and appropriateness of the newly acquired model is supported by *KBST-BM* which together with *GMA* provides fuller support throughout the modelling life cycle.

10.3 Comparison with Other Support Tools

As mentioned previously in Section 2.5, two types of modelling tools are currently available: those which primarily provide drawing and documentation facilities, and those which also provide process simulation functionalities. This section looks at two representative modelling support tools and compares them with *KBST-BM* (and *GMA*). The rationale of our selection of tools was based on the relevance of the domain that the tool was built for as well as the acceptance of the selected tool by practitioners in the business modelling community. I have firstly chosen *Rose Business Process Link* which is a business modelling tool based on an extended method which is a part of *UML*. *UML* is one of the most widely used *Object-Oriented (OO) modelling languages*. OO methods are well established and widely used by software engineers and more recently by business modellers. I have also chosen the *AIO WIN* business process modelling tool. *AIO WIN* is a "knowledge-oriented" tool which is developed and distributed by *Knowledge Based Systems Inc. (KBSI)*, a reputable company in both software engineering and knowledge management communities.

Both tools are well established and widely accepted by their users. An introduction to each tool is given, followed by a brief comparison between these tools and the tools presented in this book. Our aim is not to determine which tool is a better one, nor will we give an extensive usability comparison. Instead, our discussion will focus on the potential support that the modelling tools can provide for the user.

10.3.1 *Rose Business Process Link* **and** *Rose Planner Link*

Rose Business Process Link (RBPL) is a business modelling tool developed by Ensemble Systems Inc. who have been closely collaborating with Rational Software Corporation (RSC) and have developed several software packages for it in the past. The tool, *RBPL*, adapts and extends the *Activity Diagram* of *UML (Unified Modelling Language)* for its business modelling method. As business modelling methods have been used to understand a business and to capture business requirements, it is often the starting point of a software system development project. This tool, therefore, is often used in practice in conjunction with *Rose Planner Link* (also developed by Ensemble Systems Inc.), and which provides a framework, the *Rational Unified Process*, for software system development.

Based on the extended method, *RBPL* enables the user to describe a business' workflow, activities, actors, business objects, responsibilities of actors, events, business decision points (branching decision for the next activities) and the synchronisation of activities. These modelling elements are organised in a hierarchical browser which allows the user to traverse the model easily. Although the facility of a simulation for the workflow is not provided, it supports a "story-boarding" facility which allows the user to step through a business workflow and therefore enhance its communication ability for its users. It also automatically generates reports and the finished model can be exported to the object-oriented modelling tool *Rational Rose*.

RBPL is a typical (conventional) modelling tool which supports specific modelling methods with its elaborated electronic record-keeping facilities. The important issues of quality assurance, extraction/derivation and presentation of embedded (linking) information, or provision of guidance for good modelling practice for the built models, which are the essence and motivations for our tool *KBST-BM*, are somewhat left out and not fully supported by *RBPL*.

10.3.2 AI0 WIN

AI0 WIN [59] is a business function and process modelling tool developed by Knowledge Based Systems, Inc. (KBSI).[6] It is based on the *Activity-Based Costing (ABC)* method which provides an evaluation means to determine the performance of a business activity and to identify the sources which cause cost and limit profits. It, therefore, provides a means for the managers to carry out activity-based cost-benefit analysis. To support the use of *ABC*, *AI0 WIN* utilises the functional modelling method *IDEF0* [80] as a framework to enable its users to capture, visualise, build and analyse a business environment. The information which is stored in *AI0 WIN* can also be exported to a set of other tools which are mostly also built by the same company: e.g. process simulation tools, spreadsheet packages, data modelling tools, cost calculation tools, and project management tools.

Among them, *ProSim*, the process simulation tool, takes the output from *AI0 WIN* and simulates the business workflow which was portrayed in *AI0 WIN*. *ProSim* uses its own process modelling language (an adaptation of *IDEF3*) to enable the user to specify business processes in more detail. Since *ProSim* is related to our work, It will be combined with *AI0 WIN* in our comparison below.

AI0 WIN is similar to *KBST-BM* in the sense that they are both business support tools and they both provide automatic support to help the user build models of an underlying business method, i.e. *ABC/IDEF0* and BSDM. They are also similar in the sense that the underlying methods are similar in principle: they are both business models; they both use graphical notations to capture "things" in the world and use natural language to define and describe these things; they both capture processes and are concerned not only with the static but also the dynamic side of the world. Above all, both tools try to provide automatic support to some degree to help the user better understand the model, avoid erroneousness, and produce higher-quality models.

ProSim takes output from *AI0 WIN* and simulates the process model using statistical simulation methods: processes are instantiated, frequencies of events assigned and resources allocated before and during the execution of a simulation. These provide a measurement for efficiency analysis on the current design and bottlenecks of the process can be identified. In order to make use of this method, additional system parameters, such as various frequencies and amount of resources have to be added. *KBST-BM*, on the other hand, makes use of symbolic reasoning techniques which infer system behaviours based on the existing business model.

A further important difference lies in the level of abstraction at which processes are modelled. The processes used by *ProSim* contain more details of the business that is modelled and can, therefore, be more easily mapped onto a company's operations. In *KBST-BM* processes are logical business processes,

---

[6] KBSI is a company which was commissioned by the U.S. Air Force to develop several parts of the IDEF method which later became a standard method for software systems development.

they are at a higher level of abstraction. Although details of data used by a process are specified clearly and the relationships between them are well described, the relationships and constraints between processes are only specified when necessary which allows more flexibility in implementing BSDM processes.

These differences are probably rooted in the different motivation for the two domains. In a process modelling domain, the modelling purpose often lies in the immediate improvement on efficiency and effectiveness of current working procedures, which are often influenced by the introduction of new machinery, products, change of practices and allocation of resources. The designed process models often take current circumstances and technologies into account and are therefore designed in greater detail. The designed processes are "immediately implementable" but will have to evolve or be abandoned as a result of changes in circumstances.

By contrast, processes which are described in a BSDM business model capture business logic which is core to a business operation. Therefore, these processes are relatively robust and can remain unchanged for a long time. They are also independent of current technologies or any other limitations that an organisation may have, e.g. no particular machinery or technology will be assumed for use in these processes. The detailed (implementation) requirements and actions within and between processes are often not specified. The resulting business models, therefore, are not limited to any particular implementation. Although the implementation details are not given in the model (by the user), it is important to note that *KBST-BM* can still simulate these processes, although at a more abstract level, and therefore gain an insight into their dynamics (the purpose of our *procedural model*).

AIO WIN, in general, focuses more on providing high-quality facilities to capture and structure business related knowledge. It also focuses on communication with other tools. It, however, does not provide guidance in model building or error correction. *KBST-BM*, on the other hand, focuses on this.

A number of other business modelling support tools are available. They mostly provide an electronic record keeping and organising system. Most of them do not provide method-dependent and/or domain-dependent verification and validation support for the built model and therefore entirely rely on the modellers' effort to produce a sound product. Some business process modelling tools when given sufficient details can produce a simulation of the process which provides verification and validation support to some degree.

The gap that is still left to be filled for all of the current tools is to provide automatic support beyond record keeping and simulation functions. The novelty of the approach and the tool developed in this book lies in the provision of a mechanism that empowers a tool to *"understand"* a model and therefore provide support at the semantic level with embedded modelling knowledge.

10.4 Conclusion

In this chapter we have evaluated *KBST-BM* and *GMA* with respect to the level of support which they provide for BSDM's business modelling method. Theoretical and empirical tests have been carried out, where appropriate. A real industrial model was obtained and used to show the fitness of *GMA*.

We have also compared *KBST-BM* and *GMA* with two other existing, representative business modelling tools. Unlike the tools developed in this book, existing industrial tools were found to have little, if any, support for pro-active model-building guidance, automatic error detection and amendment. They also did not provide continuous support throughout the modelling development life cycle. Furthermore, these industrial tools lacked *KBST-BM*'s ability to provide adaptive support that evolves through time to provide a better quality of modelling guidance to its users.

It was shown that based on a logical formal method, we are able to form a coherent knowledge base which integrates expertise of different resources, which allows us to provide model guidance, verification and validation, development life cycle management, and can improve its knowledge through time (by updating and enriching its case library in *GMA*).

10.5 Exercises

1. What are the evaluation criteria for testing *KBST-BM*? Are they generic? Do they apply to other modelling tools?
2. General speaking, there are two types of testing that one can carry out on a tool – theoretical and empirical testing. In your view, which categories do those tests (for *KBST-BM*) fall into?
3. In the Completeness Assessment, a table of user requirements were used. Discuss its organisation and its significance in helping to build a correct tool. (You may need to refer to earlier chapters.)
4. Explain the tests carried out on the Model Rules and Guidelines. Interpret the test outcomes of Exact, Partial and No Match.
5. One of the knowledge sharing components of *KBST-BM* is its CBR engine, *GMA*. Explain the test being carried out on it.
6. Discuss the different types of past models being included in the evaluation for *GMA* and their different roles in the test.

10.6 Advanced Exercises

1. List user requirements for yourself as a modeller and user of a similar modelling tool. Try to prioritise and categorise them.
2. Do you know any other modelling tools? Compare those tools with *KBST-BM*. What are your criteria for comparison?

3. You may have heard of black- and white-box testing from the discipline of Software Engineering. How will you compare those with the evaluation techniques used in this chapter for *GMA*?

11

Conclusion

Enterprise Modelling (EM) methods are interesting to the business community, because they offer ways of analysing and "redesigning" an organisation that may lead to significant improvement in business performance. They are also interesting to the academic research community, because despite of their wide acceptance and potential benefits for businesses, there are still a variety of open problems that are not satisfied by any single existing EM method.

One particular problem is quality assurance of the produced models. Several reasons for this problem are explained below:

- *Availability of expertise:* A modern enterprise today is a virtual entity which consists of many sub-organisations which are distributed across different geographical areas, each possessing different expertise. Hence, it may not be possible to have all of the persons with the right expertise (who are normally senior and/or middle-level managers) available for model development. Furthermore, the required expertise may change as companies have to react – adapting their goals and processes – to today's fast changing global economies.

- *Lack of comprehensive evaluation method:* Most EM modelling methods do not provide a comprehensive evaluation method for the models they build. As a result, a standardised evaluation and appraisal of the quality of models cannot easily be obtained. Therefore, the quality of the model cannot be ensured.

- *Informal or semi-formal modelling context:* Since parts of such methods incorporate natural language text, it is difficult to perform detailed verification and validation on the models (due to the ambiguities inherited from the informality of natural language).

- *Lack of modelling support facilities:* An enterprise-sized model is often domain-specific, knowledge-rich and comparatively complex. In addition, the modellers need to keep in mind the technical details of the method they are using. Since few people possess good knowledge of both, to achieve an efficient and effective modelling process, a proper (software) tool should ideally provide the knowledge required for the specific business domain as well as direct support for the method. There is currently a lack of such tools, which means that more generic, domain-independent tools need to be used instead.

- *Flexibility in representing a domain:* As is the case in most modelling activities, there is no single correct way to describe a domain. Several different models may all be acceptable and describe a domain sufficiently correctly. The decision of which model is better suited for a domain may, therefore, not be a clear-cut one. This also contributes to the difficulties in determining a good model since several different models may be rated similarly.

- *Time pressure:* Very few projects can enjoy the luxury of not having to deal with strict time constraints. In the model-building context this means that after the model has been created there is often not sufficient time to carry out systematic and comprehensive model validation and verification, since due to the lack of appropriate tools this would take a significant amount of time, especially when dealing with model dynamics (see below).

- *Lack of efficient and effective knowledge transfer means:* Enterprise modelling methods are intended to help knowledge transfer through their models, but this requires sufficiently wide use of a particular method that people can communicate through. However, most methods do not have wide usage at this stage. A tool that conveys the semantics of the model using alternative intuitive visualisation or simulation techniques can ease the communication between people and could thus be very helpful in the transfer of knowledge.

- *Dynamic aspects of a model are complex:* An enterprise modelling method normally captures the static structure of the targeted domain, but often also implies and/or prescribes the actual activities to be carried out. As many of these dynamic activities may be happening concurrently and interacting with each other, to understand the impact of them becomes in general a task that is too complex for unaided human reasoning. It is therefore important that these processes can be simulated and their effects demonstrated clearly by a software tool.

All the above problems are shared by many EM methods. This is not surprising considering that they have a common fundamental characteristic: they are either informal or semi-formal, i.e. a large part of their models are described in natural language. To provide a highly expressive EM language which captures and describes any versatile (business) domain, a certain degree of informality is perhaps unavoidable. The informality existing in the modelling method provides the flexibility necessary to model any domain and express anything worth mentioning, but it at the same time also introduces uncertainty to its quality. As a result, the semantics of these models may be interpreted differently by different people. Furthermore, two different models may seem to be describing the same scenario, i.e. the interpretation of the two models can be the same.

The interesting issue here is, therefore, to understand how one can introduce formality to such an informal method without disturbing the practice of the original method, or in other words, how can one gain the benefits of a formalised approach without having to cope with the disadvantages that usually come with it?

11.1 A Formal Approach

The primary objective of this research was to develop an approach for using AI techniques to improve the model development process in informal modelling methods, with particular emphasis on the process for quality evaluation and assurance. Despite its importance for the EM field, very little work has been done in this area so far.

A *lightweight formal approach* was proposed in this book, i.e. instead of applying a comprehensive formalisation of all aspects of an informal modelling method, formalisation was carried out where it is appropriate. This approach avoids the prohibitively high cost normally associated with a "heavyweight" formal approach, but still enjoys the benefits of precision gained from applying a formal approach. It can also be argued that a heavyweight formal approach would not be feasible in this domain, since not all necessary knowledge is available for formalisation. The proposed lightweight formal approach is based on a new formal language, *DefBM*, which was adapted from the *PIF* core class hierarchy. Since *PIF* is one of the more accepted process languages, business processes described in *DefBM* inherit this generality. It will, therefore, be easier to communicate with other process models.

DefBM is a formal language based on First-Order Predicate Logic (FOPL). FOPL was chosen because it offers a declarative, precise and concise notation which promotes intuitive understanding of the described semantics. These characteristics are effective in clarifying ambiguities exhibited in the informal method. Furthermore, FOPL is supported with a sound inference mechanism that allows automated deduction to be naturally performed on the acquired information.

The lightweight formal approach proved to be useful: it captures valuable knowledge effectively and facilities the integration of different types of knowledge. The use of this knowledge can help reduce the time required to design and refine new business models, and the quality of models can be improved, since through the formalisation of the models using *DefBM* errors that previously would have been very difficult to discover can now be found through automated deductions.

A disadvantage of deploying FOPL is that not all of the informal knowledge can be formalised and used for automated reasoning. This disadvantage, however, may not be avoidable even if a different computational method were used, since such support often requires background knowledge that may not be available. One other disadvantage of using FOPL is that the users require training before they can understand the formal representation – this also applies to any other computational languages used. Nevertheless, this drawback is not very significant, if a suitable user interface and explanation facility is provided. In that case, the user may never need to see the underlying formal representation, as is true in the case of *KBST-BM*.

To address the problem that not all modelling knowledge can be captured using a formal method, *Case-Based Reasoning* techniques were employed. *CBR* provides us with two main benefits: 1) modelling knowledge that is not well understood can be inferred and used by referring to standardised and past models, 2) modelling knowledge is enriched and critiquing abilities improved by collecting a large set of models over time. The disadvantage of applying *CBR* in our experience is the difficulty of acquiring a large set of real industrial models. It was, thus, very useful that BSDM provides a catalogue of standard models. However, more reference models are needed to take full advantage of *CBR* techniques. To overcome this problem, a few realistic business models have been developed for selected domains which provide examples for using and testing the approach. Within a company making use of business modelling, this problem is not likely to be serious, as they can add their own models over time.

Based on the above formal approach a three-layer framework was created to fit BSDM's modelling activities. This framework was useful because it not only suggests a structure as to where and which AI techniques fit in the modelling activities, it also extends the existing BSDM modelling activities to an automated execution phase without disturbing the practice of the original method. This framework adds value to applying BSDM, because the modellers receive method-specific guidelines and critiques without extra effort, and alternative modelling options are suggested where appropriate as a part of the framework.

11.2 The System: *KBST-BM*

KBST-BM was built as a proof of concept for the proposed formal approach. Before building *KBST-BM*, a few issues had to be considered. For instance, what type of automated support is useful to the modellers? What kind of knowledge is needed to provide such support? Is this knowledge available? Is it generic or method- and/or application-domain dependent? If such knowledge is available, can it be formalised and realised in a computational tool? What kind of support would the user be particularly interested in? To obtain answers to some of these questions, user requirement meetings were held regularly with the main user type for the tool, a BSDM business modeller, during the early stages of tool development. During these, user requirements were drawn up and prioritised which provided a useful and reliable foundation for building the initial tool.

The next task was to collect standard and practical modelling knowledge that AI techniques can manipulate to provide useful automated support. The modelling knowledge was found embedded in several different sources: the method, the business models, the modelling experts and the domain experts (when a specific application is involved), and all of them were informal. The next task was, therefore, to formalise the knowledge as far as possible and to apply suitable AI techniques which take full advantages of them. This process was very much an experimental task, as there is no clear guideline for which knowledge will be useful for which modelling task and how the various modelling support may fit together. After several iterations through the development process, the combined tools of *KBST-BM* and *GMA* were produced.

This work has demonstrated how key components of an originally informally specified method, BSDM, and its business models can be formalised using first order predicate logic and realised in a support tool, *KBST-BM*. Having achieved this transition from an informal to a formal representation of models and modelling rules it was possible to provide guidance and consistency checking during the life cycle of a model – making use of techniques such as case-based reasoning. The tool was also able automatically to derive knowledge from the model which was initially not known. For example, business process dependencies and their partial execution order constraints can automatically be determined. It also allowed us to complement the original method with a model execution phase – using the *Procedural Model*. This extends the scope of BSDM and, more importantly, it adds to our understanding of how this kind of seemingly informal method can fit into parts of the design life cycle which require formal models.

The underlying formal representation of the model and the modelling knowledge together with the appropriate inferencing engines provide the modeller with support throughout the iterative *Plan-Build-Test-Refine* process, i.e. the planning, building, testing, error correcting and refining of the models are all supported. The modeller can use *WorkFlow Diagrams* to keep track of the model development process. To gain a quick head start in model-building, the *Generic Model Advisor, GMA*, can be used to provide standard and past models for the current business domain. During model-building, the automated model management and verification facilities of the tool can be of assistance. *GMA* is used to retrieve similar models from a case library and compare them with the newly built model. Advice is given to the user, if any discrepancies are found. The modeller can repeat the iterative *Plan-Build-Test-Refine* cycle as often as necessary.

To explore the system dynamics of the built model, i.e. how the processes interact with each other and change the business world, *Process Dependency and Partial Execution Order* diagrams are automatically drawn to provide an initial overview. Since this knowledge has not previously been available to the method and does not require any additional input from the user, this is a direct benefit of using formal methods. A simulator was built to further explore and demonstrate the dynamic behaviours of models, which is based on a model extension, the *Procedural Model*.

Throughout the model development life cycle, the developed tools provide significant aid for modellers wanting to achieve a high level of confidence in their models. This is possible because of the incorporation of domain-specific knowledge about business modelling into the system, which in turn allows much of the complex and often tedious work of model validation and verification to be pushed into the software.

It should be noted that none of the basic techniques applied here are specific to business modelling. Hence, other modelling domains that need to deal with informal and/or semi-formal information may benefit from the same approach. The results of this research have proved useful and sufficiently generic when a similar approach was successfully used in a later project, AOEM [56], which extended *KBST-BM* to *KBST-EM* to include in total seven different types of enterprise models, including *BSDM, IDEF3, Role Activity and Communication Diagram (RACD)* [18] and *UML*. Overall around 80 diagrams and 200 pages of textual documentations have been produced which also proved the extendibility of the above tool. Under the same project, *KBST-BM* was used as a working tool to build a real industrial business model which consisted of 41 BSDM business diagrams describing 162 different types of entities and 28 different types of processes.

11.3 Evaluation of *KBST-BM*

KBST-BM was built as a proof of concept to test the idea, proposed in the book, that based on a logic-based approach useful automated support can be provided for informal methods. The intended users for the tool are mainly BSDM business modellers. To help build, refine and then evaluate the developed tools, a set of business models have either been collected or newly created for different domains.

A business model, the *DAI* model, which describes course management and evaluation of student performance for the former Artificial Intelligence Department, the University of Edinburgh, was initially built to provide a realistic business model that makes use of the tool. In addition, standard and example business models provided by the method, an industrial business model which was developed by IBM for its client in the sector of automobile parts distribution, and a generic business model that was developed by myself for small and medium-sized restaurants have also been used to test the rule-based and case-based engines and other peripheral facilities in *KBST-BM*. All of the above models are stored in the *Generic Model Library* which provides reference models for the *Case-Based Reasoning* engine, *GMA*.

Theoretical and practical evaluations have been carried out on the tool using the above models. Although other models are also included, the *DAI* model was mainly used to test general facilities in *KBST-BM*. The rest of the models were primarily used to test the ability of the *Generic Model Advisor (GMA)*, since they describe similar business domains. Furthermore, to test the capabilities of *GMA*, an integrated part of *KBST-BM*, the Althoff et al. [3] evaluation framework was adapted and used.

To evaluate *KBST-BM*, four criteria were considered. Firstly, *Completeness Assessment*: how well the tool covers the user requirements which are needed to apply the BSDM method. At the early stages of tool development, meetings were held regularly with a real business modeller, the intended type of user for the tool. Feedback was collected from the user during these meetings and used to refine the tool. At the end of these initial stages, an evaluation was carried out. Since most of the requirements were successfully implemented and the additional tool support features did not disturb the original modelling practice, the review of this part of the evaluation was highly satisfactory.

Secondly, an evaluation of the *Model Verification* support was carried out to determine the coverage of tool support compared with guidelines provided by the method. The *DAI* model was chosen as the test case and was injected with errors using *error-injection* techniques [115]. Three types of test results were identified: *Exact, Partial* and *No Match*. Exact and Partial Match are model rules (and guidelines) that are explicitly given in the method and which were successfully formalised. No Match is the case when model rules are not formalisable. Exact and Partial Match rules are implemented in the tool for error-detecting and advice-giving: Exact Match rules discover all of the included errors, whereas Partial Match rules discover part of them.

The reason for the inability to detect all possible errors is the fact that it is impossible to record all knowledge which is necessary to detect all kinds of modelling errors and for all kinds of business organisations. In particular, since business circumstances differ between companies and contradicting practices may exist between them, it is not possible to generalise rules such that they apply to all companies.

No Match model rules tend to be quite high level which therefore require (commercial) experience and relevant generic and specific background knowledge to make a good judgement. Unfortunately, as mentioned earlier, it is impossible to obtain this. In fact, it is probable that different business modellers may make a different or even contradicting recommendation for the model. One further obstacle identified during the evaluation is that much information is given in the informal description of the business model. To formalise this would require sophisticated natural language processing ability equipped with sound background knowledge as mentioned above, which is outside the scope of this book.

It is fair to say that it is probably *impossible* to provide a complete quality proof for a business model. Hence the motivation during this research to provide partial verification and validation based on a *lightweight formal approach*, and not to attempt to formalise every aspect of the method and the produced model. The overall test results were nevertheless encouraging. The majority of model rules (85%) detected all of the targeted errors. A smaller portion of model rules (15%) only partially detected errors. Such model rules provide quality control beyond pure syntactical checking. They extended model checking to include model semantics, which made the developed tools superior compared with model support that is currently available in other existing tools.

Thirdly, theoretical analysis was carried out to determine the extent to which the tool support covers the different stages of the business model development life cycle. BSDM is an *incremental, sequential, iterative* and *flexible* method. These properties were also found to be the case for *KBST-BM*, which provides the concept of a workflow diagram to capture the various steps in

BSDM's development life cycle to provide a framework for using the tool in the context of BSDM modelling.

As an integrated part of *KBST-BM*, the use of the tool was found to be fully compliant with the principles of the BSDM development method. The designer can *sequentially* follow the workflow diagrams and use the tool to *iteratively* build a business model. The built knowledge can be *incrementally* added to using the tool. It also gives the designer the *flexibility* to choose which part of the business area to work on, and when and how to fix an error. *KBST-BM* merely gives suggestions which allows the designer to make the final decision.

KBST-BM was found not only to provide full support for BSDM model development, but also to promote effective management during model building exercises by providing facilities for recording design rationale and current working status (which was not originally supported by the method).

Finally, a series of test were carried out to determine the degree of tool support for integration and sharing of modelling knowledge that is scattered across different resources. This part of the test was primarily focusing on the *CBR* engine, *GMA*.

Three issues were of main concern: (1) to which extent can the tool help building a new model; (2) how capable is the tool in helping to detect model errors by retrieving the appropriate reference models; (3) how well can the system help to retain new knowledge and store it for future reuse? In short, the test was to determine how well the tool can help to speed-start model-building, encourage good modelling practice and accumulate model-building knowledge. The evaluation method was adapted from Althoff et al.'s [3] evaluation framework.

In our experiments, we found that *GMA* can provide relevant reference models given only little, discrete information. This means that new, usually smaller, models can get a head-start by learning from existing standard models. The matching ability was sound and consistent throughout multiple tests, and appeared robust against noisy data. All similarities and differences between the new model and the retrieved reference models are listed, each with reasons and remedy provided. One real industrial model was obtained for testing. It showed that although its scale and domain is much different from the cases in our library, similarities could still be identified, thereby demonstrating the value of reusing knowledge and the usefulness of *GMA*.

It has also been shown that knowledge that exists in different knowledge sources can been integrated and used to provide a "collective" knowledge base for advice and reuse – this was demonstrated by a combinational use of *GMA* and *KBST-BM*. A part of the vital cycle of *CBR* is the retention and reuse of newly acquired knowledge. We were able to retain all parts of the industrial model using *KBST-BM* and integrate it in the case library, thus making it available in the full modelling system *KBST-BM*.

In addition, a comparison of *KBST-BM* with other similar existing tools was carried out. We coarsely divided existing modelling support tools into two categories: the type of tools that primarily provide capturing and report-generating functions for specific modelling methods, and the type of tools which, in addition to the above functions, also provide simulation facilities. In particularly, two typical modelling tools of each category, the *Rose Business Process Link* (from Ensemble Systems Inc.) and *AIO WIN* and *ProSim* (Knowledge Based Systems, Inc.) were looked at in detail.

In general, in both categories of tools there is very little, if any, exploitation of the knowledge that is implicit in the models that have been captured through the corresponding documentation features of the tools. This is primarily due to the fact that there is no underlying formalisation and logical representation of models and model-building knowledge built into these tools. Consequently, they are unable to provide the type of semantics-based modelling support that is offered by *KBST-BM* and *GMA*.

While most other tools only provide support at the beginning of the development life cycle, leaving the task of verification, validation and refinement of the built model to the modellers, simulation tools, such as *ProSim* provide V&V to some extent. However, the simulation is carried out at a lower level of abstraction and requires a significant additional input from the user. In comparison, *KBST-BM* extracts the necessary information for process simulation from the model already developed. Its processes are also at a higher level of abstraction and therefore less prone to changes in company procedures or use of specific technologies.

In summary, *KBST-BM* provides useful automated support which fits well with the BSDM model development process. The advice given was sound and adequate, as it adheres to BSDM guidelines. The support has proved to be useful and time-saving. It has been successfully used for a later project, *Air Operations Enterprise Project* [56] and is currently used in the IRC AKT project [1]. In both projects, *KBST-BM* has been extended using a similar formal approach and tool design rationale to the ones describes in this book.

Although the work described in this book makes a valuable contribution towards building better business models, the possibility of errors remains. Unless there is a way of making sure that all domain and modelling method knowledge has been built into a tool such as *KBST-BM* and all informal aspects of EM methods can be eliminated, absolute proof will not be possible. For these reasons, we believe that similar type of work should not focus on achieving the elusive goal of absolute correctness, but that further research should be carried out in applying similar techniques described here to the domain of software development methods. Since increasingly business models are built as a first step of building a software system, there may be great benefits in investigating the link between these two activities and how the formalisation approach presented in this work could be exploited.

11.4 Exercises

1. Based on your overall knowledge of the book, discuss the value of Business or Enterprise modelling for an organisation. How do they complement

business practice and improve performance? Can you find examples in the real world to support this?

2. Discuss whether automated support is useful for business or enterprise modelling. What are the main contributions? What do we lose without such support?

3. Discuss how logical methods may play a part in providing automated support. Can such methods be used in other circumstances?

A

Generic Business Models

This appendix and Appendix B include generic and example business models that are similar to those in IBM's BSDM [51] when describing similar business circumstances. A generic business model that was built for small and medium-sized restaurants for the evaluation purpose of *GMA* is given in Appendix D.

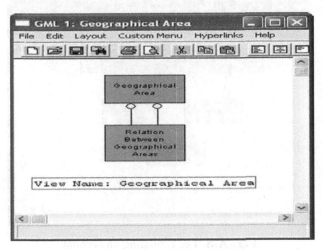

Fig. A.1. Geographical area

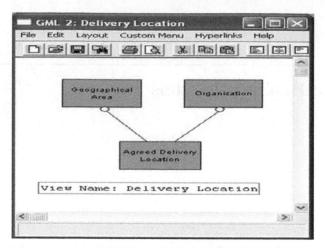

Fig. A.2. Delivery location

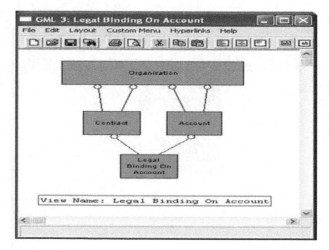

Fig. A.3. Legal binding on account

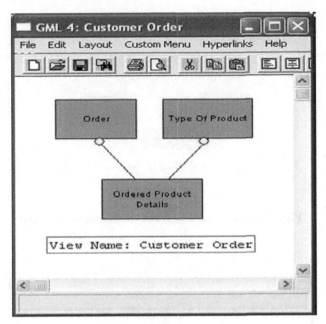

Fig. A.4. Customer order

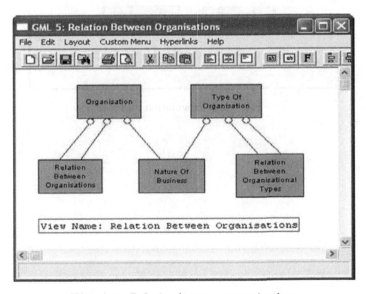

Fig. A.5. Relation between organisations

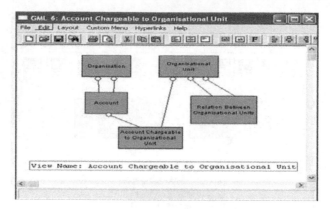

Fig. A.6. Account chargeable to organisational unit

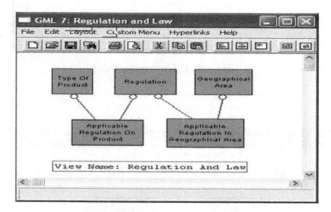

Fig. A.7. Regulation and law

B

Example Business Models

Those are example business models that are coherent to BSDM modelling practice and are similar to those models in BSDM when describing similar business circumstances [51].

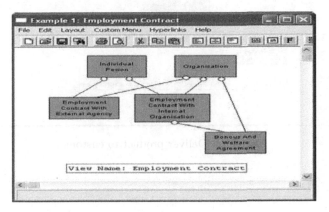

Fig. B.1. Employment contract

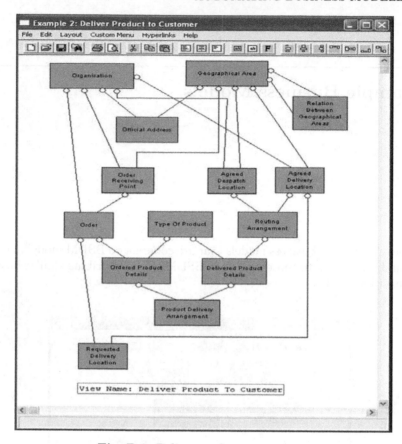

Fig. B.2. Deliver product to customer

C

An Industrial Model

Obtaining business models which are developed and used by the industry is difficult. This is mainly due to the large cost for industry in building them and, for those which have been built, their content is usually confidential (as it often conveys a business' trade secrets). However, we were fortunate to gain the permission of one company which is in the sector of automobile parts distribution[1] and obtain a small portion of their model.

This model is valuable because it is a realistic model which was independently built and used by a commercial company. It is also intriguing because it gives insights to business operations in a specialised context, in this case, in the domain of automobile parts distribution. As a result, it contributes to both the realism and "specialisation" properties of *GML*.

The source model was described in two parts: a graphical model which is presented in several diagrams and a separate supporting textual document for the model which is written in English. Both of the notational and textual information are captured in *KBST-BM*.

An example textual information of an entity, "Customer Order", from the source document is given below:

```
Entity Name: Customer Order

Description: a request to supply one or part types and
services that WE* are prepared to offer, which once confirmed,
becomes a contract. It may not be a recognised part number. It
must be a recognised customer to take order.

Inclusion: Forward Orders, Advanced Orders.

Life Cycle: Received, Accepted, Rejected, Cancelled.

Note: the rules by which a received order is validated prior
to acceptance can vary significantly according to the type
```

---

[1] The company wishes to keep their name confidential.

of order.

This textual information of the corresponding notation, in this case the entity "Customer Order" is associated with the entity itself using the Definition Form facility of the tool.

Four business areas of the model have been selected and stored in the *GML*: "order", "parts", "rules" and "marketing information". The reason that these business areas have been chosen is that they are more commonly seen across industries. Although as an international automobile company it follows specialised business logic which fits its requirements, nevertheless one expect to find some common features between these models and our generic models. There are in total four *views* involved, where each view describes a particular business area. Adapted versions of those models are included below for readers' interest.

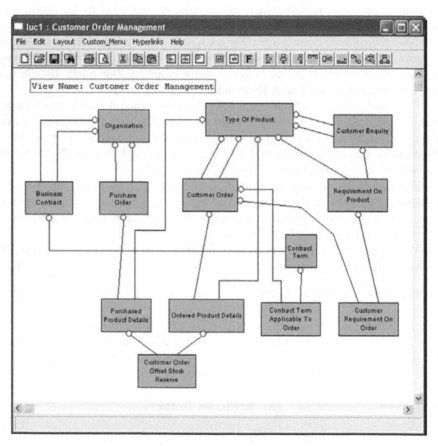

Fig. C.1. Customer order management

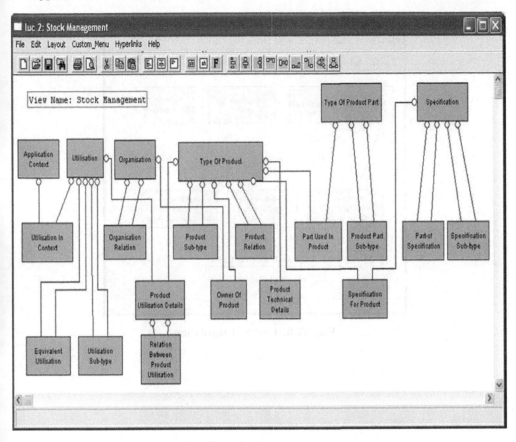

Fig. C.2. Stock management

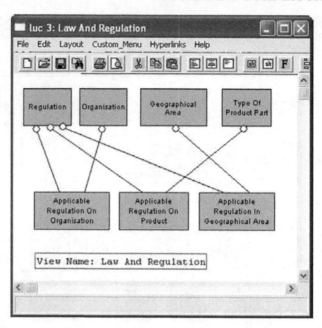

Fig. C.3. Law and regulation

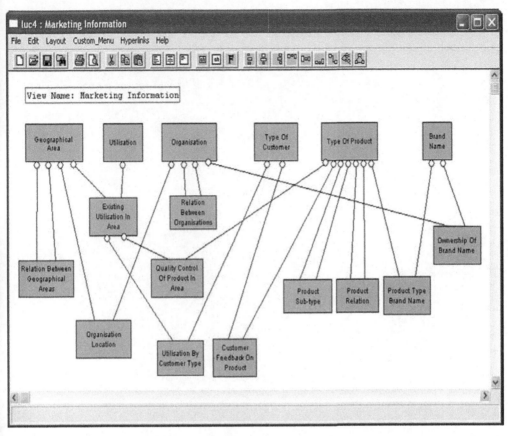

Fig. C.4. Marketing information

D

A Model for Family Restaurants

I have chosen to build a generic business model for small and medium-sized family restaurants. The reason for selecting an example in this industry is firstly that we had access to the stake holders of the business which was essential in building realistic business models. Secondly, and perhaps more importantly, a small business such as the one of a family restaurant covers important and essential business aspects. Their business operations are also simpler, compared with the complications of a large company. The resulting business model is likely to be easier to understand, and may be more generic and hence more relevant to other business (since they cover a simpler version of the essential business operations such as customer ordering and purchasing).

Several interviews were conducted with former restaurant owners here in Edinburgh, in an attempt to build a realistic but generic business model for small–medium sized family restaurants. Five common and important business areas were identified: Customer Order, Purchase Invoice, Stock Control, Employment Management and Tax Payment. Each business area is described in one or two BSDM diagrams.

Prior to the meetings with our business correspondents (the restaurant owners), an initial business model was developed. Because of the simplicity of the model and time limitation, we took a simple approach in interviewing the businessmen. There were two stages in the meetings. During the first stage, a short introduction to BSDM was given. In the second stage, the already developed model was presented to the businessmen, the semantics of the model were explained, and example business scenarios described by the model illustrated.

The focus and aims of these meetings were two-fold: (1) to gain positive confirmation of the correctness of the developed model and to identify miscaptures in the model, and seek and make appropriate modifications to the model based on the feedback on our business correspondent in order to make the model as realistic as possible and at the same time as generic as possible; (2) to identify any important aspects in the business which were left out in the model, those aspects were added to the model as appropriate.

The resulting business model consists of six diagrams which cover the above five business areas. The model is relatively small in scale compared with a full-

sized business model from a large company which has complex business requirements and covers wider services, but since I have chosen a rather simple and
straightforward business environment – a small–medium sized family restaurant – the resulting model is satisfactory to our stakeholders in describing the
necessary issues for their business operations.

The graphical part of the business model is given below.

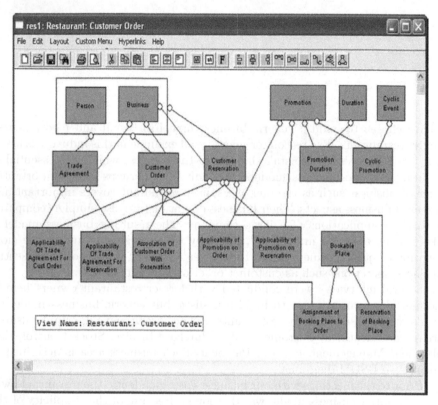

Fig. D.1. A model for family restaurants (1)

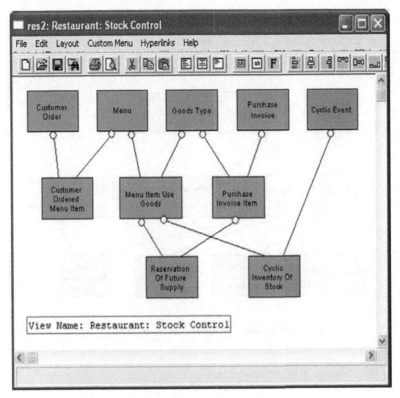

Fig. D.2. A model for family restaurants (2)

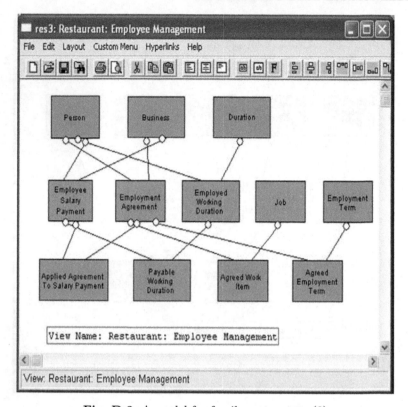

Fig. D.3. A model for family restaurants (3)

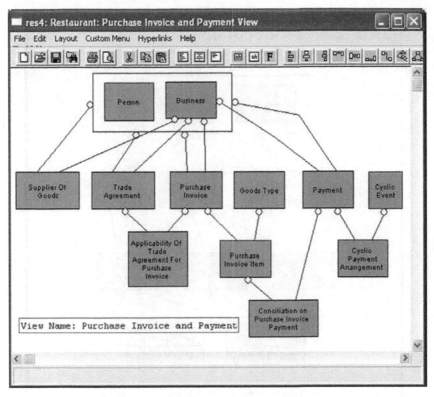

Fig. D.4. A model for family restaurants (4)

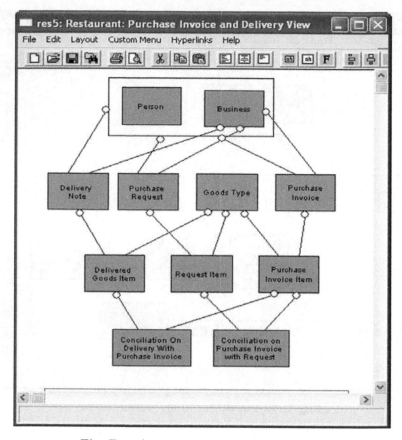

Fig. D.5. A model for family restaurants (5)

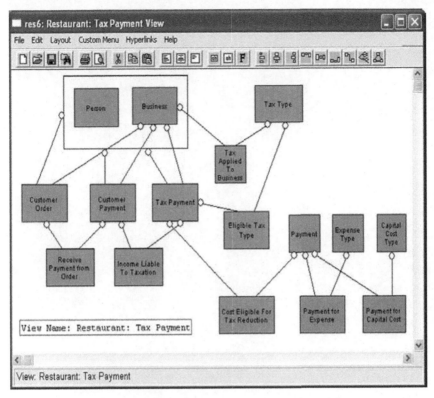

Fig. D.6. A model for family restaurants (6)

E

A Model for Academic Environments

The *DAI* business model was built based on the Department of Artificial Intelligence here in the University of Edinburgh.[1] There are in total 35 diagrams included in five different business areas which are: Module Evaluation, Course Evaluation, Degree Evaluation, Course Structure and Personnel Management. Among them, three areas, Module, Course and Degree Evaluation, have been developed in more detail. Each of these three areas describes the architecture and processes for evaluating undergraduate and postgraduate students performance and assigning marks for the taken module, course, or project and eventually the awarding of a degree.

This appendix gives some example diagrams from the model.

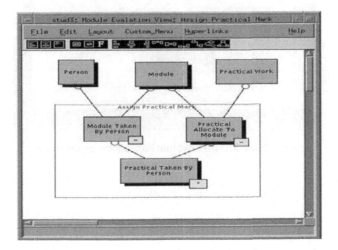

Fig. E.1. Module evaluation: assign practical mark

---

[1] Now incorporated into the Division of Informatics.

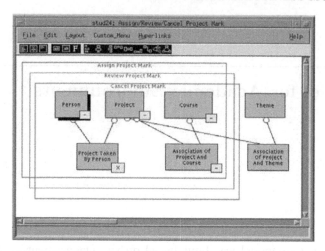

Fig. E.2. Module evaluation: assign/review/cancel project mark

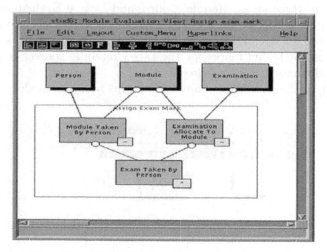

Fig. E.3. Module evaluation: assign exam mark

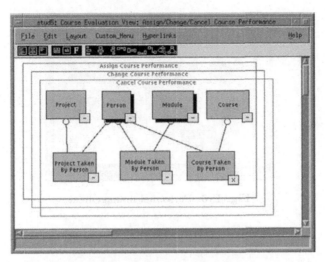

Fig. E.4. Course evaluation: assign/change/cancel course performance

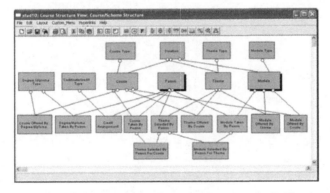

Fig. E.5. Overview of course structure in DAI

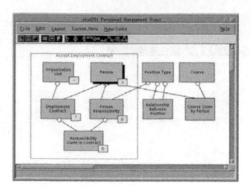

Fig. E.6. Personnel management

F

The Formal Operators in *DefBM*

The formal representation used in this book is based on an extended version of First Order Predicate Logic. We use a Prolog-like syntax for argumentation in our logical expressions. The following operators, naming conventions and predicate names are used throughout the devised formal language, *DefBM*.

F.1 Notation and Language Conventions

This book follows the naming conventions of Prolog: constants start with lower-case letters; whereas variables start with capital letters. Model rules are described in terms of First-Order Predicate Logic. To avoid any possible ambiguity, some symbols used in this documents are defined below.

- True: true
  The term "true" will be used to denote something that is true.
- False: false
  The term "false" will be used to denote something that is false.
- Inference Symbol: $\Rightarrow$
  $\Rightarrow$ is the normal inference symbol. A $\Rightarrow$ B means if A is true, then B must be true.
- Bi-directional Inference Symbol: $\Leftrightarrow$
  $\Leftrightarrow$ is semantically equivalent to two normal inference symbols $\Rightarrow$. A sentence "A $\Leftrightarrow$ B" means that if A is true, then B must be true, and that if B is true then A must also be true.
- Weak Inference Symbol: $\triangleright$
  $\triangleright$ is the weaken inference symbol which indicates the possible leading conclusion. A $\triangleright$ B reads "if A is true, then B should be true".
- Membership Symbol: $\in$
  $\in$ represents the membership of a list/set. For example, $E \in S$ means E is an element of set/list S. Therefore, if S is a list consisting of many lists, then E can be one of the lists. For instance, the statement $[1,2,3] \in [[1,2,3],[4,5,6]]$ is true, and $business(ibm) \in [business(hp), business(ibm)]$ is also true.

- Time Operators: $<, >, =<, >=, =$
  The above operators represent the time sequence in the system. For example, time-unit T6 $<$ time-unit T8, if T6 happens before T8.
- Empty set/list: [ ]
  Following the Prolog convention, [ ] used in this document represents an empty set or list.
- iff: if and only if
  The word *iff* is sometimes used in the English text when explaining a logic expression. Its logical meaning is "if and only if" or the bidirectional implication symbol $\Leftrightarrow$. A statement "A iff B" is true only when both statements "if A is true, then B is true" and "if B is true, then A is true" are true.

G

Entity Model Rules and Guidelines

In its manual, BSDM defines an entity model and recommends good practices in developing a business model [51]. There are also other modelling rules which are not documented in the manual, but are standard practice or natural deductions from the method. Some of these recommendations are necessary to follow to build a sound business model, others are circumstantial rules.

This appendix catalogues the recommendations relevant to entity modelling, the first activity toward developing a business model. According to the strength of enforcement of these recommendations, they are divided into two main categories: model rules and guidelines. A user-defined business model will be checked upon using these model rules and guidelines at the request of the user. Model rules are strong recommendations which if not followed, will probably cause an error in the business model or cause *KBST-BM* to behave wrongly. Model guidelines, on the other hand, should be followed most of the time, but there can be exceptions depending on the business' circumstances.

The formal language chosen to describe these rules is First Order Predicate Logic complemented with the argumentation convention of Prolog, i.e. arguments starting with capital letters are variables, otherwise, constants. The actual implementation of these rules is introduced in Chapter 9.

A strong inference symbol $\Rightarrow$ is used to represent the stronger enforcement of rules, whereas $\triangleright$ is used to represent the weaker enforcement of guidelines.

G.1 Entity Model Rules

- **An entity is not isolated** No isolated entity is allowed in the model, i.e. each entity must be linked with at least one other entity via a dependence relationship. Since a dependence relationship is represented in a predicate *parent_type* in the formalism, this rule can be interpreted as "each entity must have at least one parent or child entity". This rule is a deduction from BSDM.

$$class(entity, Entity)$$
$$\Rightarrow$$
$$\exists X. \left(\begin{pmatrix} parent\_type(Entity, Set\_of\_parents) \wedge \\ X \in Set\_of\_parents \end{pmatrix} \vee \\ \begin{pmatrix} parent\_type(X, Parents) \wedge \\ Entity \in Parents \end{pmatrix} \right) \qquad (1)$$

- **No circular dependence link** Any circular dependence relationship (an entity being depended on its own descendents via dependence links) are not allowed in a business model. To describe this rule, we define `ancestor(Q, P)` to mean that `P` is either a parent entity of `Q`, formally defined by the `parent_type` predicate, or that it is an ancestor entity of `Q` through the transitivity property of the `parent_type` predicate. The "circular dependence" rule is then represented by the expression below. This rule is also a deduction from the method.

$$class(entity, X) \Rightarrow \neg ancestor(X, X) \qquad (2)$$

The *ancestor* predicate can be described formally in the two expressions below:

$$parent\_type(X, Y) \wedge E \in Y$$
$$\Rightarrow$$
$$ancestor(X, E)$$

$$parent\_type(X, Y) \wedge$$
$$E \in Y \wedge$$
$$ancestor(E, Z)$$
$$\Rightarrow$$
$$ancestor(X, Z) \qquad (3)$$

- **An entity must be defined** Every entity must be given a definition statement by the modeller about the context and boundary of this entity. Since an entity definition is the most fundamental means to define the nature, purpose and relationships to its parent entities, it is essential to have each entity defined. This is a derived BSDM model rule from the entity manual (page 34 [51]).

$$class(entity, Entity\_type)$$
$$\Rightarrow$$
$$\exists Definition\_content.$$
$$\begin{pmatrix} property(Entity\_type, definition, Definition\_content) \wedge \\ Definition\_content \neq nil \end{pmatrix} \qquad (4)$$

- **A child entity occurrence must be created after its parents** The occurrence of a child entity cannot exist, unless the corresponding occurrences of its parent entities already exist (Note that parent and child entity occurrences can be created at the same time within the same process by BSDM, and this is ensured by the execution of a process.) Occurrence of an entity is represented by an occ(`Entity_type`, `Occ_name`, `Parent_occurrences`) predicate, where Entity_type is the entity type name of the occurrence, Occ_name is the name of the occurrence, and Parent_occurrences is the set of the corresponding parent occurrences. Predicate occ_exists(P) is defined to be true if occurrence P exists in the system.

$$occ(Entity\_type, Occ\_name, Parent\_occurrences)$$
$$\Rightarrow$$
$$\forall P.(P \in Parents\_occurrences \land occ\_exists(P)) \tag{5}$$

- **All entities are unique** Every entity included in a business model must be unique and used consistently throughout the model (page 32 [51]). In a business model, operations of a business area are usually shown through a "view" or several "views" of the business model. Each view includes the relevant entities and processes. Quite often an entity appears in several views, for reference and/or to introduce a new entity function in another process.
  It is hence important that the same entity has not been redefined in different views. The consistency checking of entity uniqueness includes consistency checking on the dependence links between entities, entity definitions, and the values of entity properties. Given that dependencies between entities is represented by a predicate parent_type(Entity, Set_of_Parents), and that an entity uses the same dependence definition throughout all views, then the rule below must hold within a business model.

$$parent\_type(Entity, Parents)$$
$$\Rightarrow$$
$$\neg\exists Parents2. \begin{pmatrix} parent\_type(Entity, Parents2) \land \\ Parents \neq Parents2 \end{pmatrix} \tag{6}$$

A set of *alternative parents* is an alternative set of entity parents which is also applied to the same entity. An entity can have alternative parents by depending itself to an *alternative parents box* in a business model. The alternative parents of an entity must also be uniquely and consistently defined throughout different parts of the model. In this document, we refer to a part of the model as a view and it is shown in a window in *KBST-BM*. The predicate alternative_parent(Entity, Alt_par) is true if Alt_par is the complete set of alternative parents to Entity.

$$alternative\_parent(Entity, Alt\_par)$$
$$\Rightarrow$$
$$\neg\exists Alt\_par2. \begin{pmatrix} alternative\_parent(Entity, Alt\_par2) \land \\ Alt\_par \neq Alt\_par2 \end{pmatrix} \tag{7}$$

Similarly, the properties of the same entity must be consistent throughout a business model. An entity's property is represented in a predicate property(Entity, Property_name, Property_content) where Entity is the name of the entity concerned, Property_content stores the value of a particular property, which is stored in Property_name.

$$property(Entity, Property\_name, Property\_content)$$
$$\Rightarrow$$
$$\neg\exists Content2. \left(\begin{array}{c} property(Entity, Property\_name, Content2)\wedge \\ Property\_content \neq Content2 \end{array} \right) \qquad (8)$$

- **An entity is a representation of real things** Entities included in a business model are the reflection of the existence of things in the real world. The role that an object plays in a business should not be captured as an entity, nor should its identifiers, documentation or representations. One way to ensure this mistake does not happen is to make sure that any entity name does not include one of those "avoided names", i.e. role names, identifiers, documentations and representations (pages 25, 27, 33, 39 [51]).

  Let predicate role_name(Name) be defined to be true if Name is a role name, such as teacher, student, customer, employee, and a predicate sub_string(String1, String2) be defined to be true if String1 is a part of String2, then the first part of the rule, "An entity name should not be a role name or incorporate a role name as part of its name", can be described formally below.

$$class(entity, Entity)$$
$$\Rightarrow$$
$$\neg\exists Name. \left(\begin{array}{c} role\_name(Name)\wedge \\ sub\_string(Name, Entity) \end{array} \right) \qquad (9)$$

Words such like 'link', 'form', 'documentation' and 'note' are either the representations or documentation of the real things, therefore they should also be avoided when naming an entity. This rule provides a safeguard to mistakenly creating entities which may be a representation of a particular implementation of a business model, instead of the higher-level abstraction of those possible implementations. Let predicate form_name(Name) be defined to be true if Name is a form name, such as link, form, documentation and note; this rule can be described formally below.

$$class(entity, Entity)$$
$$\Rightarrow$$
$$\neg\exists Name \left(\begin{array}{c} form\_name(Name)\wedge \\ sub\_string(Name, Entity) \end{array} \right) \qquad (10)$$

- **Derivable attributes must have derivation means** Attributes are the properties of an entity occurrence; some attributes are derivable from attributes of other entity occurrences. The corresponding deriving rules are given by the user, therefore the derivable attribute is defined, and can be calculated when the reference data is available (page 55 [51]).

The attribute rule is stored in a predicate attribute_rule(Entity, Attribute_name, Variable_list, Attribute_rule) where Entity is the name of the entity, Attribute_name is the name of the attribute, Attribute_rule is the logical and mathematical means of deriving the attribute value; the data for reference is stored in the Variable_list.

The expression below states that if an Attribute_name, denoted as in derive_attribute, is a derivable attribute of Entity, then there must exist an attribute_rule which defines how its value can be calculated.

$derive\_attribute(Entity, Attribute\_name)$
$\Rightarrow$
$\exists Variable\_list, Attribute\_rule.$
$attribute\_rule(Entity, Attribute\_name, Variable\_list, Attribute\_rule)$ (11)

- **An entity should be associated with the entity families** Any entity in a business model can be an existing entity recorded in the entity family or a specialised type of an existing entity in the entity family (page 26 [51]). Entity families are the standard entities which are common to many businesses and therefore have great reusability when developing new business models. The entity families are organised in an entity family hierarchy in *KBST-BM*: each entity in the hierarchy is represented in a predicate entity_family(Entity). The predicate special_type_of(General, Special) is defined to be true if the Special entity is a special type of the more General entity type.

Although a complete association between entities in a business model and standard entities in the entity families is not required by the user in BSDM, this establishment, however, is necessary in order to make use of the contextual information embedded in entity families, and to utilise CBR techniques to help building, verification and validation of a new business model (refer to Chapter 8). The established association between newly identified entities and standard entities is therefore strongly recommended in *KBST-BM*, and is represented as a model rule.

The model rule below states that each newly identified entity must be an existing standard entity in the entity families, or a specialised type of it.

$class(entity, Entity)$
$\Rightarrow$
$entity\_family(Entity) \vee$
$\exists General\_entity. \begin{pmatrix} entity\_family(General\_entity) \wedge \\ special\_type\_of(General\_entity, Entity) \end{pmatrix}$ (12)

The predicate special_type_of is defined by is_a relation links. An entity family hierarchy includes entities as nodes which are connected by is_a relationship. This relationship is one-directional and transitive. A more formal definition for predicate special_type_of based on transitive is_a relational links is given below.

$$entity\_family(General\_ent) \wedge$$
$$class(entity, Special\_ent) \wedge$$
$$is\_a(General\_ent, Special\_ent)$$
$$\Rightarrow$$
$$special\_type\_of(General\_ent, Special\_ent) \qquad\qquad (13)$$

$$entity\_family(General\_ent) \wedge$$
$$entity\_family(Special\_ent) \wedge$$
$$is\_a(General\_ent, Special\_ent)$$
$$\Rightarrow$$
$$special\_type\_of(General\_ent, Special\_ent) \qquad\qquad (14)$$

$$special\_type\_of(General\_ent, Special\_ent) \wedge$$
$$class(entity, New\_ent) \wedge$$
$$is\_a(Special\_ent, New\_ent)$$
$$\Rightarrow$$
$$special\_type\_of(General\_ent, New\_ent) \qquad\qquad (15)$$

- **Each entity must be given at least two life statuses** Processes are responsible for originating entity occurrences, creating their initial life statuses, and transferring their current life statuses to the next ones. The life status of an entity indicates not only the state of an entity occurrence but also that of the corresponding process occurrence which creates or updates it (page 41 [52]).

  To represent the life status of an entity occurrence, at least two (landmark) values must be used, i.e. the starting and ending life statuses. If no significant life status has been identified then at least two life status: "valid" and "invalid" should be given to an entity. This forms the advice of this rule and is not given in the logical expression below.

  The predicate *life_cycle_start_status(Entity, Life)* is defined to be true if *Life* is a valid start life status for all entity occurrences of entity type *Entity*. The predicate *life_cycle_transit(Entity, Life1, Life2)* is defined to be true for all entity occurrences with entity type *Entity* whose life status may be propagated from *Life1* to *Life2*.

There must be a start life status for each entity and this life status must be transferable The expression below states that for each entity, there must exist (at least) one start life cycle status, denoted as *Life*, and that it must be transferable to another life status – which means that there must exist at least one transition possibility which transfers it to another life status *Next_life*.

$class(entity, Entity)$

$\Rightarrow$

$\exists Life, Next\_life. \left(\begin{array}{l} life\_cycle\_start\_status(Entity, Life)\wedge \\ life\_cycle\_transit(Entity, Life, Next\_life) \end{array} \right)$ (16)

There must be an end life status for each entity and this life status must be reachable The expression below states that for each entity, there must exist (at least) one terminating life cycle status, which is defined as the argument End_life, and that it must be reachable – this means that there must exist at least one life status $Life$ which leads to this ending life status End_life.

$class(entity, Entity)$

$\Rightarrow$

$\exists End\_life, Life. \left(\begin{array}{l} life\_cycle\_end\_status(Entity, End\_life)\wedge \\ life\_cycle\_transit(Entity, Life, End\_life) \end{array} \right)$ (17)

Detecting of error life status transition BSDM has offered key words for denoting the ending life status of an entity, e.g. cancelled, terminated and closed (pages 55, 71 [52]). We have represented them together with "invalid" as the key words to denote the standard ending life statuses of an entity occurrence in the system. Those ending life statuses are stored in the $terminated\_life\_status$ predicate. The user can also define the specific ending life status for an entity; this is stored in the $life\_cycle\_end\_status$ predicate. The expression below states that any transition which transfers a standard *ending* life status or a user-defined *ending* life status to any other life status is not allowed.

$life\_cycle\_transit(Entity, From\_life, End\_life)$

$\Rightarrow$

$\neg terminated\_life\_status(From\_life) \wedge$

$\neg life\_cycle\_end\_status(From\_life)$ (18)

The expression below states that any transition which transfers a life status to a *start* life status is not allowed.

$life\_cycle\_transit(Entity, From\_life, End\_life)$

$\Rightarrow$

$\neg life\_cycle\_start\_status(End\_life)$ (19)

G.2 Entity Model Guidelines

As we have previous mentioned, some model rules which are in or derived from BSDM are with flexibility, that is their compliance is only relative to the circumstances. Those model rules are represented as model guidelines in the formalism using a weaker inference symbol ▷. When a guideline is violated, advice given to the user is with milder warnings compared with a normal model rule.

- **A business model should be within 4 layers** Certain entities are very common that they are being reused in different modelling projects. It is therefore useful to look for them when considering entity candidates. Independent entities are at the top level of the entity family hierarchy. Contract entities are generally at level two. Content type entities are at level three. Reconciliation type of entities are often at level four (page 26 [51]).
  BSDM recommends that the depth of an entity model should not be more than 4 layers, i.e. 4 steps through parent links. This is to prevent a model from being over-constrained by several layers of dependencies through levels of entities (pages 26 and 77 [51]). This rule is formally described below.

$$property(Entity, level, N) \rhd N < 5 \tag{20}$$

- **Null or two parents only** BSDM promotes the practice that each entity should only depend on zero or two parent entities. This rule, however, is not strictly enforced in all situations. There are, in fact, exceptions that the user may choose to use one-parent entities. The user is, however, generally encouraged to create only zero or two-parent entities. This rule is therefore represented as a guidelines. (pages 18 and 43 [51])

$$parent\_type(Entity, Parents)$$
$$\rhd$$
$$member\_no(Parents) = 0 \vee$$
$$member\_no(Parents) = 2 \tag{21}$$

- **Entity names should be short** Entity names should be as short as possible (page 33 [51]), e.g. less than 20 characters.

$$class(entity, Entity)$$
$$\rhd$$
$$string\_length(Entity) =< 20 \tag{22}$$

- **Entity names should be general** Entity names should be as general as possible therefore to provide the maximum flexibility for the business to cover all cases, i.e. all possible occurrences must be covered by the entity class (page 33 [51]).
  A possible way to accomplish the above check is to match entities to the entity family hierarchy, which can give some contextual information about those entities to detect any possible generalisation to the identified entities. In the expression below, each Entity is the highest possible generalisation of entities, and there isn't another entity Special_ent in the model which together with the Entity can become a more general entity name. Note that there are situations when a general entity needs to be specialised, therefore

this is only a recommendation.

$$class(entity, Entity) \land$$
$$special\_type\_of(General\_ent, Entity)$$
$$\triangleright$$
$$\neg \exists Special\_ent. \begin{pmatrix} class(entity, Special\_ent) \land \\ special\_type\_of(General\_ent, Special\_ent) \land \\ Special\_ent \neq Entity \end{pmatrix} \quad (23)$$

- **Entity names should be singular nouns** The entity name should always be a single noun or noun-phrase, because each occurrence of an entity represents a single object or thing in the real business world. The user must avoid words which end with -s, -es and -ies. This rule is described formally below using a predicate string_ending to identify the ending words of a string. The predicate string_ending(String, Ending) is defined to be true when Ending is the ending string of String. One can find exceptional words with ending -s, -es or -ies that still represent singular noun, therefore this rule again is a recommendation.

$$class(entity, Entity)$$
$$\triangleright$$
$$\neg \begin{pmatrix} string\_ending(Entity,' s') \lor \\ string\_ending(Entity,' es') \lor \\ string\_ending(Entity,' ies') \end{pmatrix} \quad (24)$$

- **Probably a mis-usage of alternative parents** A possible error of using alternative parents is to allow more than two sets of alternative parents for an entity. Since this is an unusual usage of alternative parents, it may be useful to remind the modeller of it. This is a derived rule from the method. The predicate alternative_parent(Entity, Alt_par) is true if Alt_par is the set of alternative parents to Entity. It is normally the case that two sets of parents are included in the Alt_par to indicate that they are alternative to each other; this is graphically denoted by one dependency linked to the *alternative-parent box* and the other linked to the one of the parent entity directly. This will be the case when three sets of alternative parents are included when both dependencies are linked to the *alternative-parent box* which is perhaps less common. More alternative parents may be included in the set if more than two entities are included in the *alternative-parent box*. The rule below formally describes that an entity normally has two sets of alternative parents, if there are any.

$$alternative\_parents(Entity, Parents)$$
$$\triangleright$$
$$member\_no(Parents) = 2 \quad (25)$$

H

Process Model Rules and Guidelines

This appendix documents the formalisation of the recommendation of business modelling in the BSDM process manual [52]. The formal language used is First Order Predicate Logic complement with the argumentation convention of Prolog, i.e. arguments that start with capital letters are variables, otherwise, constants.

BSDM defines a process model and recommends good practices in developing a sound business model [51]. There are also other modelling rules which are not documented in the manual, but are standard practice or natural deductions from the method. Some of these recommendations are necessary to follow to build a correct business model, others are circumstantial rules. Similarly to those given in Appendix G, according to the strength of enforcement of the recommendations on models, they are distinguished into two main categories: model rules and guidelines. A user-defined business model will be checked using these model rules and guidelines at the request of the user. Model rules are strong recommendations which if not followed will probably cause an error in the business model or cause *KBST-BM* to behave wrongly. Model guidelines, on the other hand, are normally followed but there can be exceptions depending on each business' circumstances.

A strong inference symbol ⇒ is used to represent the stronger enforcement of rules, whereas ▷ is used to represent the weaker enforcement of guidelines.

H.1 Process Model Rules

- **Each process must have a trigger** A BSDM process is identified by its trigger and (entity) functions (pages 10, 30, 62 [52]). Therefore, each process must be given at least one trigger by the modeller.

$class(process, Process)$
$\Rightarrow$
$\exists Trigger\_content.trigger(Process, Trigger\_content)$ \hfill (1)

- **Each process must include at least one entity** Each process must include at least one entity in its scope. Assuming each entity is given an entity function, this rule is represented below:

$class(process, Process)$
$\Rightarrow$
$\exists Entity\_function, Entity.$
$entity\_function(Entity\_function, Process, Entity)$ (2)

- **There are only seven different kinds of entity functions** Each process may include one or more entity functions in its scope. Those entity functions are pre-determined and can only be one of the following seven different kinds: originate focal, normal and if-flight entity functions, change focal and normal entity functions, and refer normal and master entity functions.

$entity\_function(Entity\_function, Process, Entity)$
$\Rightarrow$
$Entity\_function = originate\_focal\_fun \vee$
$Entity\_function = originate\_normal\_fun \vee$
$Entity\_function = originate\_if\_fun \vee$
$Entity\_function = change\_focal\_fun \vee$
$Entity\_function = change\_normal\_fun \vee$
$Entity\_function = refer\_normal\_fun \vee$
$Entity\_function = refer\_master\_fun$ (3)

- **Each entity must be included in at least one process** It is sensible to state that each entity in the model must be included in at least one process with one of the permitted entity functions. For this, we use the following rule:

$class(entity, Entity)$
$\Rightarrow$
$\exists Process, Entity\_function.$
$entity\_function(Entity\_function, Process, Entity)$ (4)

- **Main purpose of an originate process** An originate process' primary purpose is to originate at least one entity occurrence in its scope (pages 14, 21 [52]). To be more precise, its main purpose is to originate the entity occurrences of its *originate focal* entity, and perhaps also its *originate normal* and *in-flight* entities, if any exist (pages 29, 30, 62 [52]).

This can be summarised as: given any process which is an *originate process* then (a) it must included an *originate focal* entity-function in scope and one of its process actions must be to create an entity occurrence of the corresponding *originate focal* entity-function; and (b) it also creates entity occurrences of the corresponding *originate normal* and *in-flight* entity-functions, if it includes any of them in scope. The predicate *process_action(create_originate_focal_entity, Process, Entity, Occurrence)* means that an action of process *Process* is to create an entity occurrence of the corresponding *originate focal* entity of that process. This entity has an entity type *Entity*, and the corresponding occurrence is *Occurrence*. The same predicate is used to denote a process action which generates entity occurrences of the corresponding *originate normal* and *originate in-flight* entities, with the replacement of the first argument of the predicate with *originate_normal_entity* and *originate_if_entity*, respectively.

The logic expressions below state that each *originate* process must include at least one *originate focal* entity function, and that it must create an entity occurrence of this entity function as a part of its process actions.

$$class(originate\_process, Process)$$
$$\Rightarrow$$
$$\exists Entity, Occ.$$
$$\left(\begin{array}{c} entity\_function(originate\_focal\_fun, Process, Entity) \wedge \\ process\_action(create\_originate\_focal\_entity, \\ Process, Entity, Occ) \end{array} \right) \quad (5)$$

The two logic expressions below state that if an *originate process* includes an *originate normal* or an *originate in-flight* entity function in its scope, then it must create or confirm the entity occurrence of this entity function as a part of its process actions. (The creation of an absent originate_if entity is handled by the business model simulator.)

$$class(originate\_process, Process) \wedge$$
$$entity\_function(originate\_normal\_fun, Process, Entity)$$
$$\Rightarrow$$
$$\exists Occ.process\_action(create\_originate\_normal\_entity,$$
$$Process, Entity, Occ) \quad (6)$$

$$class(originate\_process, Process) \wedge$$
$$entity\_function(originate\_if\_fun, Process, Entity)$$
$$\Rightarrow$$
$$\exists Occ.process\_action(confirm\_originate\_if\_entity,$$
$$Process, Entity, Occ) \quad (7)$$

- **Main purpose of a change process** A change process' primary purpose is to change attributes of at least one entity occurrence in its scope (pages 14, 22 [52]). To be more precise, its main purpose is to change attributes of entity occurrences of its *change focal* entity, and also its *change normal* entities, if any exist (pages 29, 30, 62 [52]).

  In other words, given any *change process*, then (a) it must include a *change focal* entity in scope and one of its actions must be to change an attribute value of an entity occurrence of its *change focal* entity; and (b) it also changes attribute values of entity occurrences of its *change normal* entity functions, if it has included any such entity function in scope. The predicate *process_action(update_change_focal_entity, Process, Entity, Att, Old, New)* means that a particular action of a process *Process* is to *update* the value of attribute *Att* from *Old* to *New* of the corresponding *change focal* entity of *Process*. The entity type is *Entity*. The same predicate is used to denote a process action which changes attribute values of entity occurrences of the corresponding *change normal* entities, with a replacement of the first argument of the predicate with *change_normal_entity*.

$$class(change\_process, Process)$$
$$\Rightarrow$$
$$\exists Entity, Att, Old, New.$$
$$\begin{pmatrix} entity\_function(change\_focal\_fun, Process, Entity) \wedge \\ process\_action(update\_change\_focal\_entity, \\ Process, Entity, Att, Old, New) \end{pmatrix} \quad (8)$$

The expression below states that if a *change* process includes a *change normal* entity in its scope, then it must include at least one process action which carries out the update of at least one attribute of this change normal entity.

$$class(change\_process, Process) \wedge$$
$$entity\_function(change\_normal\_fun, Process, Entity)$$
$$\Rightarrow$$
$$\exists Att, Old, New.$$
$$process\_action(update\_change\_normal\_entity,$$
$$Process, Entity, Att, Old, New) \quad (9)$$

- **Focal originate entity applies only to originate processes** A *focal originate* entity function constitutes the primary purpose of an *originate* process. By definition, this process must be an *originate* process and cannot be any other kind of process (page 30 [52]).

$$entity\_function(originate\_focal\_fun, Process, Entity)$$
$$\Rightarrow$$
$$\forall Process\_type. \begin{pmatrix} class(Process\_type, Process) \wedge \\ Process\_type = originate\_process \end{pmatrix} \quad (10)$$

- **Each entity in the process scope must have an entity function** Each entity which is physically drawn within a process scope, must be assigned with an entity function for this process. On the other hand, any entity may not have any functional relationship (entity function) with a process unless it is within the process scope of that process (pages 29, 30, 62 [52]). A bi-directional symbol ⇔ is used here which is equivalent to two ⇒ which enforce the property of the other one once one property is true.

$$process\_scope(Process, Entity)$$
$$\Leftrightarrow$$
$$\exists Entity\_function.entity\_function(Entity\_function,$$
$$Process, Entity) \tag{11}$$

- **One entity function per entity in a process** Each entity which is physically drawn within a process scope must be assigned with an entity function for this process. Furthermore, this entity function should be the unique one which was assigned to the entity, i.e. an entity cannot play two roles in a process therefore cannot bear more than one different entity functions within a process (pages 29, 30, 62 [52]).

$$entity\_function(Entity\_function, Process, Entity)$$
$$\Rightarrow$$
$$\neg\exists Entity\_function2.$$
$$\left(\begin{array}{c} entity\_function(Entity\_function2, Process, Entity) \wedge \\ Entity\_function \neq Entity\_function2 \end{array}\right) \tag{12}$$

- **Derivable attributes are not the primary purpose of a change process** A derivable attribute alone is not considered to be independent and sufficiently significant for a BSDM business process – a change of its value can always be derived whenever it is needed. Therefore, a process must not be created such that its primary or sole purpose is to produce or update the value of a derivable attribute. When a change of the derivable attribute is important to the business, the values which cause the changes are important. A derivable attribute should be dynamically recalculated if any of the calculation basis has been changed (pages 15, 22, 58, 60 [52]).
  The above rule can be interpreted as: for any attribute-updating action where the updated attribute is a derivable attribute, there must be another primary action carried out by this process.

$$process\_action(update\_change\_focal\_entity, Process, Entity, Attribute, Old, New)$$
$$\wedge$$
$$derive\_attribute(Entity, Attribute)$$
$$\Rightarrow$$
$$\exists Attribute2, Old2, New2.$$
$$\left(\begin{array}{c} process\_action(update\_change\_focal\_entity, \\ Process, Entity, Attribute2, Old2, New2) \wedge \\ Attribute2 \neq Attribute \end{array}\right) \tag{13}$$

- **The calculation base for derivable variables must be in the process scope** If a process has an *originate focal* or *originate normal* or *originate in-flight* entity function in scope, then it will need to produce this entity's attribute values when it creates this entity. If any of these originated attributes is a derivable attribute, then those other entities, whose attribute values are used as a calculation basis in the derivation rule, must be included in the scope of the process (pages 28, 58 [52]).

$class(process, Process) \land$
$\exists Entity, Attribute.$
$$\left(\left(\begin{array}{l} entity\_function(originate\_focal\_fun, Process, Entity) \lor \\ entity\_function(originate\_normal\_fun, Process, Entity) \end{array} \right) \land \atop derive\_attribute(Entity, Attribute) \right)$$
$\Rightarrow$
$\exists Att\_value, Referred\_entities, Attribute\_rule\_content.$
$$\left(\begin{array}{l} attribute\_rule(Entity, Attribute, Att\_value, Referred\_entities, \\ \qquad\qquad\qquad\qquad\qquad\qquad Attribute\_rule\_content) \end{array} \right) \land$$
$\forall X, \exists Process\_scope.$
$$\left(\begin{array}{c} X \in Referred\_entities \land \\ process\_scope(Process, Process\_scope) \land \\ X \in Process\_scope \end{array} \right) \qquad\qquad (14)$$

- **Consistency checking between Life Cycle Diagram and Process Model** If a process has been included in an entity's *Life Cycle Diagram* then this must be reflected in the process scope. This means that if an originate process has been identified in an entity's *Life Cycle Diagram* (denoted as in the *orgprocess* predicate), then this entity must be originated by that process, i.e. it must either be an *originate focal, normal* or *in-flight* entity in that process; if a change process has been included in an entity's *Life Cycle Diagram* (denoted as in the *chgprocess* predicate), then that entity must be changeable by the process, i.e. it must be a *change focal* or *normal* entity in that process. These two rules are described formally below.

$orgprocess(Process, Entity, Life)$
$\Rightarrow$
$$\left(\begin{array}{l} entity\_function(originate\_focal\_fun, Process, Entity) \lor \\ entity\_function(originate\_normal\_fun, Process, Entity) \lor \\ \quad entity\_function(originate\_if\_fun, Process, Entity) \end{array} \right) \qquad (15)$$

$chgprocess(Process, Entity, Start, End)$
$\Rightarrow$
$$\left(\begin{array}{l} entity\_function(change\_focal\_fun, Process, Entity) \lor \\ entity\_function(change\_normal\_fun, Process, Entity) \end{array} \right) \qquad (16)$$

H.2 Process Model Guidelines

- **Each process should have a business rule** A BSDM process is also defined by its business rules(page 10 [52]). Therefore, it is recommended that each process should be given at least one business rule by the modeller.

$$class(process, Process)$$
$$\triangleright$$
$$\exists Rule\_content.business\_rule(Process, Rule\_content) \tag{17}$$

- **Each entity should be originated by at least one process** Each entity should be originated (created) by at least one process (pages 41, 63 [52]). Each entity included in a business model is of significance and therefore theoretically, the origination of an entity occurrence should be controlled and described in a business process. However, since the modeller may decide that the creation of some particular entity occurrence lies outside the scope of his/her modelling activities, this forms a guideline, rather than a strict model rule. The guideline states that each entity must either be an *originate focal*, *originate normal* or *in-flight* entity in at least one process (note that this is a more specific version of model rule 2).

$$class(entity, Entity)$$
$$\triangleright$$
$$\exists Process.$$
$$\left(\begin{array}{c} entity\_function(originate\_focal\_fun, Process, Entity) \vee \\ entity\_function(originate\_normal\_fun, Process, Entity) \vee \\ entity\_function(originate\_if\_fun, Process, Entity). \end{array} \right) \tag{18}$$

- **Naming convention of a process** BSDM has recommended a convention for naming a process to ensure that the name of a process is meaningful and consistent throughout the model. A process name should indicate what the process does and the main affected entity (page 24 [52]).
  The rule for naming is "a verb followed by a simple noun". The noun used can be an entity name, written in capitals, e.g. "Take CUSTOMER ORDER", or "Open CUSTOMER ACCOUNT". The simple process name can also be extended to give more information about the process, e.g. "Accept BUSINESS as Trading Partner", or "Discontinue Trade with BUSINESS", or "Accept PAYMENT against CUSTOMER ACCOUNT". Commonly used verbs are access, confirm, propose, define, make, transform, assemble, move, predict, issue, receive, take, open, close, discontinue, create.
  In short, a standardised process name should begin with a simple verb followed by a capitalised entity name. Therefore, we formalise it below.

$$class(process, Process\_name)$$
$$\triangleright$$
$$\exists Begin\_word, Entity\_name.$$
$$\left(\begin{array}{c} begin\_string(Process\_name, Begin\_word) \wedge \\ simple\_verb(Begin\_word) \wedge \\ class(entity, Entity\_name) \wedge \\ sub\_string(Entity\_name, Process\_name) \end{array} \right) \tag{19}$$

- **Unique focal entity in a process** It is generally recommended that only one *focal originate* or *focal change* entity is included in a process which forms the primary reason for the existence of the process. The expression below states that each process can have one and only one *originate focal* entity function in its scope.

$$entity\_function(originate\_focal\_fun, Process, Entity)$$
$$\triangleright$$
$$\neg\exists Entity2. \begin{pmatrix} entity\_function(originate\_focal\_fun, \\ Process, Entity2) \wedge \\ Entity \neq Entity2 \end{pmatrix} \qquad (20)$$

The expression below states that each process can have one and only one *change focal* entity function in its scope.

$$entity\_function(change\_focal\_fun, Process, Entity)$$
$$\triangleright$$
$$\neg\exists Entity2. \begin{pmatrix} entity\_function(change\_focal\_fun, \\ Process, Entity2) \wedge \\ Entity \neq Entity2 \end{pmatrix} \qquad (21)$$

- **Parents of focal and normal entities** In any process, if any of its *focal* and *normal* entities are dependent entities, then when their entity occurrences are to be created or changed, the occurrence of its parent entities may also be needed for the process execution. Their parents can be in one of the three possibilities: (1) the parent entity occurrence will always already exist, (2) the parent entity occurrence will usually exist but not always be present, (3) the parent entity occurrence will normally not be present but is created as a part of the process. It is a prerequisite in the method that parent entity occurrences must be created before or at the same time when the dependent entity occurrence is created, so that the necessary information from the parent entity occurrence can be used for the creation.

There are three different ways to model the parent entities in the process. In the first situation, as a *reference* entity function in the process, since the required information already exist. In the second case, an *originate inflight* because it sometimes already exist, but can be originated if absent. In the third case, as an *originate change* entity function, because it is always co-created during the process of originating the initial *originate focal* and *normal* entities. This rule, however, does not have to be strictly followed, since the assignment of an entity function is business dependent and modelling project dependent (i.e. it may lie outside the scope of the modelling project) (page 29 [52]).

An *originate* process is responsible for the origination of entity occurrences in addition of merely referring to those entity occurrences. The above rule is formalised in two expressions which deal with parents of an *originate focal* and *originate normal* entity.

$entity\_function(originate\_focal\_fun, Process, Entity) \wedge$
$parent\_type(Entity, Parents)$

$\triangleright$

$$\forall X.X \in Parents \wedge \left(\begin{array}{c} entity\_function(refer\_normal\_fun, Process, X) \vee \\ entity\_function(refer\_master\_fun, Process, X) \vee \\ entity\_function(originate\_if\_fun, Process, X) \vee \\ entity\_function(originate\_normal\_fun, Process, X) \end{array} \right) \tag{22}$$

$entity\_function(originate\_normal\_fun, Process, Entity) \wedge$
$parent\_type(Entity, Parents)$

$\triangleright$

$$\forall X.X \in Parents \wedge \left(\begin{array}{c} entity\_function(refer\_normal\_fun, Process, X) \vee \\ entity\_function(refer\_master\_fun, Process, X) \vee \\ entity\_function(originate\_if\_fun, Process, X) \vee \\ entity\_function(originate\_normal\_fun, Process, X) \end{array} \right) \tag{23}$$

As a *change* process primarily modifies existing entity occurrences, we assume that parent entity occurrences of the *focal* and *normal* entity occurrences always already exist. Therefore, we only need to refer to them. This is formalised below.

$entity\_function(change\_focal\_fun, Process, Entity) \wedge$
$parent\_type(Entity, Parents)$

$\triangleright$

$$\forall X.X \in Parents \wedge \left(\begin{array}{c} entity\_function(refer\_normal\_fun, Process, X) \vee \\ entity\_function(refer\_master\_fun, Process, X) \end{array} \right) \tag{24}$$

$entity\_function(change\_normal\_fun, Process, Entity) \wedge$
$parent\_type(Entity, Parents)$

$\triangleright$

$$\forall X.X \in Parents \wedge \left(\begin{array}{c} entity\_function(refer\_normal\_fun, Process, X) \vee \\ entity\_function(refer\_master\_fun, Process, X) \end{array} \right) \tag{25}$$

- **Identification of subsumed process** If there are two processes whose process actions are identical, or the actions of one are subsumed by the other one, then there may be a chance of overlapping the definition of these two processes (page 62 [52]).

$process\_action\_set(Process, Actions)$

$\triangleright$

$$\neg \exists Process2, Actions2. \left(\begin{array}{c} process\_action\_set(Process2, Actions2) \wedge \\ Actions \subseteq Actions2 \end{array} \right) \tag{26}$$

- **Identification of complementary process** If two processes are raised (triggered) by the same event and each carries out a part of the activities which together belong to a bigger process, then these two processes should be combined into a larger process (page 62 [52]).

The representation of the above rule is not straightforward, because of the difficulties in identifying the above situation. The above situation cannot be identified using only process actions, because each will be different as a partial process and complementary of each other; nor can the situation be identified using the trigger alone, i.e. to find the two partial processes by identifying processes which share the same trigger.

A more accurate judgement would take both factors into account. To determine if two process are complementary to each other, we can probably consider the primary purpose of each process, i.e. the *focal* entities of each process. We can then describe this as: if there are two processes which are invoked by the same trigger, and the primary purpose of one process is either to originate or change the direct parent or child entity of the primary focal entity of the other process, then these two processes might be combined.

To translate the above observation into formal representations, we can again rewrite this as: if one can find two processes which are invoked by the same trigger, and that the focal entity of one is the direct parent (or child) entity of the other process' focal entity, then these two processes may be combined. The final judgement of whether two processes should be kept separate or combined is again made by the individual business. We represent this rule as a guideline in the two expressions below, each dealing with an *originate* and a *change* process.

$$trigger(Process, Trigger\_content) \land$$
$$entity\_function(originate\_focal\_fun, Process, Entity) \land$$
$$parent\_type(Entity, Parents)$$
$$\triangleright$$
$$\neg \exists Process2, Entity2.$$
$$\left(\begin{array}{c} trigger(Process2, Trigger\_content) \land \\ Process \neq Process2 \land \\ entity\_function(originate\_focal\_fun, Process2, Entity2) \land \\ Entity2 \in Parents \end{array} \right) \quad (27)$$

$trigger(Process, Trigger\_content) \wedge$
$entity\_function(change\_focal\_fun, Process, Entity) \wedge$
$parent\_type(Entity, Parents)$
$\triangleright$
$\neg \exists Process2, Entity2.$

$$\left(\begin{array}{c} trigger(Process2, Trigger\_content) \wedge \\ Process \neq Process2 \wedge \\ entity\_function(change\_focal\_fun, Process2, Entity2) \wedge \\ Entity2 \in Parents \end{array} \right) \qquad (28)$$

- **All important attributes are covered by processes** If an entity has an attribute which is of importance to a business, it is essential to document how the attribute values are changed. This is particularly true when changes in an attribute value reflect changes in the status of the entity occurrence, i.e. life cycle status of an entity occurrence. In other words, one or more change processes should be defined to carry out the changes of this value (pages 22, 41 [52]).

  The formal expression below states that for each entity *Entity*, if its life cycle status can be changed from one state *Old* to the other *New*, then there should exist at least one change process *Process* which includes the *Entity* either as its *change focal* or *change normal* entity and that one of its process actions should be to change this entity's life cycle status from *Old* to *New*.

$life\_cycle\_transit(Entity, Old, New)$
$\triangleright \exists Process.$

$$\left(\begin{array}{c} \left(\begin{array}{c} entity\_function(change\_focal\_fun, Process, Entity) \wedge \\ process\_action(update\_change\_focal\_entity, Process, Entity, \\ lifestatus, Old, New) \end{array} \right) \vee \\ \left(\begin{array}{c} entity\_function(change\_normal\_fun, Process, Entity) \wedge \\ process\_action(update\_change\_normal\_entity, Process, Entity, \\ lifestatus, Old, New) \end{array} \right) \end{array} \right) \qquad (29)$$

Other important attributes can be identified by the modeller and represented in a predicate *important_attribute(Entity, Attribute)*. This predicate is defined to be true, iff *Attribute* is an "important" attribute to entity *Entity* and the business being modelled. The decision about whether an attribute is important or not is determined by each business, therefore is not discussed here.

The logical sentence below states that all important attributes must be handled by at least one change process which updates it. (The attributes may be given at the creation of the entity occurrence therefore are not specified here.)

$important\_attribute(Entity, Attribute) \wedge$

$\triangleright$

$\exists Process, Old, New.$

$$\left(\begin{pmatrix} entity\_function(change\_focal\_fun, Process, Entity) \wedge \\ process\_action(update\_change\_focal\_entity, Process, Entity, \\ Attribute, Old, New) \end{pmatrix} \vee \atop \begin{pmatrix} entity\_function(change\_normal\_fun, Process, Entity) \wedge \\ process\_action(update\_change\_normal\_entity, Process, Entity, \\ Attribute, Old, New) \end{pmatrix} \right) \quad (30)$$

For those important attributes whose values are specified in the attribute _transit predicate, the above rule is formalised below.

$important\_attribute(Entity, Attribute) \wedge$
$attribute\_transit(Entity, Attribute, Old, New)$

$\triangleright$

$\exists Process, Actions.$

$$\left(\begin{pmatrix} entity\_function(change\_focal\_fun, Process, Entity) \wedge \\ process\_action(update\_change\_focal\_entity, \\ Process, Entity, Attribute, Old, New) \end{pmatrix} \vee \atop \begin{pmatrix} entity\_function(change\_normal\_fun, Process, Entity) \wedge \\ process\_action(update\_change\_normal\_entity, \\ Process, Entity, Attribute, Old, New) \end{pmatrix} \right) \quad (31)$$

- **Deadlock prevention among processes** *Deadlock*, in the context of process modelling, is the situation when two or more processes cannot be executed because the information which is needed for execution is absent and will have to be generated by other process(es); however, the execution of these process(es) can only be done if the initial process is already executed. Since all of these processes depend on each other's information for execution, no processes can be carried out.

  In BSDM, the prerequisite for executing a process is through the *originate in-flight* entity function and the ability of triggering another process to generate it, which if not careful may invoke a chain of invocation for processes. This interdependency of process execution can be described in the *inflight_chain* predicate.

$$\left(\begin{array}{c} entity\_function(originate\_focal\_fun, Process\_name, X) \wedge \\ entity\_function(originate\_if\_fun, Process\_name, Y) \wedge \\ entity\_function(originate\_if\_invoke, Process\_name) \end{array} \right)$$
$\Rightarrow$
$inflight\_chain(X, Y)$

$$\left.\begin{array}{l} originate\_focal\_fun(Process\_name, X) \wedge \\ originate\_if\_fun(Process\_name, Y) \wedge \\ originate\_if\_invoke(Process\_name) \wedge \\ inflight\_chain(Y, Z) \end{array}\right)$$

$$\Rightarrow$$

$$inflight\_chain(X, Z) \tag{32}$$

Given the definition of the predicate *inflight_chain*, the guideline which detects the possibility of *deadlock* between processes can be formally given below.

$$\left(\begin{array}{c} entity\_function(originate\_focal\_fun, Process\_name, X) \wedge \\ entity\_function(originate\_if\_fun, Process\_name, Y) \wedge \\ entity\_function(originate\_if\_invoke, Process\_name) \end{array} \right)$$

$$\triangleright$$

$$\neg(inflight\_chain(X, X)) \tag{33}$$

A more detailed explanation about what *deadlock* is in BSDM and these rules is given in Section 6.5.

- **Inconsistent handling of entities** We could perhaps assume that normally a business policy is carried out consistently even in different business operations. Based on this assumption, we may expect that two closely related entities play similar roles even in different processes.

For instance, if an entity occurrence Y is always created when an entity occurrence X is created, then when expressed in a process scope, entity X will be the *originate focal* entity, and Y will be the *originate normal* entity. We may then think it is inconsistent with the standard practice if there is another process, Process_name2, which specifies X be the *originate normal* entity and Y be the *originate focal* entity. If this is applicable, a similar principle can also be applied to the relationships for *change focal* and *change normal* entity functions. These are the extended guidelines which are a natural deduction from BSDM. They are described formally below.

$$\left(\begin{array}{c} entity\_function(originate\_focal\_fun, Process, Entity1) \wedge \\ entity\_function(originate\_normal\_fun, Process, Entity2) \end{array} \right)$$

$$\triangleright$$

$$\neg \exists Process2.$$

$$\left(\begin{array}{c} entity\_function(originate\_focal\_fun, Process2, Entity2) \wedge \\ entity\_function(originate\_normal\_fun, Process2, Entity1) \end{array} \right) \tag{34}$$

$$\left(\begin{array}{c} entity\_function(change\_focal\_fun, Process, Entity1) \wedge \\ entity\_function(change\_normal\_fun, Process, Entity2) \end{array} \right)$$

$$\triangleright$$

$$\neg \exists Process2.$$

$$\left(\begin{array}{c} entity\_function(change\_focal\_fun, Process2, Entity2) \wedge \\ entity\_function(change\_normal\_fun, Process2, Entity1) \end{array} \right) \tag{35}$$

I

An Interpreter for User-Defined Rules

```
%%%%%%%%%%%%%%%%%%%%%%%%%%%%%%%%%%%%%%%%%%%%%%%%%%%%%%%%%%%%%%%%%
% File: derive.pl                          1999-6-17
%
% This document records the design for derivation methods for
% entity attributes.
%%%%%%%%%%%%%%%%%%%%%%%%%%%%%%%%%%%%%%%%%%%%%%%%%%%%%%%%%%%%%%%%%

%%%%%%%%%%%%%%%%%%%%%%%%%%%%%%%%%%%%%%%%%%%%%%%%%%%%%%%%%%%%%
%% Main Program (1)
%%%%%%%%%%%%%%%%%%%%%%%%%%%%%%%%%%%%%%%%%%%%%%%%%%%%%%%%%%%%%

%%%%%%%%%%%%%%%%%%%%%%%%%%%%%%%%%%%%%%%%%%%%%%%%%%%%%%%%%%%%%%%%%
% statement --> verb_phrase + noun_phrase +
%               adj_phrase  + adv_phrase  +
%               closing_phrase
%%%%%%%%%%%%%%%%%%%%%%%%%%%%%%%%%%%%%%%%%%%%%%%%%%%%%%%%%%%%%%%%%
%%%% Type 1: statement

statement([type1, function(Function),   attname(Attname),
          att_value(Att_list),  res(Result)] )
        --> vp(Function, Attname),
            adj_p(Entity), adv_p(Entity, [], EntOccs),
            closing_statement(Result),
            {find_all_attvalues(Attname, EntOccs, Att_list),
            compute(Function, Att_list, Result)   }.

%%%% Type 2: statement

statement([type2, function(Function), res(Result)] )

        --> vp(Function),
            vp_content(Result),
```

```
            call_statement(Function),
            {(\+ var(Function), call(Function);
            var(Function) ) }.

%%%% Type 3: statement

statement([type3, function(Function), res(Result)] )

        --> vp(Function),
            s1_block(Result),
            call_statement(Function),
            {(\+ var(Function), call(Function);
            var(Function) ) }.

%%%% Type 4: statement


statement([type4, function(Function), res(Result)] )

          --> vp(Function),
              s1_block(Res1), vp_content(Res2),
        call_statement(Function),
              {(\+ var(Function), call(Function);
               var(Function) ),
               append(Res1, Res2, Result) }.

%%%%%%%%%%%%%%%%%%%%%%%%%%%%%%%%%%%%%%%%%%%%%%%%%%%%%%%%%%%

s1_block([type1|Result]) --> statement([type1| Result]).

s1_block([type1|Result]) --> statement([type1| Res1]),
                             [and],
                             statement([type1| Res2]),
        {append(Res1, [type1| Res2], Result) }.


%%%%%%%%%%%%%%%%%%%%%%%%%%%%%%%%%%%%%%%%%%%%%%%%%%%%%%%%%%%

vp_content([Result]) -->
     vp2(Attname), adj_p(Entity),
     adv_p(Entity, [], EntOccs),
     closing_statement(Result),
        {write(EntOccs),nl,
         write(Entity),write(ID),nl,
         member( (Entity, ID), EntOccs),
         dyn(ent_occ_att(Entity, ID, Attname, Result)) }.
```

```prolog
vp_content(Result) -->
      vp2(Attname), adj_p(Entity), adv_p(Entity, [], EntOccs),
      closing_statement(Res1),
          vp_content(Res2),
          {member( (Entity, ID), EntOccs ),
           dyn(ent_occ_att(Entity, ID, Attname, Res1)),
           append([Res1], Res2, Result) }.
```

```
%%%%%%%%%%%%%%%%%%%%%%%%%%%%%%%%%%%%%%%%%%%%%%%%%%%%%%%%%

% (1) Verb and Verb Phrase
```

```prolog
verb --> [calculate], {write('verb'),nl}.
verb --> [compute],   {write('verb'),nl}.
verb --> [use],       {write('verb'),nl}.
verb --> [search],    {write('verb'),nl}.
verb --> [find],      {write('verb'),nl}.
```

```
%%%%
```

```prolog
vp(Function, Attname) -->
verb, [the, Function, of, attribute, Attname],
                {write('vp'),nl}.

vp(Function) --> verb, [the, Function, for], noun,
                {nl, write('vp'),nl}.

vp(Function, Attname) -->
verb, [the], function(Function),
                [of, attribute, Attname],
                {write('vp'),nl}.

vp2(Attname) --> verb , [attribute, Attname],
                {write('vp2'),nl}.
```

```
%%%%%%%%%%%%%%%%%%%%%%%%%%%%%%%%%%%%%%%%%%%%%%%%%%%%%%%%%
% (2) Noun and Noun Phrase
```

```prolog
noun --> [computation].
noun --> [calculation].

function(average)  -->  [average].
function(summation) --> [summation].
```

```
%%%%%%%%%%%%%%%%%%%%%%%%%%%%%%%%%%%%%%%%%%%%%%%%%%%%%%%%%
```

```
% (3) Adj Phrase

adj_p(Entity)--> [for, every, entity, Entity],
                 {write('adj_p'),nl}.
adj_p(Entity)--> [for, entity, Entity], {write('adj_p'),nl}.

%%%%%%%%%%%%%%%%%%%%%%%%%%%%%%%%%%%%%%%%%%%%%%%%%%%%%%%%%%
% (4) find all relevant Entity Occurrences

%% find a special set of ent occs.
adv_p(Entity, InOcc, OutOcc) -->
    [with, condition, entity-ancestor, ParOcc],
      {write('adv_p1'),nl,
        find_all_ent_occ(Entity, ParOcc, InOcc, OutOcc)}.


adv_p(Entity, InOcc, OutOcc) -->
    [with, condition, entity-ancestor, ParOcc, and],
      adv_p(Entity, InOcc, MidOcc),
      {write('adv_p2'),nl,
        find_all_ent_occ(Entity, ParOcc, MidOcc, OutOcc)
      }.

%% know the particular entity occ
adv_p(Entity, InOcc, OutOcc) -->
    [with, condition, entity-id, EntID],
      {write('adv_p1'),nl,
        find_one_ent_occ(Entity, EntID,
        InOcc, OutOcc)}.

%%%%%%%%%%%%%%%%%%%%%%%%%%%%%%%%%%%%%%%%%%%%%%%%%%%%%%%%%%
% (5)
closing_statement(Result) -->
          [when, finished, save, the, result, in, Result],
          {write('close'),nl}.
%%%%%%%%%%%%%%%%%%%%%%%%%%%%%%%%%%%%%%%%%%%%%%%%%%%%%%%%%%
% (6)
call_statement(Function) --> [call, Function],
      {\+ var(Function), write('call statement'),nl}.

call_statement(Function) --> [call, Function],
      {var(Function),
        write('Error: User defined function is not given !'),
        nl}.

%%%%%%%%%%%%%%%%%%%%%%%%%%%%%%%%%%%%%%%%%%%%%%%%%%%%%%%%%%
```

```
% find_all_ent_occ(Entity, ParOcc, InOcc, OutOcc)
%
% Given Parent Occurrence, find all relevant entity occurrence.
%
% Output = [(Entity, ID), (Entity2, ID2),...]
%%%%%%%%%%%%%%%%%%%%%%%%%%%%%%%%%%%%%%%%%%%%%%%%%%%%%%%%%%%%%%%%%

find_all_ent_occ(Entity, ParOcc, InOcc, OutOcc) :-
        findall( (Entity, ID),
                    ( dyn(ent_occ(Entity, ID, _)),
                       ancestor( (Entity, ID), ParOcc)
                    ),
                    NewOcc ),
        append(InOcc, NewOcc, Mid),
        set(Mid, OutOcc).

find_all_ent_occ(Entity, _, InOcc, InOcc) :-
        dyn(ent_occ(Entity, _, [])),
        write('An Error was found: The Entity "'),
        write(Entity),write('"'),nl,
        write('is without a parent.'),nl.

find_all_ent_occ(Entity, [], InOcc, InOcc) :-
        write('An Error was found: The Entity "'),
        write(Entity),write('"'),nl,
    write('cannot be found without given parent occurrences.'),
        nl.


%%%%%%%%%%%%%%%%%%%%%%%%%%%%%%%%%%%%%%%%%%%%%%%%%%%%%%%%%%%%%%%%%%%
% find_one_ent_occ(Entity, EntID, InOcc, OutOcc)
%
% Given the Entity name and Entity ID, the particular Ent Occ is
% retrieved and added to InOcc and return in Outocc.
%%%%%%%%%%%%%%%%%%%%%%%%%%%%%%%%%%%%%%%%%%%%%%%%%%%%%%%%%%%%%%%%%%%

find_one_ent_occ(Entity, EntID, InOcc, OutOcc) :-
    dyn(ent_occ(Entity, EntID, _)),
    append(InOcc, [(Entity, EntID)], Out),
    set(Out, OutOcc).

find_one_ent_occ(Entity, EntID, InOcc, InOcc) :-
    \+ dyn(ent_occ(Entity, EntID, _)),
    write('Warning: An entity occurrence is required for the
derivable attribute rule, but it does not exist.'),nl,
    write('The entity Name: '), write(Entity),nl,
    write('The entity ID:   '), write(EntID),nl.
```

```
%%%%%%%%%%%%%%%%%%%%%%%%%%%%%%%%%%%%%%%%%%%%%%%%%%%%%%%%%%%%%%%%%%
%      find_all_attvalues(Attname, EntOccs, Output_list),
%%%%%%%%%%%%%%%%%%%%%%%%%%%%%%%%%%%%%%%%%%%%%%%%%%%%%%%%%%%%%%%%%%

find_all_attvalues(Attname, EntOccs, Output_list) :-

        findall( AttValue,
                 ( member( (Ent, ID), EntOccs),
                   dyn(ent_occ_att(Ent, ID, Attname, AttValue)) ),
                 Output_list).


%%%%%%%%%%%%%%%%%%%%%%%%%%%%%%%%%%%%%%%%%%%%%%%%%%%%%%%%%%%%%%%%%%%%
%    compute(Function, Input_list, Result)
%%%%%%%%%%%%%%%%%%%%%%%%%%%%%%%%%%%%%%%%%%%%%%%%%%%%%%%%%%%%%%%%%%%%

compute(average, [], 0) :- !.

compute(average, Input_list, Result) :-

        compute(summation, Input_list, R1),
        length(Input_list, Len),
        Result is R1 / Len.

%%%%%%%%%%%%%%%%

compute(summation, [], 0) :- !.

compute(summation, Input, Result) :-
        my_sum(Input, 0, Result).

%%%%%%%%%%%%%%%%%

my_sum([], Res, Res) :- !.

my_sum([X|List_of_data], Input, Res) :-
        Sum is X + Input,
        my_sum(List_of_data, Sum, Res).
```

J

Model Rules and Guidelines by Category

This appendix categories all of the model rules and guidelines described in the book in four categories and list them in four tables.

Explanation of the four categories of model rules and guidelines are given below:

1. *Exact Match:* These model rules/guidelines are given in the method explicitly and all errors described by such rules are detectable by the tool and *correct* advice can be given.
2. *Partial Match:* These model rules/guidelines are given in the method explicitly, but only a part of the specified errors are detectable by the tool with *correct* advice given.
3. *Folklore Rules:* This type of rules are not explicitly stated in the method, but assumed or inferable from it and are normally used by practitioners. Folklore model rules are modelling rules which are normally applied in practice. Although they are not explicitly stated in the method, they can be inferred from BSDM guidelines.
4. *Enhanced Rules:* The use of enhanced modelling rules is only possible when applying *DefBM* or *KBST-BM*. This is due to the extension of *BSDM* that is made available in our modelling framework. Such extensions are the provision of the *Entity Conceptual Hierarchy*, *Process Dependency and Partial Execution Order Diagrams*, extended *Life Cycle Diagrams*, *Procedural Model* and the checking functionalities provided by the business model simulator.

The model rules and guidelines are described in the following sections. The IDs of the model rules and guidelines are used correspondingly in Appendices G and H.

J.1 Entity Model Rules

Rule ID	Entity Model Rules	Category
1	No entity should be isolated	1, 3
2,3	No circular dependency is allowed	1, 3
4	Each entity must be defined	1
5	A child entity occurrence must be created only after its parent occurrences are created	1, 4
6,7,8	Each entity is unique	2
9,10	Each entity represents real things	2
11	Each derivable variable must have a derivation mean	1
12,13,14,15	Each entity should be associated with members in the entity families	1, 4
16	Each entity must have a start life status	1,4
17	Each entity must have a terminating life status	1,4
18,19	Each entity must have a correct life cycle transition	1,4

J.2 Entity Model Guidelines

Guideline ID	Entity Model Guidelines	Category
20	An entity model should be within 4 layers	1
21	None or two entity parents only	1
22	Entity name should be short	1
23	Entity name should be general	2, 4
24	Entity names are singular nouns	2
25	One dependency to an alternative box only	1, 3

J.3 Process Model Rules

Rule ID	Process Model Rules	Category
1	Each process must have a trigger	1
2	Each process must include at least one entity	1
3	There are only seven different kinds of entity functions	1
4	Each entity must be included in at least one process	1
5	Each originate process must define the creation of its originate focal entity	1, 4
6	An originate process must define the creation of its originate normal entity if it has any	1, 4
7	An originate process must define the creation of its originate in-flight entity if it has any	1, 4
8	A change process must define the creation of its change focal entity	1, 4
9	A change process must define the creation of its change normal entity, if it has any	1, 4
10	Originate focal entity is only applicable for originate process	1
11	Each entity in a process must be assigned an entity function	1
12	Each entity can only have one entity function in any process	1
13	Creation and modification of values of derivable variables cannot be the primary purpose of a process	1
14	The calculation base for derivable variables must be included in the corresponding process scope	1
15, 16	Consistency checking for life cycle diagrams and processes	2, 3, 4

J.4 Process Model Guidelines

Guideline ID	Process Model Guidelines	Category
17	Each process should include least one business rule	1
18	Each entity should be originated by at least one process	1
19	Process name should obey the standard naming convention	1
20	There is only one originate focal entity in an originate process	1
21	There is only one change focal entity in a change process	1
22,23	Parent entities of originate entities in a process may also be included in the same process	1
24,25	Parent entities of change entities in a process may also be included in the same process	1
26	Checking for subsumed processes	2
27	Checking for the possibility of combining originate processes	2
28	Checking for the possibility of combining change processes	2
29	The transition of all life statuses should be handled by at least one process	1, 4
30	Important attributes should be handled by at least one process	1, 4
31	Known transition of attribute values should be handled by at least one process	1, 4
32,33	Deadlock by process definitions	1,3,4
34,35	Inconsistent handling of entities	1,3,4

K

Test Results of Model Rules and Guidelines

K.1 Test Results of Entity Model Rules

Number	Error Description	Error Found	Rule ID
1	An entity without definition	41	4
2	An entity with different parents defined in different cards	1	6
3	An entity with inconsistent class attribute values	2	8
4	Add an isolated entity	1	1
5	Insert two dependencies from Duration to its descendant to create a circular dependency	4	2
6	An entity occurrence was created but its parent occurrences were not created	-	5*
7	Name an entity "Registration Form"	1	10
8	Entities not associated with entity families	52	12
9	Entities not specifying its starting life status	56	16
10	Entities not specifying its ending life status	56	17

11	Transferring the ending life status of an entity to another life status	1	18
12	Give an entity a start life status but does not give it a transition means to another status	1	16
13	Give an entity an ending life status but does not give it a transition means to arrive it	2	17
14	Give an entity a life status transition cycle which does not end	1	18

* *This error is only checkable in the dynamic business card, and is prevented in the business model simulator.*

K.2 Test Results of Entity Model Guidelines

Number	Error Description	Error Found	Guideline ID
1	Insert a one-parent entity	1	21
2	Insert a three-parent entity	1	21
3	Long entity names	1	22
4	Two entities which divide the concept of place in two entities	1	23
5	A plural entity name is used	1	24
6	Too many layers due to circular dependencies placed in the model	26	20
7	Without planted the error of circular dependencies but with one extra entity injected at the button of the model	1	20
8	One entity which is dependent on alternative parents box only	1	25

K.3 Test Results of Process Model Rules

Number	Error Description	Error Found	Rule ID
1	Processes not defined a trigger event	37	1
2	Process not include an entity	1	2
3	Entities which are not included by at least one process	37	4
4	Originate process without defining its originate focal actions	11	5
5	Originate process without defining its originate normal actions	2	6
6	Originate process without defining its originate in-flight actions	3	7
7	One change process not having a change focal entity	1	8
8	Change processes not specifying its change focal actions	29	8
9	Change processes not specifying its change normal actions	2	9
10	One originate focal entity is added in a change process	1	10
11	Assign an entity to a process, but do not give it an entity function	1	11
12	Assign an entity with two entity functions in a process	1	12
13	A process was specified to originate an entity's life status in the LCD*, but is not specified in the corresponding process scope	1	15
14	A process was specified to change an entity's life status in the LCD*, but is not specified in the corresponding process scope	1	16

* LCD stands for Life Cycle Diagram.

K.4 Test Results of Process Model Guidelines

Number	Error Description	Error Found	Guideline ID
1	Define a process but does not specify a business rule for it	41	17
2	Creates entities in the model, but does not define any process to originate them	43	18
3	Define two originate focal entities in a process	1	20
4	Define two change focal entities in a process	1	21
5	An entity which is with inconsistent parents, but is also at the same time being an originate focal entity for a process	4	22
6	An entity which is with inconsistent parents, but is also at the same time being a change focal entity for a process	4	24

L

Example Use of GMA

This appendix gives an example use of GMA and the generated reports.

L.1 Input User Model

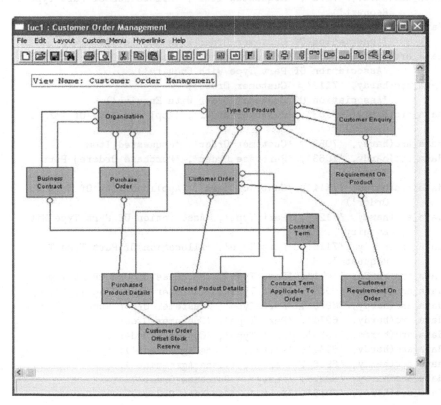

Fig. L.1. The example input model for *GMA*

L.2 Representation of the User Model

```
data_ent(hardy, 'Reservation Of Future Supply').
data_ent(hardy, 'Association Of Customer Order With Enquiry').
data_ent(hardy, 'Applicability Of Term To Order').
data_ent(hardy, 'Allocation Of Part Type To Request').
data_ent(hardy, 'Purchase Ordered Part Type').
data_ent(hardy, 'Association Of Part Type With Enquiry').
data_ent(hardy, 'Requested Item').
data_ent(hardy, 'Customer Order Enquiry').
data_ent(hardy, 'Customer Order').
data_ent(hardy, 'Purchase Order').
data_ent(hardy, 'Trade Agreement').
data_ent(hardy, 'Contract Term').
data_ent(hardy, 'Part Type').
data_ent(hardy, 'Party').
data_view(hardy, 'Order').
data_arc(hardy, '7143', 'Allocation Of Part Type To Request',
         'Reservation Of Future Supply').
data_arc(hardy, '7139', 'Purchase Ordered Part Type',
         'Reservation Of Future Supply').
data_arc(hardy, '7075', 'Requested Item', 'Allocation Of Part Type To
         Request').
data_arc(hardy, '7135', 'Customer Order Enquiry',
         'Association Of Customer Order With Enquiry').
data_arc(hardy, '7131', 'Customer Order Enquiry',
         'Association Of Part Type With Enquiry').
data_arc(hardy, '7119', 'Customer Order',
         'Association Of Customer Order With Enquiry').
data_arc(hardy, '7103', 'Customer Order', 'Applicability Of Term To
         Order').
data_arc(hardy, '7059', 'Customer Order', 'Requested Item').
data_arc(hardy, '7063', 'Purchase Order', 'Purchase Ordered Part
         Type').
data_arc(hardy, '7111', 'Contract Term', 'Applicability Of Term To
         Order').
data_arc(hardy, '7127', 'Part Type', 'Association Of Part Type With
         Enquiry').
data_arc(hardy, '7115', 'Part Type', 'Allocation Of Part Type To
         Request').
data_arc(hardy, '7071', 'Part Type', 'Purchase Ordered Part Type').
data_arc(hardy, '6982', 'Part Type', 'Customer Order Enquiry').
data_arc(hardy, '6978', 'Part Type', 'Customer Order Enquiry').
data_arc(hardy, '6974', 'Part Type', 'Customer Order').
data_arc(hardy, '6970', 'Part Type', 'Customer Order').
data_arc(hardy, '6934', 'Party', 'Trade Agreement').
data_arc(hardy, '6926', 'Party', 'Trade Agreement').
data_arc(hardy, '6922', 'Party', 'Purchase Order').
data_arc(hardy, '6918', 'Party', 'Purchase Order').
```

L.3 Dialogue using GMA

```
merlin[myprolog] SICStus 3  #5: Tue Aug 26 10:14:51 BST 1997
| ?- [cbr].
{consulting /hame/jessicac/kbst-bm/myprolog/cbr.pl...}
{consulting /hame/jessicac/kbst-bm/myprolog/case.db...}
{/hame/jessicac/kbst-bm/myprolog/case.db consulted, 80 msec
26896 bytes}
{consulting /hame/jessicac/kbst-bm/myprolog/enthrc.db...}
{/hame/jessicac/kbst-bm/myprolog/enthrc.db consulted, 40 msec
19968 bytes}

******* Welcome to KBST Generic Model Advisor *******
Please type "run." to take the specific input from Hardy.
Press control+d to quit the program. Bye for now.
{/hame/jessicac/kbst-bm/myprolog/cbr.pl consulted, 250 msec
87104 bytes}
yes

| ?- run.
{consulting /hame/jessicac/kbst-bm/myprolog/cbr.db...}
{/hame/jessicac/kbst-bm/myprolog/cbr.db consulted, 10 msec
3184 bytes}

************** Retrieving User Model ****************
**** Matching Generic Models in the Case Library ****
******* Choose Similarity Assessment Method *********

All of the relevant cases to the user model have been retrieved,
and will be presented to you in order. The sequence of display
can be given by default order. Alternatively, if you wish,
you can influence the sequence of the cases which are presented
to you by changing the weight on the selected features.

  How would you like to optimise the solution presentation:

  (1) Use The Default Method
  (2) Redefine The Optimisation Method
|: 1.
******* Finished Optimising Solution ********

**********       Stage Report No. 1      **********
**********  Fitness Measure of Matching **********

(A) The matched CASE model is: Restaurant: Customer Order
    The similar assessment ratio is: 0.50

* Matching View Name: yes
* The link matching ratio of the retrieved CASE model: 0.29
  The entity matching ratio of the retrieved CASE model: 0.39
```

```
There are 7 links matched,
and there are 17 links not matched.
There are in total 24 links in the CASE model.

There are 7 entities matched,
and there are 11 entities not matched.
There are in total 18 entities in the CASE model.
```

(B) The input USER model is: Order

* The link matching ratio of the USER model: 0.33
* The entity matching ratio of the USER model: 0.5

```
There are 7 links matched,
and there are 14 links not matched.
There are in total 21 links in the USER model.

There are 7 entities matched,
and there are 7 entities not matched.
There are in total 14 entities in the USER model.
```

```
********        Stage Report No. 2        *********
********    Result Analysis & Suggestion  *********
```

(1) The selected matching case model is: Restaurant:
    Customer Order

  - The input USER model is: Order

(2) Matching of entities:
 - There are 7 sets of entities found matched:

 - The Entity "Allocation Of Part Type To Request"
   in the USER model was found to be matching with
   the Entity "Association Of Customer Order
   With Reservation" in the CASE model

 - The Entity "Applicability Of Term To Order"
   in the USER model was found to be matching with
   the Entity "Applicability Of Trade Agreement For
   Customer Order" in the CASE model

 - The Entity "Contract Term" in the USER model.
   was found to be matching with
   the Entity "Promotion" in the CASE model

 - The Entity "Customer Order" in the USER model.
   was found to be matching with
   the Entity "Customer Order" in the CASE model

- The Entity "Customer Order Enquiry" in the
  USER model was found to be matching with
  the Entity "Customer Reservation" in the
  CASE model.

- The Entity "Party" in the USER model.
  was found to be matching with
  the Entity "Business" in the CASE model

- The Entity "Trade Agreement" in the USER model.
  was found to be matching with
  the Entity "Trade Agreement" in the CASE model

(3) An independent architecture matching:

- Matching a Valid Dependency:
  The link from entity "Customer Order Enquiry" to
  "Association Of Customer Order With Enquiry"
  in the USER model MATCHES with
  the link from entity "Customer Reservation" to
  "Association Of Customer Order With Reservation"
  in the CASE model.

- Matching a Valid Dependency:
  The link from entity "Customer Order" to "Association
  Of Customer Order With Enquiry"
  in the USER model MATCHES with
  the link from entity "Customer Order" to "Association
  Of Customer Order With Reservation" in the CASE model.

- Matching a Valid Dependency:
  The link from entity "Customer Order" to "Applicability
  Of Term To Order"
  in the USER model MATCHES with
  the link from entity "Customer Order" to "Applicability
  Of Trade Agreement For Customer Order"
  in the CASE model.

- Matching a Valid Dependency:
  The link from entity "Party" to "Trade Agreement"
  in the USER model MATCHES with
  the link from entity "Business" to "Trade Agreement"
  in the CASE model.

- Matching a Valid Dependency:
  The link from entity "Party" to "Trade Agreement"
  in the USER model MATCHES with
  the link from entity "Business" to "Trade Agreement"
  in the CASE model.

- Matching a Valid Dependency:
  The link from entity "Party" to "Purchase Order"
  in the USER model MATCHES with
  the link from entity "Business" to "Customer Order"
  in the CASE model.

- Matching a Valid Dependency:
  The link from entity "Party" to "Purchase Order"
  in the USER model MATCHES with
  the link from entity "Business" to "Customer Order"
  in the CASE model.

(4) Unmatched dependencies:

- There is a link from entity "Trade Agreement" to
  "Applicability Of Trade Agreement For Customer Order"
  in the case model which could not be matched with any
  links in the data model.

  Analysis: because the corresponding entities of
  "Trade Agreement" and "Applicability Of Trade Agreement
  For Customer Order" in the data model could not be found.

  << ... details omitted ... >>

============== End of Report ==============
Do you want to see an alternative matching ? (y. or n.)
|: y.
Show an alternative solution:

******* Finished Optimising Solution ********
**********   Stage Report No. 1   **********

********** Fitness Measure of Matching **********

(A) The matched CASE model is: Subject Of Transaction:
    Ordered Batch
    The similar assessment ratio is: 0.66

* Matching View Name: yes
* The link matching ratio of the retrieved CASE model:
  1.0
  The entity matching ratio of the retrieved CASE model:
  1.0

  There are 2 links matched,
  and there are 0 links not matched.
  There are in total 2 links in the CASE model.

```
There are 3 entities matched,
and there are 0 entities not matched.
There are in total 3 entities in the CASE model.
```

(B) The input USER model is: Order

* The link matching ratio of the USER model: 0.10
* The entity matching ratio of the USER model: 0.21

```
There are 2 links matched,
and there are 19 links not matched.
There are in total 21 links in the USER model.

There are 3 entities matched,
and there are 11 entities not matched.
There are in total 14 entities in the USER model.
```

```
********        Stage Report No. 2     *********
********    Result Analysis & Suggestion  *********
```

(1) The selected matching case model is: Subject Of
    Transaction: Ordered Batch

  - The input USER model is: Order

(2) Matching of entities:
 - There are 3 sets of entities found matched:

 - The Entity "Customer Order" in the USER model.
   was found to be matching with
   the Entity "Customer Order" in the CASE model

 - The Entity "Part Type" in the USER model.
   was found to be matching with
   the Entity "Product Type" in the CASE model

 - The Entity "Purchase Ordered Part Type" in the USER model.
   was found to be matching with
   the Entity "Ordered Batch" in the CASE model

(3) An independent architecture matching:

- Matching a Valid Dependency:
  The link from entity "Part Type" to "Purchase Ordered
  Part Type" in the USER model MATCHES with
  the link from entity "Product Type" to "Ordered Batch"
  in the CASE model.

- Matching a Valid Dependency:
  The link from entity "Purchase Order" to "Purchase Ordered
```
```

Part Type" in the USER model MATCHES with
the link from entity "Customer Order" to "Ordered Batch"
in the CASE model.

(4) Unmatched dependencies:

- All dependences in the Case Model are matched.

============== End of Report ==============

Do you want to see an alternative matching ? (y. or n.)
|: y.
Show an alternative solution:

******* Finished Optimising Solution ********
**********   Stage Report No. 1   **********

********** Fitness Measure of Matching **********

(A) The matched CASE model is: BSDM: Customer Order And
    Delivery The similar assessment ratio is: 0.32

* Matching View Name: yes
* The link matching ratio of the retrieved CASE model: 0.09
  The entity matching ratio of the retrieved CASE model: 0.21

  There are 2 links matched,
  and there are 20 links not matched.
  There are in total 22 links in the CASE model.

  There are 3 entities matched,
  and there are 11 entities not matched.
  There are in total 14 entities in the CASE model.

(B) The input USER model is: Order

* The link matching ratio of the USER model: 0.10
* The entity matching ratio of the USER model: 0.21

  There are 2 links matched,
  and there are 19 links not matched.
  There are in total 21 links in the USER model.

  There are 3 entities matched,
  and there are 11 entities not matched.
  There are in total 14 entities in the USER model.

********   Stage Report No. 2   ********
******** Result Analysis & Suggestion ********

(1) The selected matching case model is: BSDM: Customer
    Order And Delivery

  - The input USER model is: Order

(2) Matching of entities:
 - There are 3 sets of entities found matched:

 - The Entity "Customer Order" in the USER model.
   was found to be matching with
   the Entity "Customer Order" in the CASE model

 - The Entity "Party" in the USER model.
   was found to be matching with
   the Entity "Business" in the CASE model

 - The Entity "Purchase Ordered Part Type" in the USER model.
   was found to be matching with
   the Entity "Product On Order" in the CASE model

(3) An independent architecture matching:

- Matching a Valid Dependency:
  The link from entity "Purchase Order" to "Purchase
  Ordered Part Type" in the USER model MATCHES with the
  link from entity "Customer Order" to "Product On Order"
  in the CASE model.

- Matching a Valid Dependency:
  The link from entity "Party" to "Purchase Order"
  in the USER model MATCHES with
  the link from entity "Business" to "Customer Order"
  in the CASE model.

(4) Unmatched dependencies:

- There is a link from entity "Business" to "Order
  Receiving Point" in the case model which could not be
  matched with any links in the data model.

  Analysis: because the corresponding entities of
  "Business" and "Order Receiving Point"
  in the data model could not be found.

  << ... details omitted ... >>

============== End of Report ==============
Do you want to see an alternative matching ? (y. or n.)
|: y.
Show an alternative solution:

<< All of the alternative solutions have been explored by
the user, but the details are omitted here. A summary
of the retrieved cases and their reports are given in
the next section. >>

L.4 Statistical Summary of All Explored Matches

A Summary Report of Matching Results
Input USER model: Order

Matching Ratios:
(1) Match-View/Match-case-ent/Match-user-ent
    Match-case-link/Match-user-link
(2) All-User-Links/Matched-Links/Unmatched-Links
    All-Case-Links/Matched-Case-Links/Unmatched-Case-Links
(3) All-User-Ents/Matched-Ents/Unmatched-Ents
    All-Case-Ents/Matched-Case-Ents/Unmatched-Case-Ents

Restaurant: Customer Order:
1   0.39/0.5   0.29/0.33
21/7/14   24/7/17
14/7/7   18/7/11

Subject Of Transaction: Ordered Batch:
1   1.0/0.21   1.0/0.10
21/2/19   2/2/0
14/3/11   3/3/0

BSDM: Customer Order And Delivery:
1   0.21/0.21
    0.09/0.10
21/2/19   22/2/20
14/3/11   14/3/11

Purchase Invoice and Payment:
0   0.42/0.36 0.38/0.29
21/6/15   16/6/10
14/5/9   12/5/7

Restaurant: Purchase Invoice And Delivery:
0   0.45/0.36   0.25/0.19
21/4/17   16/4/12
14/5/9   11/5/6

Restaurant: Stock Control:
0   0.6/0.43   0.3/0.14
21/3/18   10/3/7

```
14/6/8    10/6/4

BSDM Manual: Employee Management:
0   0.4/0.14   0.33/0.10
21/2/19    6/2/4
14/2/12    5/2/3

Restaurant: Tax Payment:
0   0.13/0.14    0.1/0.10
21/2/19    20/2/18
14/2/12    16/2/14

Business Function: Delivery:
0   0.33/0.07    0/0
0/0/0    2/0/2
14/1/13    3/1/2

Contract and Account:
0   0.25/0.07   0/0
0/0/0    6/0/6
14/1/13    4/1/3

Inter-Business Relationship:
0   0.2/0.07     0/0
0/0/0    6/0/6
14/1/13    5/1/4

Contract And Organisation Management:
0   0.2/0.07     0/0
0/0/0    6/0/6
14/1/13    5/1/4

Application Of Law:
0   0.2/0.07     0/0
0/0/0    4/0/4
14/1/13    5/1/4

Restaurant: Employee Management:
0   0.08/0.07    0/0
0/0/0    14/0/14
14/1/13    12/1/11
```

M

Example Use of Simulator

This example is given as a supportive document to the illustration given in Section 9.5.

```
SICStus 3  #5: Tue Aug 26 10:14:51 BST 1997
{compiling /hame/jessicac/kbst-bm/simulator/top.pl...}
{consulting /hame/jessicac/kbst-bm/simulator/library.pl...}
{/hame/jessicac/kbst-bm/simulator/library.pl consulted,
10 msec 3456 bytes}
{consulting /hame/jessicac/kbst-bm/simulator/store.pl...}
{/hame/jessicac/kbst-bm/simulator/store.pl consulted,
0 msec 400 bytes}
{consulting /hame/jessicac/kbst-bm/simulator/conflict.pl...}
{/hame/jessicac/kbst-bm/simulator/conflict.pl consulted,
20 msec 10336 bytes}
{consulting /hame/jessicac/kbst-bm/simulator/cond.pl...}
{/hame/jessicac/kbst-bm/simulator/cond.pl consulted,
30 msec 9936 bytes}
{consulting /hame/jessicac/kbst-bm/simulator/exe.pl...}
{/hame/jessicac/kbst-bm/simulator/exe.pl consulted,
20 msec 8816 bytes}
{consulting /hame/jessicac/kbst-bm/simulator/model.pl...}
{/hame/jessicac/kbst-bm/simulator/model.pl consulted,
10 msec 3696 bytes}
{consulting /hame/jessicac/kbst-bm/simulator/derive.pl...}
{/hame/jessicac/kbst-bm/simulator/derive.pl consulted,
20 msec 12848 bytes}
{consulting /hame/jessicac/kbst-bm/simulator/data/cond.db...}
{/hame/jessicac/kbst-bm/simulator/data/cond.db consulted,
0 msec 3408 bytes}
{consulting /hame/jessicac/kbst-bm/simulator/data/dyn.db...}
{/hame/jessicac/kbst-bm/simulator/data/dyn.db consulted,
0 msec 1344 bytes}
{consulting /hame/jessicac/kbst-bm/simulator/data/entity.db...}
{/hame/jessicac/kbst-bm/simulator/data/entity.db consulted,
0 msec 2528 bytes}
```

```
{consulting /hame/jessicac/kbst-bm/simulator/data/process.db...}
{/hame/jessicac/kbst-bm/simulator/data/process.db consulted,
0 msec 6224 bytes}
{consulting /hame/jessicac/kbst-bm/simulator/data/trigger.db...}
{/hame/jessicac/kbst-bm/simulator/data/trigger.db consulted,
10 msec 2864 bytes}
************************************************************
Welcome to The Business Model Simulator for BSDM
This simulator is a part of the tool KBST-BM
Please activate this program by typing top(X).
Where as X is the number of steps required for simulation.
At the end of the simulation type look to see results.
************************************************************
{/hame/jessicac/kbst-bm/simulator/top.pl compiled,
260 msec 79824 bytes}
| ?- top(1).
>>>>> Searching for Processes
>>>>> Searching for Triggers
>>>>> Searching for Triggers
End Time: 0
Step left: 0
Would you like to add new occurrences to the system? (y./n.)
|: n.
End of simulation, Simulation stops at time: 1
****** export_data_to_archive ******
System States are saved in sim.out

yes
| ?- look.
------- report dynamic system state -------
Shown State: 0  State Time: 0. It is now time: 0

ent_occ('Practical', p1, []).

ent_occ('Practical Assign To Module', 'ES-p2',
[('Practical',p2),('Module','ES')]).

ent_occ('Practical Assign To Module', 'ES-p1',
[('Module','ES'),('Practical',p1)]).

ent_occ('Practical', p2, []).

ent_occ('Module', 'ES', []).

ent_occ('Person', 'John', []).

ent_occ_att('Practical', p1, lifestatus, valid).

ent_occ_att('Practical Assign To Module', 'ES-p2', lifestatus, valid).
```

```
ent_occ_att('Practical Assign To Module', 'ES-p1', lifestatus, valid).

ent_occ_att('Practical', p2, lifestatus, valid).

ent_occ_att('Module', 'ES', lifestatus, valid).

ent_occ_att('Person', 'John', lifestatus, valid).

occ_begin('Person', 'John', 1).

occ_end('Person', 'John', 2).

current_state(0).

state(0, time(0)).

ent_fun('Acknowledge Handed-in Practical', '111',
originate_focal_entity,
dyn(ent_occ('Practical Tun In By Person','John-ES-P1',
[('Practical Assign To Module','ES-p1'),('Person','John')]))).

ent_fun('Acknowledge Handed-in Practical', '111',
refer_normal_entity,
dyn(ent_occ('Module','ES',[]))).

ent_fun('Acknowledge Handed-in Practical', '111',
refer_normal_entity,
dyn(ent_occ('Person','John',]))).

ent_fun('Acknowledge Handed-in Practical', '111',
refer_normal_entity,
dyn(ent_occ('Practical Assign To Module','ES-p1',[('Module','ES'),
('Practical',p1)]))).

state_id(0).
agenda(process('Acknowledge Handed-in Practical','111',
[originate_focal_entity('Practical Turn In B Person','John-ES-P1'),
add_att('Practical Turn In By Person','John-ES-P1', lifestatus,
'handed-in'), refer_normal_entity('Person','John'),
refer_normal_entity('Module','ES'),refer_normal_entity(
'Practical Assign To Module','ES-p1')],(0,2))).

change((0,0), ('Acknowledge Handed-in Practical','111'),
[dyn(trigger(0,'Acknowledge Handed-in Practical','111',
[originate_focal_entity('Practical Turn In By Person','John-ES-P1'),
add_att('Practical urn In By Person', 'John-ES-P1', lifestatus,
'handed-in'),
refer_normal_entity('Person','John'), refer_normal_entity('Module',
'ES'),
refer_normal_entity('Practical Assign To Module','ES-p1')]))],
```

```
[dyn(agenda(process('Acknowledge Handed-in Practical','111',
[originate_focal_entity('Practical Turn In By Person','John-ES-P1'),
add_att('Practical Turn In By Person','John-ES-P1',lifestatus,
'handed-in'),refer_normal_entity('Person','John'),
refer_normal_entity('Module','ES'),refer_normal_entity(
'Practical Assign To Module','ES-p1')],(0,2))))]).

current_time(1).

skip_process(no).

yes
| ?- top(2).
>>>>> Searching for Processes
>>>>> Searching for Triggers
End Time: 1
Step left: 1
Would you like to add new occurrences to the system? (y./n.)
|: n.
>>>>> Searching for Processes
*********************************************
All processes in the Agenda are given below:

Acknowledge Handed-in Practical,111

*********************************************
* Searching for contradictory processes...
  No contradictory processes found.

*********************************
Would you like to execute process:

Acknowledge Handed-in Practical
Trigger ID: 111
*********************************
Execution? (y/n) y.

*********************************
    Process Execution Phase
*********************************
* Checking the triggers....
  checking triggers succeed.
* Checking then preconditions....
  checking precond succeed.
* Checking the referred attributes...
  checking referred attributes succeed.
* Checking the adding attributes...
  checking adding attributes succeed.
* Checking for the changing attributes...
  checking changing attributes succeed.
```

```
* Executing the process ...
  Process execution succeed.
* Verifying the postconditions...
  Verifying postconditions succeed.
>>>>> Searching for Processes
>>>>> Searching for Triggers
End Time: 2
Step left: 0
Would you like to add new occurrences to the system? (y./n.)
|: n.
End of simulation, Simulation stops at time: 3
****** export_data_to_archive ******
System States are saved in sim.out

yes
| ?- look.
------- report dynamic system state -------
Shown State: 1  State Time: 2. It is now time: 2

ent_occ('Practical', p1, []).

ent_occ('Practical Assign To Module', 'ES-p2',
[('Practical',p2),('Module','ES')]).

ent_occ('Practical Assign To Module', 'ES-p1',
[('Module','ES'),('Practical',p1)]).

ent_occ('Practical', p2, []).

ent_occ('Module', 'ES', []).

ent_occ('Person', 'John', []).

ent_occ_att('Practical', p1, lifestatus, valid).

ent_occ_att('Practical Assign To Module', 'ES-p2', lifestatus, valid).

ent_occ_att('Practical Assign To Module', 'ES-p1', lifestatus, valid).

ent_occ_att('Practical', p2, lifestatus, valid).

ent_occ_att('Module', 'ES', lifestatus, valid).

ent_occ_att('Person', 'John', lifestatus, valid).

occ_begin('Person', 'John', 1).

occ_end('Person', 'John', 2).

state(0, time(0)).
```

```
change((0,0), ('Acknowledge Handed-in Practical','111'),
[dyn(trigger(0,'Acknowledge Handed-in Practical','111',
[originate_focal_entity('Practical Turn In By Person','John-ES-P1'),
add_att('Practical urn In By Person','John-ES-P1',lifestatus,
'handed-in'), refer_normal_entity('Person','John'),
refer_normal_entity('Module','ES'), refer_normal_entity('Practical
Assign To Module','ES-p1')]))], [dyn(agenda(process(
'Acknowledge Handed-in Practical','111',
[originate_focal_entity('Practical Turn In By Person',
'John-ES-P1'), add_att('Practical Turn In By Person',
'John-ES-P1',lifestatus,'handed-in'), refer_normal_entity(
'Person','John'),refer_normal_entity('Module','ES'),
refer_normal_entity('Practical Assign To Module','ES-p1')],(0,2))))]).

ent_occ('Practical Turn In By Person', 'John-ES-P1',
[('Practical Assign To Module','ES-p1'),('Person','John')]).

occ_begin('Practical Turn In By Person', 'John-ES-P1', 2).

change((0,1), ('Acknowledge Handed-in Practical','111'), [],
[dyn(ent_occ('Practical Turn In By Person','John-ES-P1',
[('Practical Assign To Module','ES-p1'),('Person','John')])),
dyn(occ_begin('Practical Turn In By Person','John-ES-P1',2))]).

ent_occ_att('Practical Turn In By Person', 'John-ES-P1',
lifestatus, 'handed-in').

change((0,1), ('Acknowledge Handed-in Practical','111'), [],
[dyn(ent_occ_att('Practical Turn In By Person','John-ES-P1',
lifestatus,'handed-in'))]).

occ_originate_focal('Acknowledge Handed-in Practical', '111',
'Practical Turn In By Person', 'John-S-P1').
change((0,1), ('Acknowledge Handed-in Practical','111'), [],
[dyn(occ_originate_focal('Acknowledge anded-in Practical','111',
'Practical Turn In By Person','John-ES-P1'))]).

occ_refer_normal('Acknowledge Handed-in Practical', '111',
'Module', 'ES').

change((0,1), ('Acknowledge Handed-in Practical','111'), [],
[dyn(occ_refer_normal('Acknowledge Handed-in Practical','111',
'Module','ES'))]).

occ_refer_normal('Acknowledge Handed-in Practical', '111',
'Person', 'John').

change((0,1), ('Acknowledge Handed-in Practical','111'), [],
[dyn(occ_refer_normal('Acknowledge Handed-in Practical','111',
```

```
'Person','John'))]).

occ_refer_normal('Acknowledge Handed-in Practical', '111',
'Practical Assign To Module', 'ES-p1').

change((0,1), ('Acknowledge Handed-in Practical','111'), [],
[dyn(occ_refer_normal('Acknowledge Handed-in Practical','111',
'Practical Assign To Module','ES-p1'))]).

pro_occ('Acknowledge Handed-in Practical', '111').

occ_begin('Acknowledge Handed-in Practical', '111', 0).

occ_end('Acknowledge Handed-in Practical', '111', 2).

change((0,1), ('Acknowledge Handed-in Practical','111'),
[dyn(agenda(process('Acknowledge Handed-in Practical','111',
[originate_focal_entity('Practical Turn In By Person','John-ES-P1'),
add_att('Practical Turn In By Person','John-ES-P1',lifestatus,
'handed-in'),refer_normal_entity('Person','John'),
refer_normal_entity('Module','ES'),refer_normal_entity(
'Practical Assign To Module','ES-p1')],(0,2)))),
[dyn(pro_occ('Acknowledge Handed-in Practical','111')),
dyn(occ_begin('Acknowledge Handed-in Practical','111',0)),
dyn(occ_end('Acknowledge Handed-in Practical','111',2))]).

change((0,1), ('Acknowledge Handed-in Practical','111'),
[dyn(ent_fun('Acknowledge Handed-in Practical','111',
originate_focal_entity,dyn(ent_occ('Practical Turn In By Person',
'John-ES-P1',[('Practical Assign To Module','ES-p1'),('Person',
'John')]))))], []).

change((0,1), ('Acknowledge Handed-in Practical','111'),
[dyn(ent_fun('Acknowledge Handed-in Practical','111',
refer_normal_entity,dyn(ent_occ('Module','ES',[]))))], []).

change((0,1), ('Acknowledge Handed-in Practical','111'),
[dyn(ent_fun('Acknowledge Handed-in Practical','111',
refer_normal_entity,dyn(ent_occ('Person','John',[]))))], []).

change((0,1), ('Acknowledge Handed-in Practical','111'),
[dyn(ent_fun('Acknowledge Handed-in Practical','111',
refer_normal_entity,dyn(ent_occ('Practical Assign To Module',
'ES-p1',[('Module','ES'),('Practical',p1)]))))], []).

current_state(1).

state_id(1).

state(1, time(2)).
```

```
current_time(3).
skip_process(no).
yes
| ?-
```

References

1. AKT Consortium. *Advanced Knowledge Technologies (AKT) Interdisciplinary Research Collaborations (IRC) EPSRC project*, 2004. http://www.aktors.org.
2. James F. Allen, Henry A. Kautz, Richard N. Pelavin, and Josh D. Tenenberg. *Reasoning About Plans*. Morgan Kaufmann, San Mateo, California, 1991.
3. Klaus-Dieter Althoff, Eric Auriol, Ralph Barletta, and Michel Manago. *A Review of Industrial Case-Based Reasoning Tools*. An AI Perspective Report. AI Intelligence, P.O.Box 95, Oxford OX2 7XL, 1995.
4. Tony Andrews, Francisco Curbera, Hitesh Dholakia, Yaron Goland, Johannes Klein, Frank Leymann, Kevin Liu, Dieter Roller, Doug Smith, Satish Thatte, Ivana Trickovic, and Sanjiva Weerawarana. *Business Process Execution Language for Web Services (BPEL)*. ed. Satish Thatte. http://www-106.ibm.com/developerworks/library/ws-bpel/.
5. Assaf Arkin. *Business Process Modelling Language (BPML)*, 2002. http://www.bpmi.org/.
6. Artificial Intelligence Application Institute. http://www.aiai.ed. ac.uk.
7. Artificial Intelligence Application Institute. *Procedural Builder, Enterprise Project*. http:// www.aiai.ed.ac.uk/project/enterprise.
8. J. Barber, S. Bhatta, A. Goel, M. Jacobsen, M. Pearce, L. Penberthy, M. Shankar, and E. Stroulia. *Integrating Case-Based Reasoning and Multimedia Technologies for Interface Design Support*. In Artificial Intelligence in Design, ed. J.G. Boston, Kluwer Academic, 1992.
9. Alfs Berztiss. *Software Methods for Business Reengineering*. Springer-Verlag New York, 1996.
10. Grady Booch. *Object Oriented Design with Applications*. Benjamin/Cummings, 1991.
11. Grady Booch, James Rumbaugh, and Ivar Jacobson. *The Unified Modelling Language User Guide*. Object Technology. Addison-Wesley, February 1999.
12. Jonathan P. Bowen. Seven more myths of formal methods. *IEEE Software*, 7(5), September 1990. pp. 11-19.
13. Jonathan P. Bowen. Ten commandments of formal methods. *IEEE Computer*, 28(4), April 1995. pp. 56-63.
14. BPR Online Learning Center: the Reengineering Directory. ProSci, January 1999. http://www.prosci.com/.
15. Ian Bratko. *Prolog Programming for Artificial Intelligence (2nd edition)*. Addison Wesley, 1986. ISBN 0-201-41606-9.

16. Alan Bundy. *The Computer Modelling of Mathematical Reasoning*. Academic Press, 1983. ISBN 0-12-141352-0.
17. CACI Products Company. Simprocess. http://www.simprocess.com.
18. Yun-Heh Chen-Burger. A knowledge based multi-perspective framework for enterprise modelling. Technical report, Informatics, University of Edinburgh., February 2001.
19. Yun-Heh Chen-Burger. Knowledge sharing and inconsistency checking on multiple enterprise models. *International Joint Conference on Artificial Intelligence, Knowledge Management and Organizational Memories Workshop, IJCAI 2001, Seattle, Washington*, August 2001. Also available as Informatics Division Technical Report, University of Edinburgh.
20. Yun-Heh Chen-Burger. *Sharing and Checking Organisation Knowledge*. Knowledge Management and Organizational Memories. ed. Rose Dieng-Kuntz, Nada Matta. Kluwer Academic, Boston, ISBN 0-7923-7659-5, 2002. http://www.cs.cmu.edu/afs/cs.cmu.edu/project/cadet/ftp/docs/CADET.html.
21. Yun-Heh Chen-Burger. *AKT Research Map, Technology Showcase*. Advanced Knowledge Technologies (AKT) Project, 2003. http://www.aiai.ed.ac.uk/jessicac/project/3-akt-res-map-tech-profile-sub/details.html.
22. Yun-Heh Chen-Burger, Dave Robertson, and Jussi Stader. A case-based reasoning framework for enterprise model building, sharing and reusing. *Proceedings of ECAI Workshop: Knowledge Management and Organizational Memories, Berlin*, August 2000.
23. Yun-Heh Chen-Burger, David Robertson, John Fraser, and Christine Lissoni. KBST: A support tool for business modelling in BSDM. *Proceedings of Expert Systems 95: Applications and Innovations in Expert Systems III, Cambridge, UK*, December 1995.
24. Yun-Heh Chen-Burger, David Robertson, and Jussi Stader. Formal support for an informal business modelling method. *International Journal of Software Engineering and Knowledge Engineering*, February 2000.
25. Yun-Heh Chen-Burger and Jussi Stader. *Formal Support for Adaptive Workflow Systems in a Distributed Environment*. ed. Layna Fischer. Future Strategies, USA. Published in association with Workflow Management Coalition., April 2003.
26. Yun-Heh (Jessica) Chen-Burger. KBST: a support tool for business modelling in BSDM. MSc thesis, Artificial Intelligence Department, University of Edinburgh, September 1994.
27. Alan M. Davis. *Software Requirements: Objects, Functions and States*. Prentice-Hall, 1993. ISBN 0-13-805763-x.
28. Delphi Group. *BPM 2002: Market Milestone Report*, February 2002.
29. Department of Defense. *Framework for Managing Process Improvement*, December 1994. http://www.dtic.mil/c3i/bprcd/3003.html.
30. Department of Defense. *ABC Guidebook*, June 1995. http://www.dtic.mil/c3i/bprcd/.
31. J.E. Dobson, A.J.C. Blyth, J. Chudge, and M.R. Strens. *The ORDIT Approach to Organisational Requirements*. Requirements Engineering: Social and Technical Issues. ed. Marina Jirotka and Joseph A. Goguen. Academic Press Professional, San Diego, CA, 1994.
32. John Dobson and Ros Strens. Organizational requirements definition for information technology systems. Technical report, Department of Computing Science, University of Newcastle upon Tyne, NE1 7RU, 1992.

33. E. Domeshek, J. Kolodner, and C. Zimring. The design of a tool kit for case-based design aids. *Proceedings of the Third International Conference on Artificial Intelligence in Design*, 1994.

34. Hans-Erik Eriksson and Magnus Penker. *Business Modeling with UML: Business Patterns at Work*. John Wiley and Sons, 2000.

35. Excel Software. Win A&D and Mac A&D, 2001. http://www.excelsoftware.com.

36. B. Faltings. *Case Reuse By Model-Based Interpretation*. Issues and Applications of Case-Based Reasoning in Design. ed. M.L. Maher and P. Pu. Lawrence Erlbaum Associates, Hillsdale, NJ, 1997. pp. 30-60.

37. International Organization for Standardization. Human centred design processes for interactive systems. *ISO DIS 13407*. http://www.iso.ch/.

38. M.S. Fox and M. Gruninger. Ontologies for enterprise integration. *Proceedings of the 2nd Conference on Cooperative Information Systems, Toronto, Ontario*, 1994. Also available at http://www.cil.utoronto.ca/enterprise-modelling/papers/index.html.

39. M.S. Fox and M. Gruninger. Enterprise modelling. *AI Magazine, AAAI press*, Fall, 1998. pp. 109-121.

40. John Fraser and Ann Macintosh. Enterprise state of the art survey, the enterprise consortium. Technical report, Artificial Intelligence Applications Institute (AIAI), University of Edinburgh, September 1994. http://www.aiai.ed.ac.uk/project/enterprise/papers/soa_svy/.

41. Michael Friedman and Jeffrey Voas. *Software Assessment: Reliability, Safety, Testability*. John Wiley and Sons, 1995.

42. Norbert E. Fuchs. Specifications are (preferable) executable. *Software Engineering Journal*, September 1992.

43. Norbert. E. Fuchs and David Robertson. Declarative specifications. *The Knowledge Engineering Review*, 11(4), 1996. pp. 317-331.

44. M.R. Genesereth and N.J. Nilsson. *Logical Foundations of Artificial Intelligence*. Morgan Kaufmann, 1987.

45. Michael Hammer and James Champy. *Reengineering the Corporation: A Manifesto for Business Revolution*. Harper Business, May 1995.

46. J.H. Harrington. *Business Process Improvement: The Breakthrough Strategy for Total Quality, Productivity, and Competitiveness*. McGraw-Hill, New York, 1991.

47. High Performance Systems. Ithink. http://www.hps-inc.com.

48. T.R. Hinrichs. Towards an architecture for open world problem solving. In *Proceedings of CBR workshop*. Morgan Kaufmann, San Francisco, 1988. pp. 182-189.

49. David Hollingsworth. *Workflow Management Coalition, The Workflow Reference Model*. Workflow Management Coalition, Avenue Marcel Thirty 204, 1200 Brussels, Belgium, 1994.

50. IBM Education Services, Sudbury, UK. *Business System Development Method: Business Mapping*, July 1994. IS03 Course Notes.

51. IBM, UK. *Business System Development Method: Business Mapping Part 1: Entities*, 2nd edition, May 1992.

52. IBM, UK. *Business System Development Method, Business Mapping Part 2: Processes*, 2nd edition, May 1992.

53. IBM, UK. *Business System Development Method, Introducing BSDM*, 2nd edition, May 1992.

54. IDS Scheer International. Aris Toolset. http://ids-scheer.com/english/index. php.

55. Ivar Jacobson, Maria Ericsson, and Agneta Jacobson. *The Object Advantage – Business Process Reengineering with Object Technology*. Addison Wesley, 1995.

56. Joint Force Air Component Commander, Defense Advanced Research Projects Agency Program. Air Operation Enterprise Modelling Project. http://www.darpa.mil /iso/jfacc/index.htm, 1999-2001.

57. Martin King. Knowledge reuse in business domains experience with IBM BSDM. Technical report, Artificial Intelligence Application Institute, 1995.

58. K. Knight. Unification: a multidisciplinary survey. *ACM Computing Surveys*, 21(1):93–124, 1989.

59. Knowledge Based Systems. http://www.kbsi.com/.

60. Knowledge Based Systems. Business Process Modelling Tool: AI0 WIN and ProSim. http://www.kbsi.com/software/ai0win.htm, http://www.kbsi.com/ software/prosim.htm.

61. Janet Kolodner. *Case-Based Reasoning*. Morgan Kaufmann, SanMateo, CA, 1993.

62. Jintae Lee, Michael Gruninger, Yan Jin, Thomas Malone, Austin Tate, Gregg Yost, and other members of the PIF working group. The PIF interchange format and framework. *The Knowledge Engineering Review*, 13(1), March 1998. http://ccs.mit.edu/pif/, http://www.aiai.ed.ac.uk/project/pif/.

63. E.J. Lemmon. *Beginning Logic*. Van Nostrand Reinhold, 1965.

64. Paul Levine, Jim Clark, Cory Casanave, Kurt Kanaskie, Betty Harvey, Jamie Clark, Neal Smith, John Yunker, and Karsten Riemer. *ebXML Business Process Specification Schema*. UN/CEFACT and OASIS, 2001. http://www.ebxml.org/specs/ebBPSS.pdf.

65. Frank Leymann and Dieter Roller. Business process management with flowmark. *IEEE*, 1994.

66. Logic Works. BPwin: Business Process Modelling Tool. http://www.shi.com.

67. Ann Macintosh, Ian Filby, and Austin Tate. Knowledge asset road maps. *Proceedings of the 2nd International Conference on Practical Aspects of Knowledge Management, Basel Switzerland*, October 1998.

68. M.L. Maher, B. Balachandran, and D.M. Zhang. *Case-Based Reasoning in Design*. Lawrence Erlbaum, 1995.

69. M.L. Maher and A. Gomez de Silva Garza. Developing case-based reasoning for structural design. *IEEE Expert, Intelligent Systems and Their Applications*, 11(3), June 1996.

70. Thomas W. Malone, John Quimby, Kevin Crowston, Abraham Bernstein, Jintae Lee, George A. Herman, Brian T. Pentland, Mark Klein, Chrysanthos Dellarocas, Charles S. Osborn, George M. Wyner, and Elisa O'Donnell. Tools for inventing organizations: Toward a handbook of organizational processes. *The MIT Process Handbook*, 2003. pp. 13-37, http://ccs.mit.edu/ph/.

71. David Martin, Mark Burstein, Grit Denker, Daniel Elenius, Jerry Hobbs, Lalana Kagal, Ora Lassila, Drew McDermott, Deborah McGuinness, Sheila McIlraith, Massimo Paolucci, Bijan Parsia, Terry Payne, Marta Sabou, Evren Sirin, Monika Solanki, Naveen Srinivasan, and Katia Sycara. *OWL-based Web Service Ontology (OWL-S)* , 2004. http://www.daml.org/services/owl-s/, http://www.daml.org/services/owl-s/1.1B/.

72. Richard Mayer, Christopher Menzel, Michael Painter, Paula Witte, Thomas Blinn, and Benjamin Perakath. *Information Integration for Concurrent Engineering (IICE) IDEF3 Process Description Capture*

Method Report.   Knowledge Based Systems (KBSI), September 1995.
http://www.idef.com/overviews/idef3.htm.

73. Richard J. Mayer, Michael K. Painter, and Paula S. deWitte. IDEF family
of methods for concurrent engineering and business re-engineering applications.
Technical report, Knowledge Based Systems, 1992. http://www.idef.com.

74. Chris S. Mellish. *Computer Interpretation of Natural Language Descriptions.*
Ellis Horwood, 1985.

75. Peiwei Mi and Walt Scacchi. A meta-model for formulating knowledge-based
models of software development. *Decision Support Systems*, 1996.

76. Microsoft. Visio, 2002. http://www.microsoft.com/office/visio/.

77. Glyn V. Morrill. *Type Logic Grammar: Categorical Logic of Signs.* Kluwer
Academic, 1994.

78. S. Narashiman, K. Sycara, and D. Navin-Chandra. *Representation and Synthesis
of Non-Monotonic Mechanical Devices.* Issues and Applications of Case-Based
Reasoning in Design. ed. M.L. Maher and P. Pu. Lawrence Erlbaum Associates,
Hillsdale, NJ, 1997. pp. 187-220.

79. NASA Johnson Space Center (JSC). *C Language Integrated Production System.
Clips 6.0 Reference Manual.* Software Technology Branch, June 1993.

80. National Institute of Standards and Technology. *Integration Definition for Function Modelling (IDEF0)*, December 1993.

81. Oracle Workflow. http://www.oracle.com/appsnet/products/procurement/ col-
lateral/ds_workflow.html.

82. Martyn A. Ould. *Business Processes: Modelling and Analysis for Re-engineering
and Improvement.* John Wiley and Sons, 1995.

83. William Perry. *Effective Methods for Software Testing.* John Wiley and Sons,
1995.

84. Platinum Technology. Paradigm plus.

85. David Profozich. *Managing Change with Business Process Simulation.* Prentice
Hall, 1998.

86. Rational Software Corporation. http://www.rational.com/index.jtmpl, 1999.

87. W. Reisig. Petri nets, an introduction. *EATCS, Monographs on Theoretical
Computer Science*, 1985.

88. Christopher K. Riesbeck and Roger C. Schank. *Inside Case-Based Reasoning.*
Lawrence Erlbaum, 1989.

89. Peter Rittgen. Paving the road to business process automation. *European Conference on Information Systems (ECIS) 2000, Vienna, Austria*, July 2000. pp.
313-319.

90. Dave Robertson and Jaume Agusti. *Software Blueprints: Lightweight Uses of
Logic in Conceptual Modelling.* Addison Wesley, May 1999.

91. J.A. Robinson. A machine oriented logic based on the resolution principle. *J
Assoc. Comput. Mach.*, 12:23–41, 1965.

92. W. Royce. Managing the development of large software systems. *IEEE
WESCON*, August 1970. pp. 1-9. Reprinted in Ninth IEEE International Conference on Software Engineering, Washington DC, Computer Society Press, 1987.

93. James Rumbaugh, Michael Blaha, William Premerlani, Frederick Eddy, and
William Lorensen. *Object-Oriented Modelling and Design.* Prentice Hall, 1991.

94. James Rumbaugh, Ivar Jacobson, and Grady Booch. *The Unified Modeling
Language Reference Manual.* Addison Wesley Longman, 1999.

95. Geary A. Rummler and Alan P. Brache. *Improving Performance: How to Manage the White Space on the Organizational Chart.* Jossey-Bass, May 1995.

96. Hossein Saiedian. An invitation to formal methods. *IEEE Computer*, April 1996.
97. SAP. SAP R/3 System, 2001. http://www.sap.com.
98. Craig Schlenoff, Amy Knutilla, and Steven Ray. Proceedings of the Process Specification Language (PSL) Roundtable. *NISTIR 6081, National Institute of Standards and Technology, Gaithersburg, MD*, 1997. http://www.nist.gov/psl/.
99. Guus Schreiber, Hans Akkermans, Anjo Anjewierden, Robert de Hoog, Nigel Shadbolt, Walter Van de Velde, and Bob Wielinga. *Knowledge Engineering and Management: The CommonKADS Methodology.* MIT Press, 2000. ISBN 0262193000.
100. R. E. Shannon. *System Simulation.* Prentice-Hall, Englewood Cliffs, NJ, 1975.
101. Julian Smart. *User Manual for HARDY.* Artificial Intelligence Applications Institute, University of Edinburgh, August 1994. http://www.aiai.ed.ac.uk/project/hardy/.
102. John F. Sowa. *Knowledge Representation: Logical, Philosophical and Computational Foundations.* Brooks/Cole, Thomson Learning, 2000.
103. Kathy Spurr and Paul Layzell, editors. *Case: Current Practice, Future Prospects.* John Wiley and Son, 1992.
104. Staffware. http://www.staffware.com/.
105. L. Sterling and E. Shapiro. *The Art of Prolog.* MIT Press, 1986. ISBN 0-262-69105-1.
106. E. Stroulia and A.K. Goel. Generic teleological mechanisms and their use in case adaptation. *Proceedings of the Fourteenth Annual Conference of the Cognitive Science*, 1992. Erlbaum, Northvale, NJ.
107. K. Sycara, R. Guttal, J. Koning, S. Narasimhan, and D. Navinchandra. Cadet: A case-based synthesis tool for engineering design. *International Journal for Expert Systems*, 4(2), 1992. pp. 157-188, http://www.cs.cmu.edu/afs/cs.cmu.edu/project/cadet/ftp/docs/CADET.html.
108. Ensemble Systems. Rose Business Process Link (RBPL), 2000. Business Modelling Support Tool Integrated with Rational Rose Tool Set, http://www.ensemble-systems.com.
109. Austin Tate. Generating project networks. *Proceedings of the 5th International Joint Conference on Artificial Intelligence*, 2, August 1977. pp. 888-893.
110. Technology Economics International. BPSimulator. http://www.reengineering.com/articles/jun96/techwtch.html.
111. U.S. Department of Defense. *Military Standard: Defense System Software Development*, June 1985.
112. U.S. Department of Defense. *Leading Change in a New Era*, May 1997.
113. Mike Uschold, Martin King, Stuart Moralee, and Yannis Zorgios. *The Enterprise Ontology.* Artificial Intelligence Application Institute, University of Edinburgh, 1995. Also available at http://www.aiai.ed.ac.uk/ entprise/enterprise/ontology.html.
114. Mike Uschold, Martin King, Stuart Moralee, and Yannis Zorgios. Enterprise ontology. *The Knowledge Engineering Review: Special Issue on Putting Ontologies to Use*, 13, 1998. Also available as technical report from AIAI, University of Edinburgh (AIAI-TR-195).
115. Jeffrey M. Voas and Gary McGraw. *Software Fault Injection Inoculating Programs Against Errors.* John Wiley and Sons, 1998.
116. Roel J. Wieringa. *Requirements Engineering – Frameworks for Understanding.* John Wiley and Sons, 1996.

117. Workflow Management Coalition. *XML Process Definition Language (XPDL)*, 2002. http://www.wfmc.org/standards/docs.htm.
118. Eric S.K. Yu, John Mylopoulos, and Yves Lesperance. Modelling the organization: New concepts and tools for re-engineering. *IEEE Expert: AI Models for Business Process Reengineering*, August 1996.
119. Pamela Zave and Michael Jackson. Four dark corners of requirements engineer. *ACM Transactions on Software Engineering and Methodology*, 6(1), January 1997. pp. 1-30.

Index